D0147706

Russ Harris, PhD, MDiv, LCSW

Christ-Centered Therapy
Empowering the Self

Pre-publication
REVIEWS,
COMMENTARIES,
EVALUATIONS . . .

"**H**ow many times have you found yourself saying, 'Part of me wants to go to the party tonight, but another part of me would rather just stay home and watch a movie?' As it turns out, you were speaking more truly than you may have known. A grand adventure of inner discovery awaits you in *Christ-Centered Therapy: Empowering the Self.* For underneath such a simple musing about how to spend an evening lies a profound, extensive personal reality: you and I really do have different parts of who we are, subpersonalities that possess a real life of their own, complete with feelings, agendas, beliefs, wounds, and roles that each play in our internal system. Our psyche is, indeed, much like an internal family, replete with the roles, needs, agendas, hopes, and conflicts experienced by external (literal) families.

For any psychotherapist, there is a minimum of two central questions that must be addressed for the sake of clinical effectiveness: What model most thoroughly and comprehensively helps us understand our client's clinical situation? And how can that model lead us into effective interventions to initiate healing change for the client? The genius of Christ-centered internal family systems is that both questions are answered in a manner that is both theoretically all-encompassing and clinically very useful and practical.

Therapeutic professionals will likely find their current approach to therapy surrounded by an outstanding model that will shed tremendous light on understanding their clients. It's easy to get lost in theory. All readers will be fascinated and empowered especially by the exercises offered at the end of each chapter, by the last four 'tools' chapters, and by the way the case studies help the reader to stay on track with Harris's actual use of CCIFS therapy.

For academics, this is a valuable textbook for courses in abnormal psychology, models of psychotherapy, and family therapy. Certainly CCIFS would be extremely valuable for any course seeking to relate Christianity and psychology. I recommend you postpone both the party and the evening movie, and flip open this book."

Rev. Jim Tilley, MDiv, PhD
Minister of Discipleship,
First Presbyterian Church,
Rochelle, Illinois

More pre-publication
REVIEWS, COMMENTARIES, EVALUATIONS . . .

"**D**r. Harris has made a rich contribution to the growing literature related to internal family systems theory and therapy. His understanding of the key concepts as developed and articulated by Dr. Richard Schwartz is evident throughout his work even as he presses the application of IFS theory into a new arena, that of a Christian context. The case studies provide a setting in which theory and practice emerge with clarity. Likewise, *Christ-Centered Therapy: Empowering the Self* will challenge the therapist who wants to develop an explicitly Christian approach to the treatment of the problems encountered by individuals, couples, and families. Therapists and clients who find themselves in contexts that allow for the full expression of life struggles and spiritual directions of therapy will find this approach both meaningful and effective.

While the first chapters provide a readable excursion through complex intrapersonal theories, the chapters on 'Christ-Centered IFS Concepts' and 'Christ-Centered Therapy' bring the integration to life as case studies depict experiences of both the pain within the parts and the healing power prompted by a relationship with Jesus.

The COAMFTE-approved marriage and family therapy program that I direct at Abilene Christian University is committed to the integration of theory and therapy with theology and spirituality. This particular book will be used in a variety of ways in that setting."

Waymon R. Hinson, PhD
*Chair and Program Director,
Department of Marriage
and Family Therapy,
Abilene Christian University,
Texas*

The Haworth Pastoral Press®
An Imprint of The Haworth Press Inc.
New York • London • Oxford

NOTES FOR PROFESSIONAL LIBRARIANS AND LIBRARY USERS

This is an original book title published by The Haworth Pastoral Press®, an imprint of The Haworth Press, Inc. Unless otherwise noted in specific chapters with attribution, materials in this book have not been previously published elsewhere in any format or language.

CONSERVATION AND PRESERVATION NOTES

All books published by The Haworth Press, Inc. and its imprints are printed on certified pH neutral, acid free book grade paper. This paper meets the minimum requirements of American National Standard for Information Sciences-Permanence of Paper for Printed Material, ANSI Z39.48-1984.

Christ-Centered Therapy
Empowering the Self

THE HAWORTH PASTORAL PRESS
Religion and Mental Health
Harold G. Koenig, MD
Senior Editor

New, Recent, and Forthcoming Titles:

Christ-Centered Therapy
Empowering the Self

Russ Harris, PhD, MDiv, LCSW

The Haworth Pastoral Press®
An Imprint of The Haworth Press Inc.
New York • London • Oxford

Published by

The Haworth Pastoral Press®, an imprint of The Haworth Press, Inc., 10 Alice Street, Binghamton,
NY 13904-1580

© 2002 by The Haworth Press, Inc. All rights reserved. No part of this work may be reproduced or
utilized in any form or by any means, electronic or mechanical, including photocopying, microfilm,
and recording, or by any information storage and retrieval system, without permission in writing
from the publisher. Printed in the United States of America.

All Bible quotes from *Today's English Version*, except where noted.
Client identities and circumstances have been changed to protect confidentiality.

Cover design by Jennifer M. Gaska.

Library of Congress Cataloging-in-Publication Data

Harris, Russ, 1938-
    Christ-centered therapy : empowering the self / Russ Harris.
        p. cm.
    Includes bibliographical references and index.
    ISBN 0-7890-1227-8 (alk. paper)—ISBN 0-7890-1228-6 (alk. paper)
    1. Counseling—Religious aspects—Christianity. 2. Psychotherapy—Religious aspects—Chris-
tianity. I. Title.

BR115.C69 H37 2001
153.5—dc21

                                                                                    2001024394

To John E. Lehman,
mentor, friend, pioneer in integrating pychotherapy
and Christian spirituality

ABOUT THE AUTHOR

Russ Harris, PhD, MDiv, LCSW, has been practicing professional counseling and psychotherapy in Evanston, Illinois, for thirty years, first as an ordained minister, then as a therapist in private practice. He has used his advanced degrees in psychotherapy, theology, and education to integrate counseling, spirituality, and experiential learning in helping clients. He is a member of the National Association of Social Workers, the National Association of Christian Social Workers, and the Paternal Family Systems Association.

CONTENTS

Acknowledgments

I am amazed as I think of the number of people who helped in significant ways over the four years of this writing project. It seems that God led me to them or sent them to me just as I needed help at each stage.

The vision for the project began with Shirley Burnside and colleagues, after I presented a Christ-centered Internal Family System (IFS) workshop for NACSW (North American Association of Christians in Social Work). They described the need for Christian therapists to be introduced to CCIFS in book form. I tried to seek God about considering this need but found myself stuck in self-doubt about the writing. Next, Hal Edwards and the others in a local pastors and therapists group to which I belong saw that I was stuck. They would not let me sidestep the issue. They helped me see that it was my own parts that were stuck in the past and helped me release them.

In the process of freeing my parts and considering if God actually wanted me to write the book, Mike Buren, one of my friends from church and a faculty member at Northwestern University, offered to edit the book if I would write it. This offer dealt with my greatest writing fear and also seemed to be another of God's ways of saying that I should go ahead. I said yes to the project.

Mike helped me organize the concepts and procedures into an outline and table of contents and write a chapter. After Mike's editing, I could see that the project could work. Also, thanks to Mike for marvelously editing all but the last chapter—eliminating the chaff and retaining the wheat.

Much of the credit for the contents and procedures goes to my clients. In their yearning for healing, they trusted God and this new process to reenter their parts' deepest pits of anguish and despair. God always showed the way through.

Major thanks goes to Dick Schwartz, the developer of the IFS model and my teacher and mentor in learning to use the model. Dick, through many workshops and personal mentoring, not only taught those of us in the IFS community to use the model, he also taught us to develop as therapists with our own selves and parts and to develop the model, an empowering experience. Dick's specific encouragement of my vision to extend IFS into Christian spirituality was a pivotal factor in my going ahead with the project.

Various other groups and colleagues have contributed to the discovery of procedures and concepts as the CCIFS model emerged. Those in our monthly IFS group, especially Betty Fisher, Dawna Gutzman, and Sally Stepath, were helpful in letting me test emerging concepts, procedures, and diagrams throughout the project. Reverend Jim and Dr. Sherry Tilley were a steady encouragement to me, showing me the need for the CCIFS model in the churches and using the concepts in their church and practice. They also supported the workshops where I tested the procedures by regularly bringing laypeople.

I am especially grateful to three Christian therapists who included me in their pioneering efforts to combine therapy and faith: John Lehman, my mentor and colleague at Reba Place Church in Evanston; the late Frank Lake, MD*; and Reverend John Bedford, both from England. Also, thanks to other Reba Place Church therapists including Paul Tretbar, Bev Wiebe, and Dan Yutzy.

Many others made special contributions along the way that I would like to acknowledge: Dave and Nita Jackson for their coaching in the writing process; Barbara Pamp for her publishing experience and skill; our daughter and son-in-law, Susanne and Peter Bergeron, for believing that I could accomplish this project and for testing the concepts; Susanne for typing some early chapters; and Hal Edwards for support throughout, sponsoring workshops, and reading the first draft of many chapters.

Special thanks goes to my expert word processor, Donna Norris, for being able to read my writing, for typing most of the chapters and a number of diagrams and tables, and even making them look attractive. Thanks to Ric Hudgens for the big job of indexing; and to Karen Fisher, Jen Durgan, Peg Marr, and the great staff at The Haworth Press for all their expert help.

To Pat, my wife, goes my biggest thanks, for being a companion in exploring our own internal families, for endlessly listening to me try

*Frank Lake authored *Clinical Theology* (1966, London: Darton, Longman and Todd).

to describe new discoveries and procedures, for believing I could do it, for steady encouragement. She even edited the last chapter, and I found she has the magic editing touch, as well. Amazingly, over the years, our selves have grown, our parts have continued healing, and our marriage has grown stronger and more joyful.

Introduction

The Need for a Breakthrough: A Personal Note

The Christ-centered internal family system model (CCIFS) introduced here is relationship centered. It is necessary, therefore, to relate how it developed in my own consciousness over a period of fifteen years as a response to prayer and deep, personal searching. During that time, I was counseling as a Christian pastor and clinical social worker with John Lehman, a clinical social worker, pastor-mentor, and colleague at Reba Place Church, Evanston, Illinois. (Lehman is one of the unpublished pioneers of integrated clinical and spiritual healing.) We saw many people healed in Christian therapy, yet were frustrated that some of the most wounded continued to be stuck in compulsive behaviors, depression, and inner anguish. They were prayed for powerfully and experienced a range of therapies; some even were living in the healing love of Christian community or twelve-step groups. Although many made progress, others continued to be stuck and hopeless. How many of us have felt frustration at not being able to help such people break through into a more functional and truly hopeful mode of living? The last dozen years of my life have been most exciting because the clinical breakthrough I was seeking finally emerged.

Early in this period, the Lord took me into my own valley and brought healing to my deepest wounds and inner conflicts. This prepared me to better walk with clients into their valleys. Then came extended clinical work with Mary Ann (all client names used are fictional), which opened a door to another kind of breakthrough. Mary Ann was approaching sixty-five at the initiation of therapy, a loving Christian woman, but one who suffered for decades with depression.

She was repeatedly in and out of mental hospitals. Her childhood and early years possessed no more than the usual amount of stress, yet here she was entering another period of depression and dysfunction. She appeared headed for another six-month period of hospitalization. I sensed an inner reason for these depressed periods but could not identify it. She had attempted nearly every mode of therapy, medication, and prayer with previous counselors and myself; yet now she was slowly slipping into depression again.

One day we were considering Mary Ann's experience of feeling strongly rejected at depression times, as if someone inside were telling her how terribly inadequate she was. I decided to take this inner dynamic seriously and to consider the rejection as coming from one source in her personality. This implied the existence of another part that believed she was inadequate and accepted the put-down. Entering into a spirit of exploration, I suggested to Mary Ann that she strive to imagine the initiating source of her depression. She immediately saw the image of a critical inner personality she called Henry; then, she perceived a second part, that of a needy three-year-old she named Denise. We began to speak and listen to the two parts. As they had an opportunity to tell their story, Mary Ann became more energized and hopeful. She also sensed her own distinctive character, somehow separate yet including these two parts.

Mary Ann did not appear to have any of the characteristics of confused identity or the significant impairment distinctive of personality disorders. Nor did she satisfy the criterion for multiple personality disorder (dissociative identity disorder), since neither personality state took control of her behavior. She was severely depressed, however; the more we communicated with her two parts, Henry and Denise, the more the put-down dynamic between them diminished. Mary Ann was greatly encouraged and did not need to be hospitalized as feared.

I asked myself: Have we experienced a new mode of understanding and treatment? My excitement grew as Mary Ann returned to part-time work and continued her social life and ministry in the church. Yet many questions were bothering me due to my background in organizational and family systems. How much are systems dynamics at work in Mary Ann's inner network of several parts? What would be the effect of entering further into her inner system? Was our success only accidental? Was it permanent? What part did the Christian faith that Mary Ann and I shared play here, the belief in a Lord who doesn't put us down or strive to have us feel inadequate? I began to think of a hierarchy of empowerment from God to Jesus to Mary Ann's *real* self all the way down to critical Henry and poor Denise (see Figure 1).

A NEW MODEL OF PERSONALITY AND TREATMENT

During the period that Mary Ann and I were relating to her two parts, I interned at the University of Illinois at Chicago, where a faculty trainer, Richard Schwartz, was developing a new model he called the "internal family system." In the process of listening to clients, Schwartz came to see the person as comprised of numerous dimensions or subpersonalities he called "parts." His book, *Internal Family Systems Therapy,** relates that he realized he was following in the footsteps of the pioneers of psychotherapy, Carl Jung and Assagioli, who theorized that the mind is composed of numerous subpersonalities.

Schwartz also brought his training and experience to assist in discovering further ways of understanding how the parts relate to one another. He noticed within each client an entity different from the parts, which manifests a capacity for judgment, self-reflection, and beneficent leadership of the parts. He refers to this entity as the "self," and the self and parts together as the "internal family system" (IFS). The parts and self function as a *system* internal to the personality; he saw that since the powerful dynamics between self and parts are un-

FIGURE 1. Mary Ann's Hierarchy of Empowerment

GOD
|
JESUS
|
MARY ANN

```
+---------------------------------------------------+
|                       SELF                        |
|                        |                          |
|          +-------------+-------------+            |
|     Henry                        Denise           |
|  (critical part)              (needy part)        |
+---------------------------------------------------+
```

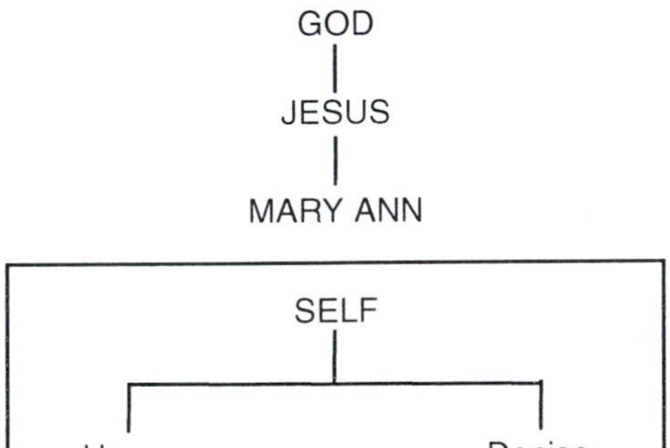

*Schwartz, R. (1997). New York: The Guilford Press.

derstandable, they are treatable. Schwartz also discovered that a respectful therapist could, with permission from the self and parts, enter the internal system to help it change. Another exciting contribution was his discovery that the therapist could serve as a "coach" for the self to grow in its leadership role in the system.

By the time I encountered Schwartz's work, he had developed a body of concepts and techniques, along with a history of treatment successes that were shared by a network of therapists and practitioners. As a model of understanding and treating the inner human struggle for change and growth, I felt the IFS model could appropriately be called a breakthrough and adopted it in my work with clients. Over the past ten years, I have found that it deserves this original estimate, as a *breakthrough in the search for ways to help stuck people.*

APPLICATION OF IFS
IN A CHRIST-CENTERED CONTEXT

Internal Family System

Following my successful experience with Mary Ann, I set about absorbing and practicing IFS theory and techniques with appropriate clients. Most of them caught on quickly and enjoyed working in the IFS style. I have always used an outcome-centered approach that strives to measure effectiveness. Thus, it immediately became clear that when using the IFS approach, my clients worked harder, progressed more quickly, and gained more self-confidence than with other models used in the past. I also discovered that the "coaching" role provided by the model was personally satisfying and allowed me to utilize my spiritual as well as clinical knowledge and skills as appropriate.

At an early point, I turned to the IFS model in a different way—for help for myself. I had over a period of time become overwhelmed with work and somewhat depressed. In addition to my clients at Reba Place Church, I had clients at the University of Illinois at Chicago; my academic work in the final year of a clinical program was demanding, and I was teaching one day a week at a local seminary. Schwartz put me in touch with Bart Mann, an IFS senior trainer at the university. With his help, I began to discover my own internal family. I found within me a "caretaker" part that pushed me into taking on too many responsibilities and a young, anxious part, "future guy," who always worried about tomorrow's responsibilities and problems (the opposite of what Jesus commended for a life of faith). Underneath them was a frightened and needy five-year-old. These parts pushed me to an overloaded schedule with the subsequent depression and loss of self-confidence.

Mann helped me to establish a caring relationship with my parts and to restore my self to its leadership role. I learned to adjust my workload and, more important, to integrate a relationship with Jesus into this new understanding of my inner family system. Since Jesus was the center of my life and the source of my creative activity, I began then to recover my original inspiration. My purpose for being a counselor became clear; it was not to rescue or fix people as my parts wanted, but to serve God and others with the clinical abilities God had given me.

With this reorientation, the unruly parts began to loosen their grip on me; my self's leadership began to be spiritual rather than just social. Since my original empowering came when I learned to center my life around Jesus, I now began to help those parts center around me as leader and around Jesus as Lord and Son of the Father. In this way, they could properly use their energy and gifts and not just be blown about by the demands of a needy world (see Figure 2).

When I introduced clients to the IFS model, I saw how their parts needed a nourishing relationship with their self, just as my parts did. With Christian clients, I saw how they, like me, needed an empowering relationship with Jesus. We discovered how eager Jesus is to be part of the healing process. Sometimes clients are afraid to revisit deep memories; but when Jesus goes back with us, they are confident enough to begin the healing process. Many times Jesus himself goes into the "scene" at the request of a part to minister to the needs of the part.

At other times, Christian clients learned to establish a deeper relationship with Jesus where previously past and present difficulties blocked the transforming power of the cross from reaching them (Ephesians 1:19-20). Together we discovered how a frightened, skeptical part can keep the self from an empowering relationship with Jesus, because it is afraid He will reject it, just as a parent may have done in the past. We saw it is possible to help the self "unhook" from the negative influence of extreme parts. With care and reassurance, parts will eventually allow the self to develop a new, transforming relationship with Jesus. Experiencing that Jesus is loving and trustworthy,

FIGURE 2. Russ' Hierarchy of Empowerment

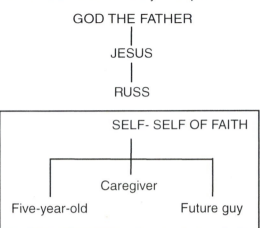

the self can then take frightened parts to Him to discover this for themselves. As healing progresses, the parts become free to change and will eventually contribute to the effectiveness of the whole personality.

There are non-Christian clients who yearn to develop a spiritual center for their lives but are blocked by doubts and fears from the past. After trust is established with the self and with me, their parts will allow the self to meet Jesus and see how trustworthy He is. Other clients are drawn directly to a relationship with God. Many times the client's self, and later the parts, discover God as the source of unconditional love and begin a spiritual pilgrimage that eventually transforms life itself.

The Holy Spirit often emerges early in the process of applying IFS in a Christ-centered context. Jesus promised he would send an Advocate and Helper (John 16:7) who is God's own spirit of compassion and power. Over time I began to see the presence of this Helper in the client's internal system as part of the leadership team with Jesus and the self. The self has the incredible task of finding a way to live in the world and yet not be of the world (John 17:15-16). Parts that are oriented around living in the world will be in conflict with the self when the self is oriented around Jesus (Romans 8:15); the Holy Spirit is needed to stay in touch with God and not be of the world. I pictured the Spirit embodied in a "self of faith" who is invited to share leadership with the self.

With these discoveries, the Christ-centered extension of IFS emerged. Later, in training other Christian therapists, I began to call the model Christ-centered internal family systems therapy (CCIFS). This new approach was consistently helping clients, both Christian and non-Christian where appropriate, in breaking through to growth and meaningful living. They urged me to make it available in book form as soon as possible.

THOSE WHO WILL FIND THIS BOOK HELPFUL

I asked colleagues: Who are the readers who would find this book useful? Initially, we considered only Christian therapists and pastors asking for help in integrating IFS with Christian spirituality. Some therapists also want to integrate their clinical work with a spiritual dimension. We realized that a wide range of caregivers, secular and religious, professional and volunteer, might find the CCIFS model valuable in their own professional and spiritual development: for example, teachers K through 12 who relate to students and their parts regularly; clergy, trainers, and group leaders in the church setting; doctors, nurses, and physical therapists who often work with people depressed or in crisis; college teachers and seminary professors; social workers and police. In addition to the many professionals who serve others, general readers would appreciate learning these new developments in clinical practice and spirituality. My colleagues also thought the book could be useful as a text in graduate clinical courses.

AN INVITATION TO A JOURNEY OF DISCOVERY

This book has several purposes best explained at the outset. It proposes to:

1. *Introduce the IFS model* to those not yet acquainted with it as a new way of understanding and changing intrapsychic systems.
2. *Explain the CCIFS model* as an extension of IFS into Christian spirituality. It will describe the new concepts and techniques with the help of case studies as appropriate.

3. *Offer four new procedures* to equip clients' selves to lead their parts in dealing with challenging life situations in creative and Godly new ways.

4. *Invite the reader into a personal journey of discovery* as you consider your own internal family, your life journey, and growth in self leadership of your parts. You need not be a Christian or even a person interested in spiritual matters to do the exercises provided to assist in this process; whenever an exercise has a Christian or spiritual slant, it offers an alternative. Each chapter in all three sections concludes with such a personal exercise.

CONTENTS AND ORGANIZATION

The first of three sections, The Internal Family System Model, describes the IFS model in two chapters: The first sets forth IFS *concepts*. The second describes the clinical techniques, IFS *therapy*. With these as a foundation, the second section presents Christ-Centered IFS (CCIFS) in two parallel chapters: CCIFS *concepts* and CCIFS *therapy*.

The third section introduces four new leadership tools for equipping clients' selves to lead their parts in meeting challenging life situations. These tools are described in four chapters. The first chapter describes the first tool, the forgiveness process. The next three tools are presented in turn in the last three chapters as three linked sequences called the flowchart. The first tool equips the self to spot the parts taking the self in a downward spiral. The second tool enables the self to unhook from the parts and empower with God. The third tool coaches the self in developing new Christ-centered responses to the situation. The result is that the self can use the three tools separately or linked together according to the self's needs to proactively meet the new situation.

My hope is that in reading *Christ-Centered Therapy: Empowering the Self* and applying the concepts to your service of others or your own inner system, you will help not only your clients through some previously stuck places but also you may be able to move through some stuck places on your own life journey. May God be with you!

EXERCISE:
BEGINNING THE PERSONAL APPLICATION

The following exercise strives to assist you in beginning the personal application. Review the sections of this introductory chapter and give responses (in thought or in writing) to the following:

1. What do you think of the presentation of the CCIFS model in the example of Mary Ann? Do you sense parts and a self in yourself?
2. What is your initial reaction to the concept of the self and the parts as an inner system? Are you aware of systemic connections between your parts?
3. Which of the following reasons do you have for reading further *and why?*

    a. To further your knowledge and skill in order to help others in some service capacity?
    b. To enhance your own self-knowledge?
    c. To advance your spiritual growth?
    d. Other reasons?

4. What plans do you have about how you might read further ahead in the book? Select certain chapters and sections? Start reading in the given chapter sequence?

SECTION I:
THE INTERNAL FAMILY SYSTEM MODEL

This section, the first of three sections, describes the IFS model. The first chapter describes the IFC *concepts,* followed by a chapter on clinical techniques, IFS *therapy.* The second section introduces the Christ-centered IFS model, CCIFS, in the parallel chapters: CCIFS *concepts* and CCIFS *therapy.* The third section presents four new leadership tools for equipping clients' selves to lead their parts in meeting challenging life situations.

Those who are familiar with IFS therapy may choose to skip Section I and go to Section II. However, it could be valuable to skim through, noticing the cartoons, exercises, and the figure, "Raymond's Internal Family."

Chapter 1

Basic Internal Family System Concepts

MULTIPLICITY AND SYSTEMS:
TWO FOUNDATIONAL CONCEPTS OF IFS

Jane had just returned from fifteen years in Asia and, before that, ten years in Africa. Yet as I listened to her ambivalence about a current job search in the United States, I could see the multiplicity in her self-description: "Part of me wants to get going on this job search before I run out of money, but another part is worried about taking time to consider what I must do at this stage and how God plans to use me." I wondered, has this IFS concept of having different parts to our personality now spread to Asia and Africa? (It does seem to be more a part of our everyday vocabulary.) I also rejoiced that Jane felt free to consider her contradictory needs. Jane did not have to see herself solely as a "practical person" and thus deny a need for a wider view of her vocational interests, nor did she consider herself only as a servant of God and deny her financial anxieties. She could hold the two aspects together and accept them both as *parts* of her. She was enjoying the freedom provided by the concept known as "multiplicity of mind."

The multiplicity paradigm views the human mind as comprised of numerous subpersonalities. Richard Schwartz, in working with clients and studying the pioneers of psychotherapy, claims that it is the nature of the human mind to be divided into subpersonalities or "parts" as he prefers to call them. A trained family therapist, Schwartz went on to apply systems thinking to his work with individuals. He noted that clients' parts interact in patterns understandable to family systems thinking; thus, he termed their interaction an "internal family system." Schwartz consistently noticed an entity different from parts within the client, which he calls the "self"; it appears to lead the parts with judgment, self-reflection, and compassion. He also discovered that a respectful therapist could, with permission from the self and parts, enter the internal system to help it change. Along with a network of therapists including myself, Schwartz developed a body of concepts and techniques that began to produce a history of treatment successes—internal family systems therapy.

A Personal Aside

My own use and development of internal family systems (IFS) therapy for the past ten years has been quite fruitful; I have found the IFS model to be a real breakthrough in my search for ways to help stuck people. As a pastor-therapist working with Christian clients, I have also extended the IFS model into the Christian's daily walk with the Lord Jesus. These efforts have developed into what I call "Christ-centered IFS" (CCIFS).

This book serves as an introduction to my spiritual application of a successful therapeutic model. This first chapter will summarize the IFS concepts for readers not already familiar with them. In the next chapter I will review the therapy techniques of IFS. With these two chapters as foundation, the remainder of the book is given to describing the concepts and techniques of CCIFS. I find the IFS model to be respectful, nonblaming, and empowering of clients. It gives them the tools to truly understand themselves and enables them to "release their stuck parts," thus mobilizing their full strengths.

Please consider reading this book to be an invitation to a clinical-spiritual adventure, either to explore new ways of helping others in a professional capacity or to discover more about your own self and parts. At the end of each chapter a short summary and exercise is included to help with this journey. If you are familiar with the characteristics and dynamics of the internal family systems model, skip forward to Section II which introduces the Christian dimension as CCIFS.

VIEWING THE INDIVIDUAL AS A SYSTEM: THE SECOND CONCEPT

Dr. Sczerny's secretary in the cartoon (see Figure 1.1) is apparently helping the doctor's clients relate to *his* internal family. In Schwartz's terms we can assume that "Dr. Sczerny" refers to his self;

FIGURE 1.1. Dr. Sczerny's Parts

Reprinted by permission of Raymond Larrett.

his "feminine side" refers to a caring or nurturing part (since he is a psychoanalyst), and we can only speculate about the "child inside him." This "child" could be playful or needy; or is it carrying wounds from childhood (like many in the helping professions), finding satisfaction through caring for others' wounded parts? We presume other parts exist in his system; perhaps he has a self-critical part and an achiever part (or he never would have gotten through grad school). He may also have an angry part that defends the child part. Together they constitute an *internal system.*

Knowing one's inner family and how the members interact with one another can help us understand much about why we suddenly become impatient, yelling at the kids; or why we at times get angry "for no reason whatsoever;" or even why we repeatedly engage in compulsive behavior, not able to stop ourselves even though it harms us or others. This is the foundation of IFS therapy: the application of multiplicity and systems thinking to the intrapsychic realm, which in turn makes our internal world far more understandable and treatable.

To understand IFS, we first must consider the characteristics of parts and the role of the self in the internal system. But first a short account of a startling encounter with some of my own parts to illustrate the characteristics.

CHARACTERISTICS OF PARTS AND SELF
IN THE INTERNAL SYSTEM

Ten years ago as I was just discovering my parts and those of my clients, I found myself one day suddenly caught in the infamous Chicago rush hour. I had just purchased a sporty little fiberglass sailboat and was towing it home to nearby Evanston when traffic seemed to swallow me up. I tried to reassure myself that I need not worry; I had only a short distance to travel and no deadline to meet. Yet I found myself cutting in and out of traffic attempting to find a slightly faster lane of travel. I soon realized, however, that changing lanes while towing a boat was a bit dangerous.

Suddenly, all lanes ground to a halt as traffic appeared to be backed up for blocks. My anxiety escalated. I spotted movement in the lane to my right; so, with a quick glance over my right shoulder, I swerved the car toward the right lane. At this point, I heard a horrible scrape of metal, the screech of brakes, and a loud male voice yelling. It did not take long to realize I was the "stupid idiot" he was yelling at. I had just put a three-feet-long crease in the fender of his car. He had been in my blind spot, and I had pulled out so hastily I had not taken the time to look carefully. I certainly felt like the "stupid idiot" he was proclaiming me to be.

I took a deep breath, got out of my car, and apologized; he eventually stopped yelling. On my way home, I shamefacedly kept asking myself, "How could I have done such a stupid thing?" At home later, after I finished blaming myself for my foolishness, I began to journal on the question of why I had been so impulsive. So far as I know, I had never acted like this before. Was it possible to understand this impulsiveness, so I could avoid repeating it another time? I recalled the anxiety proceeding the accident and began to sense a very young part within me who feels it is his job to energize me in tight spots and emergencies. Apparently, he perceived the traffic jam as an emergency. When he observed the traffic closing in, he triggered a strong impulse to action to escape being swallowed up. After the collision, a second part within was activated, who agreed with the other driver that I was indeed a "stupid idiot." This part I recognized as my critical part. Then a third part emerged who felt the embarrassment and guilt for doing such a "stupid thing."

As I began to see how my various parts had been triggered, the entire sequence of behaviors made more sense. Fortunately, in the midst of it, I had not lost touch inwardly with the God who loves me for myself and not for my performance. Furthermore, I was able to talk to my parts, reassure them, and consider with them how to prevent this from happening again. Eventually, I was able to see the incident as comparatively cheap learning experience that could help to prevent a more serious accident in the future. And, painfully, I saw that I needed to work much more with the young "panic part" within me.

In attempting to understand my reactions to the entire incident, I recalled some of the characteristic patterns of behavior that Schwartz had described earlier in my studies with him. They are listed as follows.

The Parts

1. *Parts are experienced by us in various ways: thoughts, feelings, sensations, desires, and behaviors.* My rising anxiety, the impulsive behavior, the condemning thoughts, and the feelings of guilt all illustrate ways my parts manifested themselves in that situation.

2. *Activated parts can set off other parts in a chain reaction (called sequences) among themselves.* My parts' reactions illustrated such a sequence: the panicked part caused the accident, which in turn triggered the critical part, causing embarrassment for the guilty part.

3. *All parts want positive things for the individual and will use a variety of strategies to bring this about.* This appears difficult to believe, considering the damage and pain caused by my panicked part and later my critical part. Yet, when seen through the eyes of the parts, the proposition makes sense. My panicked part was trying to rescue me from being "swallowed up and crushed" by the traffic jam; for him, it was the same as being swallowed up and crushed by angry parents. The critical part was trying to get me to meet people's expectations, so I would be liked; and the guilty part was carrying the shame and embarrassment for the whole inner family, so the rest of us wouldn't be disabled. To my adult mind, these are not healthy strategies, but at the time it was the best the parts knew to do.

4. *When not extreme, parts can be creative and use their innate gifts to contribute to the well-being of the whole.* Not illustrated by my traffic mishap, this point is nonetheless important. A goal of therapy is to free parts from their burdens and extreme states, so they can contribute their gifts to the whole. How can such a transformation happen? Schwartz notes that the self has the capacity to lead the inner family wisely, so that each part does not have to struggle for control for fear that other parts will take over.

The Self

1. *The self, at a different level than the parts, has innate qualities giving it a perspective that encompasses the whole individual.* As I was changing traffic lanes before the accident, I had at times a clear and realistic perspective—that there is no need to hurry, that the rapid lane changing could be dangerous. This was the more balanced perspective of my self.

2. *The self can be overwhelmed by the parts, by the speed of their reactions, and the intensity of their emotions.* This is what seemed to cause the crash. My self was momentarily overwhelmed by the panic part and the more balanced perspective of the self was lost.

3. *When the self is unhooked (differentiated) from the parts, its leadership qualities are available: self-awareness, perspective, balanced judgment, empathy, and compassion. It can then be competent, self-assured, and relaxed. Thus, the self can lead the internal system, bringing the parts into a harmonious relationship with one another. Each part then feels safe and can make an appropriate contribution to the well-being of the whole inner family.* During and after the accident, my parts felt very unsafe; they had good reason to fear the power of the panic part. They could easily have developed dislike and anger toward the panic part and looked for ways to punish and keep him from influencing my driving again. Fortunately, my self did not stay overwhelmed long, but soon after the accident appraised the situation and apologized to the other driver. Later, I reflected on the situation, discovered the panic part, and reassured each internal part. The harmony and well-being of my inner family was gradually restored, and my parts did not stay extreme and polarized against one another.

4. *The self can learn to unhook from the parts and to teach them to respect and not overwhelm the self.* My capacity to take charge after

the accident, analyze the situation, and respond appropriately suggests that the parts had stepped back to let my self lead the process of straightening out the mess. Later, when I discovered the panic part, I hoped to discover what triggered his reaction. This way I could help him find a less damaging way of letting me know he was distressed. I also wanted to find a way to prevent being overwhelmed by him in the future, especially in traffic. Situations where parts regularly distrust the self and take control will be addressed in the next chapter.

THE THREE-GROUP SYSTEM OF PARTS

Schwartz organizes the parts around three categories of roles that we use to help ourselves cope with trauma and stress. He names these "exiles," "managers," and "firefighters." We see the *exiles* illustrated well in the Jules Feiffer cartoon (see Figure 1.2). The man, head slumped down, observes to himself that he is "deeply depressed." Perhaps it is this recognition of depression that moves him to talk with an "inner child." Such a nurturing decision seems to come from the self. In frames two, three, and four he finds the child "digging his way toward his heart" because, as he claims, the man "abandoned him at 12." The child part says that the man treats him "worse than he does his 3 kids." Because of the child's reference to abandonment, we can surmise that the man neglects his children as well as his own inner child. This fits with the child's desire to tunnel to the man's heart, considered to be the seat of love. Perhaps the child is starved for attention and love.

The child has the qualities of an exiled part; as a young part that has experienced trauma, an exile can become isolated from the family system in an effort to protect the individual from feeling the painful emotions it is carrying. Exiles can become even more extreme over time in an effort to be cared for and "get their story out." Frame three suggests that some type of abandonment occurred at twelve years of age that is still unresolved. The other parts appear to have exiled the child part, probably because the pain he carries is too great to remain in consciousness. He seems to have gotten quite extreme in his effort to be cared for.

In frame five the child part implies he is afraid that someone (the self or another part) is trying to bury him, and in desperation says he will torture the man until he dies. In frame six it appears that the man

20

FIGURE 1.2. The Depressed Man and His Parts

FEIFFER © 1992 JULES FEIFFER. Reprinted with permission of UNIVERSAL PRESS SYNDICATE. All rights reserved.

is being conciliatory toward the child part by inviting him to play ball. In frames seven and eight, however, we realize that the playful invitation is a disguised trick: the man rejoices and pronounces himself "cured." The reader is left with a sense of horrible confusion, as the realization comes that the invitation to play is actually a diabolical assassination attempt.

Who pulled off the trick? Would the self have tried to get rid of the child part? No. It has already been noted that the character of the self when unhooked from the parts is secure, relaxed, and capable of compassionate, competent leadership of the parts. It is more likely that a part with a hidden agenda has blended with the self. The self believes it is leading the way in talking with the child part; the definitive clue is that the positive leadership capacity of the self has been lost. What kind of part would want to get rid of an exiled part? One possibility is a manager part.

Managers are parts that conduct our day-to-day life, trying to keep the exiles in captivity so that their painful agenda is kept from consciousness. They accomplish this by controlling events, people, and other parts with such strategems as striving for goals, caretaking and pleasing, criticizing, avoiding, etc. It is likely that the invitation to the child in frame six is from a manager speaking through the self. He is doing his job of protecting the system by dealing with the perceived threat of the extreme child.

The final category of parts is the firefighters. *Firefighters* are parts that work hard to control and even extinguish the strong feelings of exiles when they break out. They do this through extreme behavior: drug or alcohol use, binge eating, sexual addiction, self-mutilation, clinical depression, physical or emotional violence. Like managers, their goal is to keep the exiles' painful agenda away from consciousness; they just use different strategies to accomplish this.

Schwartz emphasizes that when firefighters are called in, the building is already "on fire." The managers have not been able to contain the exiles' threat to the system in exposing painful feelings and making the individual vulnerable and fragile. One panel hints that a firefighter is involved in the cartoon situation: the reference in frame one to deep depression. A firefighter might depress the man to dampen painful feelings that an exile is trying to bring into consciousness. The firefighter seems compelled to act from a lack of confidence in a manager's ability to contain the exile. He thinks depressed feelings are safer than alcohol, drugs, sex, gambling, or whatever.

The three categories of parts (exiles, managers, and firefighters) carry different responsibilities in maintaining and protecting the equilibrium of the inner family, and it is essential to understand their roles in working with the dynamics of the inner system. The cartoon illustrates also the extreme states that parts can attain when struggling against one another. What follows is a description of two common extreme states—polarization and burdens.

PARTS STUCK IN EXTREME STATES

Polarization is an unfortunate dynamic between parts occurring when they become rigidly stuck in a posture of opposition to each other. A noticeable dynamic in the cartoon is the powerful enmity between the child and the manager parts. As they strive to exterminate each other, each feels that if it backs down, the other will dominate and the system will be severely damaged. What is not so clear in this vicious circle of escalation is that a firefighter causing the depression is polarized against them both. He takes on the child because of the threat of abandonment feelings being dumped into consciousness; he is polarized against the homicidal manager as well, because he considers him incompetent. The firefighter must outescalate the other two to do his job, and he might accomplish this by deepening the depression to the point of suicidal thoughts and the need for hospitalization.

What about the leadership capacities of the self to bring harmony? In the Feiffer cartoon, the self cannot help the parts depolarize because it has been co-opted by the manager in trying to lure the child into traffic to eliminate him. By siding with the manager, the self demonstrates to the child that he must escalate further to get his needs met. Thus, the self has now become part of the problem rather than the solution. A *burden* is a constraint given to a part to carry for the inner family, such as a traumatic memory, a core belief such as worthlessness, a hopeless or resentful attitude, or a harmful protective role within the inner family. The child in the cartoon is the part most likely to be carrying a burden. The clue Feiffer gives us is that the child experienced some kind of "abandonment" at age twelve. Did the father or mother die or leave him? From the severity of the polarization, it appears something this serious happened. Schwartz notes that where such trauma occurs, if needed love and comfort is not given, the vulnerable part becomes "frozen in time" with the traumatic event, doomed to live it out thereafter as if fixed in that terrible situation. Other parts then distance that part from the self and themselves to keep the trauma from reaching them. The frozen part is thus *burdened* with carrying the trauma for the system. Other parts are also burdened with protective managerial roles or compensatory roles in which they also feel stuck. This could be the case in the cartoon: the child carrying the pain of the abandonment forever stuck at the twelve-year-old stage, with the other parts organized to keep him exiled from them and from the self.

When vulnerable, parts can take on additional burdens such as extreme ideas, behaviors, or feelings. When abused or neglected by a critical or unaffirming parent figure, for example, a child may conclude that he or she is lacking in value and never will meet parents' expectations. This belief of worthlessness and unlovability will stay for good, regardless of love subsequently given by others. Such convictions, known as "core beliefs" in clinical literature, can be used by the inner system in reorganizing the parts toward powerful coping styles.

One such coping style is the need for "redemption from worthlessness." The parts become desperate for redemption in the eyes of the person who gave the worthless message. Schwartz says the person on whom the child depends becomes a redeemer and the parts constantly seek the "lifting of what feels like a curse of unlovability." Other parts may take on the qualities of that person or another substitute. Then parts mimic the behavior or ideas of the important person or substitute, and strive to find ways to meet their expectations in the hope of winning approval and finally becoming redeemed and acceptable.

We can imagine that the cartoon character's child carries some of this deep-seated burden. Perhaps the outward sign, the depression, will serve as a wake-up call for family, friends, or employer to encourage him to get help. Schwartz, with the use of internal family systems therapy, has discovered powerful ways to help people find and release such burdens and to help parts back away from polarizations. The self can then be elevated to its proper position of leadership, where its gifts will be used to enhance the mutual functioning of the whole inner family.

CHAPTER SUMMARY

This chapter has attempted to explain basic internal family systems concepts as a foundation for understanding IFS therapy and for presenting Christ-centered IFS therapy. It began by explaining two foundational concepts, multiplicity and systems. *Multiplicity* asserts that it is the nature of the human mind to be divided into subpersonalities called parts. *Systems* as a concept views the personality as a living system of parts meaningfully organized in a family relationship, thus the name "internal family system." With the use of these two concepts, inner psychic relationships are more understandable and thus more treatable.

The chapter noted that the *self* is a different entity from the parts, and has the innate capacity for a broader perspective. When unhooked from the parts, it can lead with wisdom so that the internal family functions harmoniously, with parts contributing their gifts to the functioning of the whole.

All *parts* want something positive for the individual; however, individual parts can become extreme and trigger destructive sequences in other parts. Parts also can become *polarized* against one another and against the self in vicious escalating cycles. In such situations, the self becomes overwhelmed as different parts try to gain influence over one another.

The chapter described how parts can be more deeply understood by observing their three role responsibilities, as exiles, managers, and firefighters. *Exiles* have experienced trauma and are assigned to carry the trauma for the system. They are isolated from the self and other parts to protect the system from painful emotions. Exiles can then become extreme and desperate to be cared for. *Managers* attempt to control our daily lives, so that the pain of the exiles remains out of consciousness. The *firefighters* react when the managers seem to fail at keeping control and isolating the exiles. They deal with urgent situations and must devise more powerful and compulsive strategies to protect the inner family. Firefighters can trigger another round of escalation among parts in which the parts become still more extreme. The chapter identified this dynamic where parts are stuck in opposition to each other as *polarization* and noted the danger of vicious cycles of escalation. Here parts become even more extreme to counter one another's escalations.

The chapter noted one additional way parts get stuck. *Burdens* are put on them, such as painful memories or core beliefs such as worthlessness. Sadly, burdened parts are stuck or frozen in time at the point where the trauma happened or the burden was put on them. The goal of therapy is not to eliminate our inner parts or even identify them as bad or problematic, but to unburden, release, and restore them to a nonextreme state where they can contribute to the internal family and to the leadership of the self. The next chapter will review the techniques developed by IFS therapy for elevating the self and freeing the parts.

EXERCISE: SEEKING YOUR INTERNAL FAMILY SYSTEM

Consider your own internal family as you ponder the usefulness of these concepts for you. Block out fifteen to thirty minutes for an interruption-free time. Have a notebook or journal and pen available. Draw a line down the center of a page to be your worksheet, following the example in Figure 1.3.

1. Begin with a few minutes of deep breathing and relaxing.
2. If you are so inclined, ask God to give you objectivity about yourself and a respect for yourself and your parts.
3. When you are ready, let yourself recall a recent stress situation that was intense, but not more intense than you wish to review at this time.
4. Describe the situation in a word or phrase at the top of your sheet.
5. Now mentally return to the situation and permit yourself to feel again the sensations of stress. Recall what you said to yourself and how you acted in the situation.
6. In the left column of your page, list each feeling, sensation, self-statement, and behavior, with one item per line.
7. When finished, consider the first feeling or response and what part may have caused it. Select a tentative name for it, and list this in the right column. You can make up a personal name or a descriptive name such as "the angry part" or "the critical part." Other common parts: achiever part, pleaser, caretaker, fearful

part, and various ages of child or adolescent parts. Firefighters can be designated by what they urge you to do: excessive eating, drinking of alcohol, sexual activity, as well as anger and violence. Avoid judgmental names such as "stupid part" or "worthless part." Select a name for each part, and list it in the right column.

8. Then consider if there are other parts which did not get activated by this situation. Add them to this list.

9. Locate around a "board of directors table" (see Figure 1.3) the parts that seek to run your life for you (managers); then away from the table, locate to one side your parts that appear to be exiles; place those that seem to be firefighters to the other side. Where would you locate your self and why?

Note: Now that you have made a systematic beginning in identifying your own internal family, you will want to reflect on the following questions:

- What do you observe about how your parts affect you, your attitudes about yourself, and your ability to conduct your life?
- Do you find you like some parts and dislike others? (You may be discovering a polarization where parts are trying to get you to join with them against other parts.)
- What kind of situations trigger your parts?
- Do you notice when your parts are activated? Is so, how do you respond to them?
- How satisfied are you with any patterns you notice?
- Do you notice any parts which are burdened or polarized? If so, would you like to help them? How could you do this?
- How much freedom do you think you have for leading your parts? or to help them?

Now try to step back from taking sides, and be equally respectful of all the parts even though you may not understand why they act as they do at this stage. Consider if you want to find an accepting friend with whom you can share some of your self-observations.

FIGURE 1.3. Seeking Your Internal Family System

A stress situation recently experienced _____

_____

Effect of the situation on me (feelings, self-statement, urges, images, actions)   Select a name for the part that is likely to be causing each effect

_____   _____

_____   _____

_____   _____

_____   _____

_____   _____

_____   _____

_____   _____

Other possible parts which did not get activated

_____

_____

_____

Seat your <u>Manager</u> parts around the table drawn below. Locate your <u>Exiles</u> to one side and your <u>Firefighters</u> to the other side. Where would you place yourself? Why?

Chapter 2

IFS Therapy:
Changing the Internal System

This chapter introduces the techniques of IFS therapy and uses one client's therapy for illustration. In doing this, it builds on the IFS concepts of Chapter 1. The two chapters can then serve as a foundation for the presentation of Christ-centered IFS therapy. The chapter concludes with a summary of the procedural steps of IFS therapy and an exercise.

RAYMOND:
A CASE STUDY OF CHANGING
THE INTERNAL SYSTEM

Raymond was an attractive forty-two-year-old single teacher. Friendly and personable, he shared an apartment with a male roommate. His concern at the beginning of therapy was an inability to relate to adult single women; he felt he lacked the "courage" for dating and sustaining relationships. He noticed that when talking about his singleness with friends or with his adult students in class, he became embarrassed, got sweaty palms, and felt panicky. All four of Raymond's siblings were married and raising families, and he felt he was missing out on an important dimension of life. In therapy, he sought help in relating to women so he could be "fully human" and "free to move toward marriage" or to choose to remain single.

INTRODUCING THE IFS MODEL

As I listened to Raymond's description of his fears and distress, I sensed different parts at work in his inner family. I assumed they had their reasons for keeping him from relating and would help us understand if we asked them. I considered how to introduce Ray to IFS language and concepts, since this is a first necessary step. Clients thereby are able to identify their inner parts and the chains that weigh them down. They then can enter into an active, collaborative role with the therapist as healing coach.

Introducing the Parts Language and Concepts

As I listened to Raymond's story, I repeated what I was hearing back to him in parts language: "It sounds like you have a part inside you that is very cautious and fearful about relating to single women, probably for very good reason. It also seems there is another part that gets down on you for lack of courage." Ray affirmed that both were true. One part is frightened—we named him "the fearful part"; the other part calls him a coward and said he is "no good"—dubbed "the critical part."

Ray had had an intuitive sense of these parts and was relieved to hear me say that we all have various parts inside us that try to take over at times or fight one another and make us feel out of control. Paraphrasing St. Paul, I said, "At times they make us do things we don't want to do or keep us from doing what we would like to do" (Romans 7:15). I told him that even though the parts become extreme at times, they really want what is good for us. I also discussed the self with its capacity to lead the parts in becoming less extreme. When I said that I could help his self learn to lead the parts, he was interested and encouraged and wanted to continue.

Determining Whether the Client Wants to Proceed with IFS Therapy

Clients quickly grasp the idea of parts existing to their personality, especially when illustrated with their own emotions, self-statements, and actions. It helps to normalize this by emphasizing that everyone has these parts, and they are often much relieved to know they are normal, not "crazy as I thought." Ray felt empowered to know that I did not think he lacked courage as his critical part believed. I made sure he realized that I saw him as a person whose parts responded in seemingly mysterious ways, yet they would reveal their reasons in time so we could help them. The IFS model with the concepts of self and parts effectively carries the message that the client has the capacity to assist the parts in dealing with problems. When this message is reinforced by the therapist's coaching attitude and behavior, the client feels greatly encouraged and empowered. It is important at this point to check with clients as to whether they want to proceed in this manner. Ray was encouraged by the parts language and did want to go forward.

GETTING TO KNOW THE TERRITORY

Identifying Parts and Determining Their Relationships

In our first session, Ray and I had identified a critical part and a fearful part; I later asked if he was aware of any others. He said that he always has had a strong urge to please his mother, who is at times opinionated and overbearing; he also often looks for approval elsewhere. This suggested the presence of a "people pleaser" part. This was confirmed by memories that while his father sat on the sidelines, his mother often tried to get the children to conform to her ideas, but his siblings resisted while Ray did not.

In high school, Ray felt restricted by his mother's ethical standards and did not feel free to experiment with dating; when he did date he found it an uncomfortable experience. In college, he did not date at all, due, he felt, to pressure for good grades and his fear of asking girls out. He told himself that he did not have the social skills and would not know what to do on a date. He regularly had feelings of loneliness and regret at the time from missing out on close relationships with women. We agreed there was probably a fourth part inside, which felt the loneliness and regret, and called it the "lonely part."

I asked if there might be an angry, resentful-at-his-mother part; Ray agreed, but added that it is usually "pushed to the side." When I asked if other parts are pushed aside, he said yes, especially one that, at times, gives him sexual impulses with lustful thoughts or fantasies. We agreed to call these parts the "angry part" and the "sexual part."

Ray and I then considered the relationship of the identified parts to one another. It seemed the critical part was pushing him to take risks in relationships with women, but the fearful part managed to block all these efforts. They seemed to be manager parts polarized against each other for control over how Ray conducted his social life. We agreed to be respectful of them and to avoid being drawn into taking sides (see Figure 2.1).

The people-pleaser part appeared to be a manager as well. The lonely part, however, was an exile pushed away by managers because of the power of the lonely part's needy feelings to push Ray into relationships. The angry part and sexual part were probably firefighters who get activated only when the lonely part is in great distress.

In making such initial assessments of parts we recognize they are only hypotheses to be tested later. It is important in therapy to let the parts speak for themselves; thus they will confirm, disconfirm, or modify the initial hypotheses. This minimizes the danger of erroneous interpretations and avoids the mistake of entering the system unknowingly by taking sides or triggering off protective or destructive parts.

After an initial reading of the parts present and their relationships is a good time to explain to the client other more subtle aspects of the model. As I described each of the following points for Ray, he quickly understood them and grew more hopeful about the possibilities of change.

1. There is a self which has the capacity to help the parts change and work together.
2. The parts themselves all are trying to accomplish something positive although it often does not work out well.
3. The parts have the capacity to change and grow.
4. All parts have a continuing place in the internal family where they can contribute to the whole.

These ideas are encouraging to most of the parts (who are usually listening) and help to calm their fears about being discarded. They also encourage the client, who begins to realize he or she has the capacity to lead. The therapist's respect for the self is also noted by the parts and helps to reinforce the parts' respect for the self.

The therapist is aware that often the parts' sense of control is threatened by elevating the self and that work must proceed carefully. He or she welcomes any parts who are interrupting and lets them express their fears and concerns about the therapy in progress. This re-

FIGURE 2.1. Raymond's Internal Family

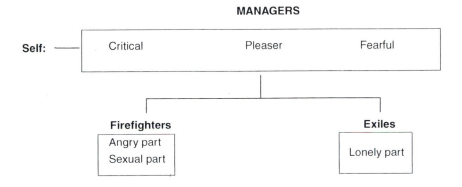

spectful approach is consistent with the goal of therapy, which is to empower the parts rather than see them as resistance to be overcome, as often is the temptation.

Consider the Safety of the Client

The last step is to assess the safety of the client's external situation. Are there circumstances or relationships on the job or at home that negatively activate the parts? Are there positive circumstances or relationships that would be threatened by a change in attitude or behavior? If necessary, the therapist and client should plan for dealing with such situations, before returning to "parts work." In Ray's case, this was not necessary, and we proceeded to work with his inner family.

ENTERING THE CLIENT'S SYSTEM

Addressing Their Concerns

In our next session, Ray described how two of his parts were activated at a recent faculty meeting when he wanted to make several points. One part felt that people would not know what he was talking about and think his comments were stupid. As a result, he felt intimidated and held back (the fearful part). Another part jumped in to complain that Ray was a coward for holding back (the critical part). Ray did make a comment but in a "wimpy voice," with little response from others.

Ray naturally felt he had done poorly. I asked which of these two parts he wanted to address first; he chose the fearful part. Schwartz notes the usefulness of starting with managers (we considered Ray's fearful part to be a manager) whose permission is normally needed to enter the system. Even when the client wants to start with an exile or firefighter, it is necessary to clear this with the managers first. If they object, the other part will have to wait until the managers are satisfied that it is safe to progress.

With Ray, we were starting with a manager, but I still had Ray ask if all the other parts approved. He did this by asking the question and assuming they would hear and respond through words or feelings. Ray was quiet for a moment. Then he said the critical part was pleased that we were going to help the fearful part stop being so wimpy; there seemed to be no hesitation from the other parts. We took this as permission to enter the system.

Unhooking the Self from Polarized and Blending Parts

I asked Ray to take a deep breath and let himself relax. When he indicated he was ready, I asked him to focus on the sense of fear or intimidation he felt at the recent faculty meeting. I requested that he put it in a room and look into that room through a window. He soon said he saw a scared eight-year-old child. This procedure, called the "room technique" by Schwartz, serves to separate the part from the self, making it possible for the self to then develop a relationship with the part before dealing with any polarized relationships the problem part may have with other parts.

It is not necessary for clients to see an actual image of the part as Ray saw the little boy, but they must be able to sense that the part is in the room. Often the part is afraid to show itself because of the presence of other parts who are polarized against it. The significance of this differentiating step is that the self can now consider the part separate from the self, a necessary first step for developing a relationship with the part.

Next, I asked Ray to consider how he felt toward the little boy in the room. He replied that he felt the boy was the source of his problem with being unassertive. I told Ray that I sensed another part was present and that I wanted him to find and ask it to trust him for a few minutes and step back. I noted that he could take the part to a different room if necessary.

DEPOLARIZING PART

Identifying Polarized Parts

This step is a continuation of the differentiating process. It seemed that the part disliked the fearful part and projected its disdain onto Ray. Unless this critical part was separated from Ray's self, the eight-year-old boy would feel the disdain as if it came from Ray himself and thus would not feel safe. Schwartz discovered that the compassionate, confident self quickly can be separated from polarized parts. Then the targeted part feels the self's compassion or interest rather than disdain. Furthermore, the self can then experience its own natural confidence when separated from the timidity of a fearful part.

Self Meets Each Part and Helps Them Negotiate

I again asked Ray how he felt toward the eight-year-old boy. This time, Ray reported anger and a desire to get rid of him. I asked Ray to take the angry part to a separate room. With this accomplished, he was curious about the boy and wished to help him.

This differentiating process continues until all interfering parts have separated and the self is free to assume its natural posture of openness and caring for the target part. The effect of these differentiating steps is to create a boundary between the self and the parts resulting in an empowerment of the self, since the self's leadership qualities are set free. Its compassion, perspective, and problem-solving abilities are now available to help the parts.

IDENTIFYING CHAINS THAT BIND THE PARTS

Questioning the Parts and Helping Them Contain Their Feelings

Once Ray's self was differentiated and available to the fearful part, I asked him if he wanted to enter the room to get to know the part. He was interested and went in to talk. I continued to coach Ray, urging him to ask if the part was worried about Ray looking stupid. The fearful part replied "yes," affirming that the critical part was always pushing Ray to speak before he was ready, and, therefore, it was up to him (the fearful part) to put the brakes on. Ray asked if he was worried about anything else. The fearful part said there was a pushing part that dangerously pushed Ray toward women.

Ray: Why was that so dangerous?

Fearful Part: Because women can control you!

Ray: Were there women who did control in the past?

(Ray had an image of a preadolescent boy feeling controlled by his mother.)

Ray: How does the mother control the boy?

(Ray then sensed that if the boy did not comply with his mother's wishes, she would criticize and not love him anymore. The fearful part was striving to protect Ray not only from his mother but from the critical part as well.)

RELEASING THE CHAINS BY UNBURDENING AND RETRIEVING A PART FROM THE PAST

The fearful part had demonstrated how effectively it could communicate with the self through pictures and feelings when the self was unhooked from the critical part and truly listening.

I had Ray ask the fearful part to consider if we could help the critical part to push less and to help the lonely part's needs get met; could the fearful part not put the brakes on so hard and instead let Ray try out new behaviors such as speaking up at meetings? The fearful part agreed to try but said he would "have to see it to believe it." We invited the fearful part to watch as we (me and Ray's self) talked with the critical part. The two parts were too polarized at that time to talk directly as in the usual method of depolarization. The fearful part had taken a step toward trusting Ray, as it sensed we were taking its fears seriously. Ray thanked this part for its helpfulness in showing us its concerns.

In the next session, Ray reported that he was less fearful and more assertive in recent social situations. We took this as a sign that the fearful part was following through with the agreement. Ray related that while playing basketball recently, the critical part told him that he had made a stupid play. Instead of dropping out of the game as he had done before, Ray told himself, "It's okay to make mistakes," and continued playing. His conversation with the fearful part had mobilized some assertiveness within his self.

Unburdening a Part

It was now time to meet the critical part. To begin, I asked Ray to focus on one of the critical part's statements and put the statement in a room. When looking into the room, all Ray saw was a mist; he sensed, however, that the critical part was also present in the room. I began the unhooking steps, asking first how Ray felt toward this part (he said "afraid"). I asked him to put the fearful part in another room.

Next, Ray found an angry part and then two other parts. Finally, the parts were separated so that the self was free to interact with the critical part. Ray was now able to go into the critical part's room and ask him why he told Ray that he was not good enough and that he was a coward. The answer came back that he was only trying to push Ray to be a better player so he would not be criticized.

Ray: Why are you so concerned about being criticized by others?

Critical Part: We would feel rejected like we did when Mother criticized us.

Ray: So, you are protecting me and my parts from rejection?

CP: Yes, this is true.

Ray: What is it like to carry so much responsibility around?

CP: I'm full of tension all the time, constantly watching.

Ray: Where is it in your body?

CP: It's a big knot in my stomach.

Ray: If I were to take responsibility for dealing with rejection and criticism, would you be able to undo the knot and just be free to do something you liked better?

CP: (no response)

Ray: What are you afraid would happen if you took out the responsibility?

CP: You wouldn't need me anymore and would get rid of me.

Ray: Guess what? You are part of the family; in our healing plan, all parts have a place. You could do something you liked, which wouldn't cause you so much tension; and the other parts would like you better, too.

CP: But I wouldn't know what else to do.

Ray: We'll help you. If you undo the burden, then we can help you find a new role.

The critical part seemed to be ready and able to do this. He decided to get rid of it by putting the responsibility knot in the "garbage." Parts often concretize the pressures symbolizing their burden as a knot, for example, because they are oriented around concrete expressions the way children are. If the critical part had not been able to "get the knot out," I would have asked the self to step in and help.

We then asked the critical part if any other burdens existed; he said no. He felt free and wanted a new job. After discussion, it became clear he wanted to be a part that instills confidence in Ray. This made sense; he had been trying to increase Ray's confidence, although in a way that did not work and terrorized the other parts. We agreed to begin calling him the "confidence part."

This, then, is the process of unburdening a part: helping the part to manifest its role and its burden; uncovering the part's fears of releasing its burden and reassuring it that it will be safe to do so; aiding in the release of the burden and finding a new role (and name, if desired). The final step is to assist other parts in accommodating to this change in the internal family system. This can be the occasion for parts reducing long-held tensions between them; once one part moves away from its extreme position, it is possible for other parts to relax their positions as well.

At this point, Ray and I sensed that it could be safe now to work with the lonely part, an exile. Exiled parts often carry pain from the past that frightens the other parts.

Retrieval of An Exile Stuck in the Past

In retrieval, we return to a past time where a part is stuck, unburden it, and bring it to the present. This involves reentering the past trauma with the part so that it can reveal the experience and the pain it has been carrying; helping the part to find a means of resolving the situation; releasing any burdens acquired; and bringing the part up to the present so that it can take its place in the internal family, free to contribute its gifts to the system. Schwartz notes that such parts are frozen in time and are living in the previous period; no matter how much attention they receive, they remain trapped with their past fear or shame. Schwartz discovered that revisiting the past to bring resolution (abreaction) can be accomplished effectively with parts as well as with the total personality.

Safeguards for Going to the Past with an Exile

Because exiles carry much pain from the past, the managers and firefighters are fearful of the self relating to exiles at all, much less revisiting the past with them. Managers especially are afraid of various consequences and must be reassured about each one; following are their main fears, which Schwartz observed in the managers:

1. *The self will be overwhelmed by the exiles flooding the system with painful feelings and memories.* This is known as "blending" and incapacitates the self from leading, rendering the system much more vulnerable. Some exiles, seeking redemption from the burden of worthlessness, may rush the client into a relationship only to be rejected and hurt. Ray's lonely part had, in the past, tried to overwhelm him with lonely remorse to push him into such relationships. The other parts had usually been successful in blocking this, but they were now worried. We assured the other parts that the lonely part had the

capacity to control the release of feelings and maintain boundaries if he believed that it was in his (the lonely part's) best interests. The lonely part was able to understand that if he did not overwhelm the self, he could get his feelings out and be understood by the self. We then talked to the lonely part about not blaming or pushing Ray into relationships; he was willing to try this in exchange for being listened to.

2. *Dangerous firefighters will be released who act impulsively and often destructively, driven by their rageful, suicidal impulses, or to get the client to indulge in alcohol, drugs, food, or sex.* Ray's managers were worried about his firefighters. They feared the angry part would jump out at people and cause more distancing and loneliness. But the managers were even more worried that to compensate for the lack of relationships, the sexual part would engage in lustful impulses, resulting in a pornography habit that would be accompanied by the displeasure of God and the loss of eternal life with God. We assured the angry part that we would listen to his concerns in time; he agreed to wait, having waited thirty years already. The sexual part had given the lonely part a way to relate to women that the managers could not block—through fantasy. It provided something for the lonely part that no one else was providing. We asked him if he would abstain from fantasy while we related to the lonely part and his wounds. The sexual part agreed to let us try but said that he would be watching to see how well we did.

3. *The therapist often is repulsed by the exiles and will distance from and lose respect for the client.* When therapists have not worked with their own exiles and the pain they carry, their own managers can cause a judgmental, controlling, or withdrawing response as exiles reveal their pain. Clients' protective parts can be triggered, which further escalates the therapists' own protective parts. This feels to clients like their original rejection and abandonment. To avoid this, therapists must assess their own capacity to accept clients' emerging exiles and reenter the exiles' past pain or abuse with a caring self. In my own work with clients, I ask myself: What is the worst I am likely to find? and Will I be able to stay in my "self"? With my parts, I review how we have been to the bottom of my own anguish, and with God's help, can go to the bottom of the client's anguish without being overwhelmed. I also remind my parts that they must let me lead. Finally, I ask God for His grace so His unconditional acceptance comes through

me. It is important that all helping professionals have a way to assess their capacity for acceptance so as to stay within their own limits.

4. *Exiles cannot change.* We assured Ray's managers and fire-fighters that even exiles can change when they have an accepting self to relate to.

5. *The client's external environment sometimes is not a safe enough place for the exiles to reveal themselves in; dangerous people may be present who will react and wound.* This was not so for Ray; he was residing in a different state from his family and possessed an adequately safe environment.

6. *Exiles may hold secrets that, when revealed, may result in dire consequences, such as further rejection or even destruction.* Ray felt that he could safely manage any secrets which might come out, and he reassured his parts.

7. *Managers could be eliminated once they are no longer needed in their overprotective roles.* We assured Ray's managers that the plan was to free them from their burdensome roles so that they could be with the other parts and the self and enjoy a freer life where they could freely contribute their gifts.

Having reassured Ray's managers and firefighters about these concerns, it seemed we were ready to proceed to the lonely part. In the next session, Ray reported that he had experienced feelings of sadness and remorse all week. We suspected that this was the lonely part. I had Ray check with the other parts to confirm that they felt it was safe enough to relate to the lonely part. I asked him to invite them to watch but to give Ray enough space to get acquainted with the exiled lonely part for himself. When they agreed, I asked Ray to take the sad feelings to a room and to come outside and look at them through the window in the room. This "room procedure" is useful, especially when meeting an exile for the first time. It minimizes the blending of an exile's feelings into the self by using the boundaries of the room to reinforce the boundary between the exile and the self.

Ray: I see a little boy in the room—looking very sad.

Therapist: How are you feeling toward him?

Ray: I feel he causes me a lot of trouble.

Therapist: Find the part that feels that and ask him to give you enough space to talk to the little boy.

Ray separated from the part and two other parts in the same manner before he felt he was "in himself" and able to help the boy in the room. This unhooking is necessary so that the exile is not revictimized by other parts' attitudes coming through the self.

Then I requested that Ray ask the sad little boy through the window not to overwhelm the self with his feelings, so that he could enter and talk with him. When the boy said he would try, I asked Ray to enter the room and see how close he could get without being overwhelmed by the boy's feelings.

Ray: I'm right alongside him.

Therapist: How are you doing?

Ray: No problem.

Therapist: Okay. Ask the boy if he is the one who has been feeling lonely and yearning for companionship with women. (This to confirm which part is in the room.)

Ray: He says he is, and he feels that if he can't be appreciated by Mother, at least he might be appreciated by other women. [to the part] Did something happen with Mother in the past that relates to your loneliness?

Lonely Part: Yes, right.

Ray: Would you take us back to that time and show us what happened?

Lonely Part: Okay.

I asked Ray to first check with the other parts to be sure that they still felt it was safe enough to do this. Then the lonely part took us back to a scene of Mother fussing at him because he did not want to practice the piano after school. I had Ray ask the part to show us whatever was needed so he could get unstuck from the scene.

Ray: What is it that's distressing about the scene?

LP: I don't like to miss out on being with my friends for one thing, but the worst is the loneliness.

Ray: What's that about?

LP: Mother doesn't care about what I'm interested in—she just wants me to do things to please her. She wants me to be a band director someday, so she makes me practice whether I want to or not.

Ray: What is the most upsetting about that?

LP: I'm not sure she wanted me in the first place, so soon after my sister was born. If she wanted me, she wouldn't have treated me this way.

Ray: What was that like for you?

LP: It's a yucky feeling inside.

Ray: Do you feel that we are listening to you and are understanding you?

LP: Yes.

At this point the part has revealed a core fear—that Mother does not love him for himself and did not want him. There may be more, but the part is not disclosing it at this point. I asked Ray to enter the scene with Mother and the lonely part.

Ray: What do you need?

LP: I'd like to know if she actually loves me.

Ray: With me to help you, could you ask her?

LP: I don't know if it's safe. She might get angry at me.

Ray: We'll help you if she gets angry.

LP [to mother]: I don't know why you make me practice so much when I want to be playing—there are other times I wouldn't mind so much, but it's like you don't care about what I want.

I asked Ray to tell the lonely part to wait and see how Mother responds. If Mother cannot listen or respond appropriately, we may need to help her separate her self from the parts in her that push the lonely part with their own agenda. The lonely part sensed that she could respond.

Mother: I guess I get too pushy at times. I'm sorry I do. I'll try to be more reasonable, discuss it with you.

This illustrates the process Jung called "active imagination" in which the self and the lonely child part sense Mother's response.

Ray [to LP]: How does her response seem to you?

LP: She's listening, but . . .

Ray: Do you want to ask her your other question about whether she actually wanted you?

LP [to Mother]: I don't know if you really wanted me—you said I came too soon after Betty (oldest child).

Mother: I know I said that I was feeling worn out and not ready when I discovered I was pregnant, but your dad and I talked it over and we prayed about it and came to feel like we could manage it and you would be a blessing—and you actually have been.

I asked Ray if he believed Mother's statement. He said yes because it was consistent with something he had previously heard from her and he sensed that she actually did love him. With this much validation, I suggested he continue with the lonely part.

Ray [to LP]: You believe what Mother said?

LP: I believe it some, but part of her wants me to perform—but underneath she does care about me and doesn't want to force me.

Ray: What about what she said about working it through and coming to want you?

LP: I don't know if I believe it.

I talked to Ray regarding the possibility of the lonely part carrying a burden that prevented him from believing this and asked Ray to investigate this further.

Ray [to LP]: How do you feel about yourself?

LP: Like I'm not worthy. If I was, she wouldn't treat me this way.

This is an example of the burden of worthlessness, which explains why the part couldn't believe Mother's response that she came to want him.

Ray: Look around inside and outside your body and find where you are carrying this.

LP: It's a yucky paste feeling in my guts.

Ray: Do you need to carry it any longer, or is it time to take it out?

LP: I'd like to get rid of it, but I don't know if I can.

Ray: See how much you can get out yourself. If you need help, I'll help.

(Pause)

LP: Okay. It's all out.

Ray: How do you feel now?

LP: Much different. I feel clean. I feel okay.

Ray: What about when Mother said that she came to love and appreciate you?

LP: I guess that's true.

Ray: Can you open your heart and let some of her love in?

The lonely part tells Mother it is okay and that he knows she loves him. He gets a hug from her and negotiates with her about practice time. He tells her he does not know what he wants to do, but he does not want to be a band conductor. Mother accepts it and hugs him.

I asked the lonely part if anything on him or in him makes him want to be with girls. The lonely part finds a strong urge in his stomach to find girls so that he can be okay. This is the burden of redemption. If he cannot measure up for mother, he may be able to measure up for other women. Ray helps him remove the burden. He now feels free and senses no other burdens in him. Ray asks him if he is interested in a new name and a new role. He and Ray decide to call him the "eight-year-old," and his new role is just to be an eight-year-old instead of having to carry such a heavy responsibility to find acceptance.

This work is completed by bringing the part back to the present time and finding a safe place for him if he needs one. Ray asked the other parts if they witnessed the events and changes in the eight-year-old. They had, and all felt happy for him. They were ready to get reacquainted with him and, under Ray's supervision, hosted a little party to welcome him; they even enjoyed playing with him. This part was delighted that after several decades of being exiled, he was now included as a valuable member of the internal family.

This last step of having the other parts receive and integrate the exiled part is important. It helps the parts that were once polarized against him to change their attitudes and accept him into relationship. With this "harmonizing" completed, the possibility of the part picking up old burdens again is reduced, and a way is opened for the part to grow and develop its capacities to contribute to the internal family. The parts will notice the new capacity of the self to enhance the well-being of the family, and the self feels more confidence in his growing ability to help free the parts and to lead them.*

Shortly after the unburdening of the fearful part, Ray began dating. At our last contact, he had made friendships with several interesting,

---

*Managers and exiles get stuck in the past just as exiles do, even though they are not the primary carriers of past pain and memories as exiles are. When they are stuck in the past, they need to be released in the same way as exiles.

enjoyable single women. He felt more comfortable with people in general and even felt free to sing and play the piano for friends and students when the occasion arose. The tension in his head and chest was mostly gone, and he was making plans for more training to develop his professional skills.

Ray and I noted his new ability to stretch himself in three new areas at once. He attributed it to the release of his self from parts with the accompanying ability to lead, and the freeing of his parts from the past so they can contribute all they have to the stretching process. Ray felt he was now making up for lost time by growing in areas he had wanted to develop but had felt unable to previously.

This concludes the presentation of the key techniques of IFS therapy. This and the preceeding chapter present the conceptual and clinical foundations of IFS therapy. Now, in the next chapter, we will build on this foundation by introducing the concepts of Christ-centered IFS therapy.

CLINICAL OUTLINE FOR WORKING WITH INDIVIDUALS

What follows is a summary of the clinical techniques described in this chapter, illustrating the main techniques in IFS Therapy. The summary, however, describes one among many possible sequences of steps. (For a more comprehensive listing, refer to the Summary Outline, Appendix A in Schwartz, 1997.)

I. Introducing the IFS model to the client
   A. The client describes the problem; therapist feeds back what client says using the language of parts.
   B. Therapist introduces basic concepts of model.
      1. Everyone has parts and self.
      2. The goal is to elevate the self to leadership and free the parts so they can get along and contribute to the whole.
      3. Therapist will coach client in the process.
      4. The process can be done safely at a respectful pace.
   C. Therapist asks whether client is interested in working this way and negotiates the process.
II. Getting to know the territory
   A. Client identifies parts he or she is aware of. Therapist and client formulate hypothesis about the relationship of parts to one

another and to the self and consider how to enter the system respectfully.

   B. They consider the safety of clients' external context of social situations and assess ability to proceed with inner work. If needed, they decide first to make the external context safer.

III. Entering the client's internal system, meeting parts and their problems.

   A. The client and therapist address the parts' concerns about going inside, especially managers' reluctance to work with exiles, and negotiate until the parts are assured that:

     1. The self will not be overwhelmed.

     2. Dangerous firefighters will not be released.

     3. The therapist will be able to accept the exiles and remain supportive.

     4. Exiles will be able to change.

     5. The external environment is safe enough.

     6. Dangerous secrets can be dealt with safely.

     7. Managers will continue to have a place in the inner family.

   B. Therapist helps client to unhook (differentiate) self from blending parts, using the room technique.

IV. Depolarizing parts as necessary to open the way for unburdening them

   A. The client and therapist identify polarized parts.

   B. The self meets each part to assess what each needs to depolarize.

   C. The self helps polarized parts get unhooked by having parts meet and negotiate with one another.

V. Identifying the chains (constraints) which bind individual parts

   A. The client's self asks each constrained part:

     1. Why does it act the way it does?

     2. What is it afraid will happen if it leaves its extreme role?

     3. What burdens does it carry and where in the past is it stuck?

   B. If the part is an exile, the self helps it to contain its feelings as the self interacts with the client.*

---

*If the part cannot contain its feelings, and danger exists that the self will be overwhelmed, the therapist may need to work with the part directly. This technique is called "direct access" and is beyond the scope of this book. See Schwartz, 1997, Chapter 5.

VI. Releasing the parts' chains through unburdening and retrieving it from the past

    A. Unburdening a part:

        1. The self asks the part if it is ready to release the extreme feeling or belief (burden). If the part feels the burden is intrinsic to itself, the self must return with the part to the time in the client's life when the burden began and unburden the part in the context of the retrieval from the past (see B following).

        2. When the part is ready, self helps it find the burden.

        3. The self helps the part remove the burden and dispose of it.

        4. The self checks with other parts to see if they're aware of the change in the part and accept it.

        5. The self helps the part find a new role and name if desired, incorporating the part's talents and goals.

        6. The part is introduced to the other parts in its new role.

    B. Retrieving a part from where it is stuck in the past:

        1. The self checks with managers about concerns they may have regarding a return to the past.

        2. Therapist assists the self in unhooking from parts and getting ready.

        3. Self asks the part to take it back to the past where the part is stuck.

        4. The part reveals to the self all necessary information about the situation until the part feels the self understands the significance of the scene.

        5. The self enters the past scene in a way that the part needed for someone to be there for it originally.

        6. Self and part check for extreme feelings or ideas to be unburdened.

        7. Self helps part consider when the situation is resolved and when the part is ready to come into present.

        8. Part and self come into the present to find a safe place for the part.

        9. The self introduces the part to other parts and monitors so that their relationship is respectful.

VII. Continual maintenance of the harmony of the internal family

The self continues to assess the needs of the internal family, noticing any remaining polarizations. It also monitors the need for synchronizing new roles so that unburdened parts fit well together. It can convene the internal family as appropriate for making decisions and problem solving together.

EXERCISE: GET TO KNOW A PART

This exercise invites you to have a conversation with one of your parts using the room and unhooking techniques. Find paper and pencil and a quiet place.

1. Breathe deeply for a minute or two. Relax your body as much as possible.
2. Consider which of your parts you want to relate to. How does that part affect you or what does the part say to you? (Note this on your worksheet.)
3. If the part is present now, take the part, a statement it is saying to you, or a feeling it is giving you, and put it in a room.
4. If the part is not present, go back to a recent situation in which it was present and put the part or statement or feeling into a room.
5. Come outside and look into the room. See or sense the part present in the room. (Note on paper its appearance, age, condition, your sense of it.)
6. Note on paper how you feel toward the part. If you experience anything except interest or compassion, another part is present. Take the other part aside. Ask it to wait as you take it to a separate room, so that you are free to relate to the first part.
7. Look through the window again. Do you feel only interest or compassion for the part, or is there still another part present? Repeat Step 6 as necessary until your self is free to relate to the part that you originally put in the room.
8. Consider if you would like to go into the room to talk to the part. If you are not comfortable in getting this close to it, then talk to the part through the window.
9. If you decide to go into the room, notice when you sense its influence to be too strong. If you begin to feel overwhelmed, step back from the part or leave the room until you can feel separate from the part again.

10. Find out as much as you can by asking the part: Why does the part do or say what it does? How does it feel toward you? Does it trust you? Does it seem polarized with any other parts? What are its extreme beliefs or feelings? Is it a manager, firefighter, or exile? What does it need to grow and contribute its gifts to your life? (Note the answers on your worksheet.)

11. Thank the part for what it has shown you and say "good-bye."

12. Reflect on your interaction with the part and record your reflections on the worksheet. Note whether it would be helpful to discuss these with a friend. Note whether you want more conversation with this part and, if so, what direction it might take.

13. Consider whether other parts exist that you want to interact with in the same manner.

SECTION II:
THE CHRIST-CENTERED IFS MODEL

Section II extends IFS therapy into Christian spirituality. It builds on the summary of IFS therapy in Section I by describing CCIFS *concepts* and CCIFS *therapy* in two consecutive chapters.

Section III introduces four new leadership tools to help equip clients' selves in leading their internal family to new responses to difficult situations in their lives. Together, Sections II and III constitute *Christ-centered therapy,* the goal of which is *empowering the self*—the title of the book.

Chapter 3

Christ-Centered IFS Concepts

> I do not understand what I do; for I do not do what I would like
> to do but instead I do what I hate.
>
> Romans 7:15

The apostle Paul in Romans describes a distressing dilemma that for Christians characterizes the struggle that all are called to. He finds himself unable to carry out his intention to serve God, and instead does those things displeasing to God. Paul might have said that parts of him want to serve God, but other parts cause him to do the very things he does not want to do.

Pam seemed to be stuck at a similar place. A struggling thirty-five-year-old single mother, Pam developed a dynamic new relationship with Jesus that brought her out of drug addiction and enabled her to take charge of her life. Now, four years later, she felt that she was failing in her role as mother and spouse; the life had gone out of her relationship with Jesus. Confused, depressed, and despairing, she felt stuck in her spiritual journey. She thought: What could be the reason for such a hopeful beginning ending up in such a depressing place? Certainly Jesus would not abandon her; would He?

Many wounded people turn to Jesus as the source of transforming love and power from God; they then experience an empowering healing to live in a more victorious way for a time. But many, like Paul, get stuck and fall back, disappointed, confused, and sometimes angry at God.

If Christ-centered IFS (CCIFS) is to be useful, it must help us understand not only how God's transforming love brings healing when our clients are walking closely with Jesus, but also when, like Pam, they are stuck and feel cut off from God's healing power.

CCIFS, AN EXTENSION OF IFS THERAPY INTO CHRISTIAN SPIRITUALITY

This chapter introduces what CCIFS has discovered about how to facilitate God's healing through Jesus and how to understand and help clients who are stuck and feel cut off from him. The following chapter will illustrate the clinical and spiritual steps needed to resolve the inner struggle; it will show how the transforming power of Jesus continues to be available over time for the client's healing journey. Together the two chapters set forth the concepts and practices of CCIFS.

Pam's Story

When Pam came for therapy, she not only was confused and depressed but she viewed her struggle as evidence of her inadequacy. She felt she had lost God's love and purpose for her life, and she blamed herself for the loss. She lost her temper often, exploding at her daughter or a friend. Although she had obtained a legal separation from her husband, she vacillated in periodic interactions with him, sometimes wanting him back and other times angrily critical of him.

Pam attended church regularly, seeking counsel from the pastor and other church leaders, but she continued to feel a failure and anger at God for withdrawing his love and support from her. Her doctor had prescribed antidepressant medications to no avail.

Pam is typical of many Christians who face significant challenges in their lives, who feel cut off from God's love and power, and who also feel overwhelmed and self-critical. What disrupted the relationship Pam had with God through Jesus Christ? How can it be restored so that she can take charge of her life again?

Using the CCIFS approach, Pam and I began by asking God to give us the humility to listen to the experience of her self and her parts. This act began to elevate Pam to a leadership role within her own internal system and to put me, as therapist, in a coaching role to help in the work. I then described the concepts of the self and the parts, along with the "self of faith" as the entity in which the Holy Spirit dwells. Pam recalled from past teaching that Jesus had promised to send

God's Spirit as a "helper" in the challenging task of leadership. Pam could thus invite the self of faith to be part of her leadership team. Together they could turn to Jesus as the way to God the Father for the needs for the whole inner family (see Figure 3.1).

I described how the parts needed a relationship with Pam's "self" and with Jesus just as Pam did. This could help them to trust Pam and Jesus, and would facilitate the healing and unburdening process in the inner system. Then we would identify and talk with her parts, allowing them to show where the relationship with God and Jesus had broken down. Pam was quite excited about the idea of her "self" as leader, aided by the self of faith, and the possibility of discovering where she got stuck with Jesus.

Pam's Parts

Pam and I began to let her parts speak for themselves and teach us about her internal family. Figure 3.2 summarizes the principal parts. The left column lists her individual parts under the three IFS categories: her *managers* (critical part and pleaser part), her *firefighters* (angry part, hopeless/depressed part, sexual part, and anesthetizing part), and her *exiles* (lonely part and unworthy part). The right column lists the behavior of each part.

Next, Pam and I located her parts on a parts map to see their relationship to each other and to her self. We observed that the parts had overwhelmed her self and her previously dynamic relationship with God. We illustrated this on the chart by locating her self off to the side of the powerful managers (see Figure 3.3).

FIGURE 3.1 Pam's Self—The Link Between God and Parts

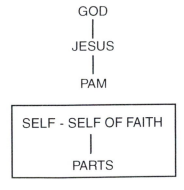

FIGURE 3.2. Summary of Pam's Parts

Managers	Behavior of the Parts
1) Critical Part	Puts Pam down: "You're not good enough" "You don't pray enough" "God doesn't love you anymore" (trying to get Pam to be perfect, to please everyone)
2) Pleaser Part	Makes Pam rush around pleasing others to fill the "inner void" Makes Pam self-conscious about others evaluating her
Firefighters	
3) Angry Part	Stores the resentment and anger of the internal system Periodically gets Pam to blow up at husband or daughter
4) Hopeless/Depressed Part	Gives Pam a sense of hopelessness about limited success of pleasing everyone to fill the inner void Makes Pam depressed to take the edge off the dominating managers
5) Sexual Part	Before marriage, got Pam into sexual relationships to fill the void Following the marriage, makes Pam feel sexually needy around her manipulative husband
6) Anesthetizing Part	Used to get Pam to use drugs to dull inner void and shame Currently gets Pam to use cigarettes only
Exiles	
7) Lonely Part (a twelve-year-old)	Carries loss of her dad after her parents divorced (when Pam was twelve years old) Gives Pam a feeling of having an inner void which needs to be filled by others
8) Unworthy Part (a five-year-old)	Carries the conviction that mother did not love her because she did not measure up and was unworthy of love Gives Pam a feeling of inner shame

As we considered the parts map and the roles of her various parts, Pam's major internal dynamics began to emerge as follows:

- *The Exiles:* The unworthy part carries a burden of worthlessness and shame and is seeking "redemption" from parents and other people. The lonely part gives Pam and the parts the feeling of the *inner void*. This multiplies the urgency of the unworthy part.

- *The Managers:* The way the managers try to fill both the redemption need and the inner void is through pleasing others. The pleaser part directs the effort to please others. The critical part tries to make Pam and the parts perfect and thus more able to please others.
- *The Firefighters:* Of the various firefighters, the sexual part had calmed down after marriage, and the anesthetizing part had been relieved of the big task of calming the pain of the inner void and the shame. Only the hopeless part and the angry part were still highly active and creating problems for Pam.

Next, Pam and I considered her spiritual journey, why it was so powerful, and why it broke down.

Pam's Spiritual and Healing Journey

At age sixteen, Pam rebelled against God and turned away from the church, putting her spiritual journey on hold. At twenty-four, after a number of sexual encounters and drug experiences leading to addiction, she married in hopes of finding happiness by establishing her own family. At twenty-six, a daughter was born. Pam realized by twenty-eight that her marriage was in trouble and sought help in Narcotics Anonymous. With help, she was able to stop her most pow-

FIGURE 3.3. Pam's Parts Map

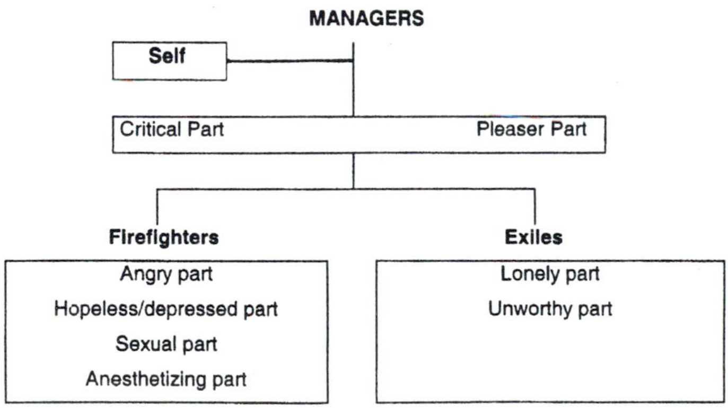

erful drug addictions, although she retained the craving for cigarettes. This seems to have been the beginning of her healing journey. Pam observed that the urgency she felt to protect her family was so strong that it united all her parts, giving her the strength to seek help and achieve victory over the drug addiction. The result was to block her anesthetizing part's main tool for dulling the shame and void within her. Pam's husband, however, had little success with his anger and drug addictions. For four years, Pam tried to help her husband find success with inpatient drug programs but none provided lasting results.

Pam's victory over addiction and her husband's lack of it propelled her forward in a search for happiness, resulting in a fuller expression of deep pain and yearning in her consciousness. Her husband's continued drug dependency and abusive behavior made the dream of a happy family even more remote. Yet the absence of drugs in Pam's life meant that the yearning and pain of her exiles could be directly projected into her consciousness. Stimulated by the urgency of the pain and her loss of hope, Pam's parts came forward with rescue plans. The sexual part wanted Pam to have an affair with a man to relieve the loneliness and offer emotional "redemption" from the burden of worthlessness. The hopeless part stood ready to lead her into depression and even suicide if necessary. The angry part, afraid of the hopeless part's plan, wanted to blow up in anger at her husband as a release for the pent-up blame and pain. Instead, influenced by a vision of a "higher power" and the offer of support from the group, Pam began a spiritual search.

To understand Pam's spiritual journey, how powerful it became, and how it got stuck, we need to consider further the organization of Pam's internal family. CCIFS has extended the IFS organization of manager parts, firefighters, and exiles to include three additional structures by which the internal family carries out its mission.

THREE FOUNDATIONAL STRUCTURES OF THE INTERNAL SYSTEM

To help clients such as Pam, it has been necessary to understand how their spiritual journeys intersect with and affect their parts and how their selves and parts affect their spiritual journeys. Three internal structures, *a survival core, a dominant coalition of parts, and a survival strategy* have proven helpful. These three undergird the managers, firefighters, exiles, and even the self; they are foundational as they form a center around which the whole IFS revolves.

The Survival Core

Schwartz described in the internal family system the operation of "burdens" as "extreme ideas or feelings carried by parts" that govern their lives. Burdens come from exposure to an external person or event. CCIFS extends this by noting that when the extreme beliefs are about one's worth or being and are so foundational as to be believed by most or all of the internal family, they then become the defining features of the personality with the power to affect one's very sense of existence and well-being. This survival core of the internal system includes core beliefs, feelings, and the core experiences that anchor the beliefs and feelings. For Pam, her survival core included her core belief (her unworthiness), her core feelings (shame and inner void), and the memories of her core experience (her mother's neglect and her father's departure from the family).

Taken together, these constitute a structure that is beyond proving or disproving for the parts. It governs the entire internal family by becoming the center around which the system organizes for survival. It is useful to picture this core as an axis around which the system rotates. Certain parts are selected to carry key roles according to the core of beliefs, feelings, and experiences. These parts then direct and control the self and the parts to carry out the mission of the system, which is to survive.

Pam's unworthy part is the primary carrier of the core experience of emotional abandonment by her mother. This produces the core belief in her unworthiness and the core feeling of shame. The lonely part carries the experience of loss of Father and the inner void. These two parts are both exiles; however, far from being remote and impotent in their exiled state, they become hidden keepers of the core. With these emotions at the center of the whole system, they are powerful and even dominant in their neediness.

For Pam, the unworthy part and the lonely part can leak out shame and urgency to fill the void in her life. The critical part and the pleaser part then must work tirelessly to seek a "redeemer" person or find a meaningful social connection. Without this, the connection to life itself seems lost. Without a "redeemer" to bestow worth, the key parts feel that the entire human community proclaims Pam unfit to exist in society. Such ontological dread, the fear of the loss of being itself, must become the axis around which every effort is organized. This illustrates the power of the survival core to organize and control the inner family. It can be pictured as a vertical axis (see Figure 3.4) around which the self, the managers, firefighters, and exiles rotate to carry out their survival mission. All are directed by the perspectives and urgencies of the survival core.

The Survival Coalition

The survival coalition is comprised of the internal family members assigned to support the survival mission of the internal system. It includes selected managers, firefighters, exiles, and usually the self, (not necessarily); for Pam, her two exiles are pivotal. In addition, two of her managers, the critical part and the pleaser part, are also included in the coalition. The pleaser part manages Pam's social interactions so that she maximizes social affirmation and minimizes rejection. The critical part anticipates others' expectations and shapes up the parts to meet them. For this she uses criticism, the main strategy of her mother's critical part, as she knows how powerful it can be in controlling Pam's self and parts. (Pam has other managers, a caretaker part and an achiever part, not included in the coalition.)

FIGURE 3.4. The Survival Core As Organizing Axis for the Internal System

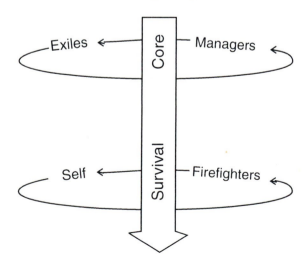

Several of Pam's firefighters were originally in the survival coalition but are now excluded. From the ages of sixteen to twenty-four, Pam's sexual part and her anesthetizer part both played key roles. The sexual part sought to fill the void and redeem the shame through relationships of sexual intimacy. The anesthetizer part was trying to dull the pain. After Pam's marriage at twenty-four, the sexual part was limited to a search for intimacy in the marriage. This restriction had the effect of moving the sexual part out of the coalition. Although she still tried to do her task within the marriage, this part was seen as ineffective by the other parts because of Pam's limited satisfaction in the marriage and because she wasn't allowed to seek satisfaction outside. At age twenty-eight, Pam ended her addiction to drugs. Thus the anesthetizer part, having lost her most potent strategy, was also removed from the coalition.

The angry part was only recently allowed in the coalition, since her managers kept a tight rein due to the need to conform to family sanctions against expressing anger.

The hopeless part, overshadowed for years by other parts, emerged when Pam realized that her marriage and family dream were in serious trouble. Since other firefighters were ineffectual and removed from the coalition, the hopeless part emerged and depressed Pam to dull the pain. It even offered suicide as an exit, in case the pain became overwhelming. Pam's self also emerged during this developmental period, with sufficient judgment and autonomy to be included in the coalition.

Pam's current survival coalition thus included her self, her critical part and her pleaser part from the managers, her hopeless part from the firefighters, and her two exiles. The self and these five parts carried the responsibility for the survival and well-being of her internal family.

The Survival Strategy

The survival strategy is the interaction style used in interfacing with the external world to meet the needs of the self and the parts. Strategies are usually given to one or more of the managers to carry out. In urban, industrial societies, individuals' survival strategies are often centered around pleasing and performing. They can also encompass opposite styles, such as aggression and withdrawal.

In Pam's case, the core strategy was to please others for approval. We noted above how this was based on the unworthy part's need for redemption and release from shame and the lonely part's need to fill the inner void.

Pam's pleaser part is the manager assigned to execute the strategy in the social world. Her critical part, by criticizing all the other parts, tries to "shape them up" to the expectations of others. It thus controls the internal dynamics while the pleaser part relates to the external relationships.

This completes the description of the three structures of the survival organization. The survival core (core beliefs, feelings, and experiences) is the axis around which the survival coalition of self and parts revolves to forward the strategy of behaviors into the external world to provide for the survival and well-being of the entire internal family system. It is useful to note that other parts exist in the internal system not included in the survival coalition. They range from playful parts to altruistic parts. Their behaviors are permitted only when energy remains from the survival requirements of the inner needs and secrets.

Just because they have common beliefs and a common strategy, all is not harmonious among the parts of the survival coalition. Rather, they are often polarized against one another in their efforts to achieve common goals, unable to trust one another or the self as they compete for control.

Respect for the Survival Organization

The internal survival organization is a creative and comprehensive adaptation to a sometimes cruel environment, especially when considering how young the self and parts are when they organize. It is appropriate for therapists to respect this system's creativity, even when the client is asking for help to change. Pam's unworthy part was assigned to carry the shame; the angry part carried and concealed the resentment so that the self and parts could relate to a mother with little capacity to love.

The Survival Organization's Inability to Meet the Core Needs of the Parts

Despite Pam's excellent survival organization and her best efforts, hopelessness and despair were growing. As we talked with Pam's parts, it was clear to them that their plan was not working. Pam's work relationships and those with neighbors and friends were discounted. The parts felt that if the people who affirmed and supported Pam actually knew their inner secret (that Pam is actually an unworthy person), they would not offer her friendship or support. Yet the parts kept on like faithful soldiers, doing what they were assigned, often worn out by constantly striving to please. The hopeless part was the only one who spoke the horrible truth about how hopeless they believed it to be. Seeds of change were planted in this despair, however, propelling Pam to seek a different kind of solution. Thus began Pam's spiritual pilgrimage.

PAM'S SPIRITUAL JOURNEY

As stated earlier, Pam and her husband had sought help for their drug habits from Narcotics Anonymous. Pam was successful in ending her habit while her husband was not. Pam soon saw the need to end her relationship with her husband and attained a legal separation, hoping he would eventually gain a victory over his habit. These steps brought two unforeseen consequences. First, since Pam's firefighters were unable to use their most "effective" strategy, drugs, the exiles' yearnings for redemption from shame and the inner void came to consciousness more forcefully than ever. Second, with her husband gone, the hope of a happy family to minister to the inner yearnings seemed more remote than ever.

With the parts increasingly distressed, great pressure existed to find a new person, such as a lover, who could be a "redeemer" for Pam's inner needs. Instead, influenced by her support group and their dependence on a "higher power," Pam and several of the parts began a spiritual search for something that would hold out more hope than the present, failing survival strategy.

Pam searched in unusual venues for years, including turning to ancient "gods and goddesses," and contemporary spirituality, such as that based on crystals. At one point, she was experimenting with crystals over her eyes and saw a terrifying image of Satan that convinced her she was pursuing the wrong paths. She told herself she needed something "solid and trustworthy." Shortly afterward, her daughter introduced her to a school friend whose father was the pastor of a lively, loving Christian congregation. They began to attend the church, enjoy the fellowship, and listen to its teaching about a God who "loves us so much he sacrificed His son not to judge us but to be our savior" (Pam's paraphrase of John 3:16 and 17). During the next year, Pam recognized that she needed a "powerful God and a powerful savior" to care for her and her daughter.

Pam's Encounter with Jesus

One day when Pam felt burdened by the hopelessness of her situation, she asked the pastor to pray with her after the worship service. Although it seemed that all her parts were resisting, she took a "tiny step of faith" and opened her heart to Jesus Christ's love for her. She soon felt a sense of Jesus' presence with her, "just accepting her as she was with all her struggles." The pastor prayed for her to receive the "Holy Spirit," and Pam experienced the "presence of God coming inside her," giving her the inner sense of peace that she had yearned for but never felt before. Later, the pastor helped her understand the Holy Spirit's role of helping her follow Jesus in her life.

Over the next months, Pam felt that some of the shame of unworthiness had been washed away. A deep personal connection with Jesus as a friend and a savior began. This relationship with Jesus along with the presence of the Holy Spirit started to fill her inner void. Pam soon joined the church and began a new hopeful period in her life. For two years, she became more clear and confident and even experienced inner serenity.

After this wonderful growth period, however, Pam began to feel blocked inside from opening her heart more fully to Jesus. She could not continue to let him fill the inner void or to bring further resolution to the inner unworthiness. Eventually, her new inner confidence eroded and she experienced hopelessness again in her struggles as a single mother and spouse of an addicted husband. At that point, she came for counseling. She asked: Why had her new relationship with Jesus not settled more deeply within her? Why had her new confidence eroded? She wanted help to regain the confidence to direct her life and get back "on track" with Jesus.

Pam and I decided we needed to understand what had happened before making a plan to get her moving again. We needed to explore. What had taken place in Pam's empowering encounter with Jesus Christ? Why did it not last? Why was Pam blocked in growing in her healing relationship with Jesus? Why did she experience such a loss in confidence in dealing with the challenges in her life?

Effects of Pam's Relationship with Jesus Christ on Herself and Her Parts

As Pam and I talked with her parts, an understanding of their experience emerged. When Pam achieved victory over drugs, she gained more control over her life, but the inner yearnings of two exile parts were forcefully projected into her consciousness (the unworthy part for redemption from shame and the lonely part for filling the relationship void). These two parts and Pam had formed a new alliance to explore a different way of meeting the yearnings—a relationship with a savior who redeems the unworthiness and bridges the loneliness.

The two manager parts, however, had different responses. The critical part feared rejection from Jesus, expecting him, as the representative of an angry God, to be as critical as Mother was. The pleaser part was afraid that Pam would be no more successful at pleasing God and Jesus than she was at pleasing people. They were both afraid of the loss of their powerful manager roles and tried to block the relationship with Jesus. Among Pam's firefighters only the hopeless part was encouraged by the spiritual search. She had earlier despaired that the survival strategy of the parts would never work. This skepticism undermined the controlling influence of the two managers to block the spiritual search, although the hopeless part of her self was so stuck in despair that she could not easily join the new alliance. The result seemed to be that Pam, the lonely part, and the unworthy part prevailed by bringing new energy and urgency to the spiritual search. Although the critical part and the pleaser part projected their fears into Pam and the two exiles, they were not able to block the spiritual steps forward.

The Emergence of the New Coalition

The first effect of the spiritual search was that Pam and the two exiles began to constitute a new coalition that led the spiritual exploration over the next year. This trio threatened the old coalition, which then tried to block the spiritual search by projecting their fears about God into Pam and the two exiles. The new group prevailed because the urgency and energy for a new solution was so strong.

After Pam opened her heart to Jesus and felt his love and acceptance, and after the pastor prayed with her and Pam felt the Holy Spirit, more change occurred. Pam's self was strengthened and elevated to the clear role as leader of her internal family system; and the Holy Spirit was invited in, creating a "leadership team" to lead the parts. It was a team with access to the healing resources of God Himself through Jesus and the Holy Spirit. This was the first of several changes in Pam's internal organization. These are summarized and described in Figure 3.5.

Healing of the Core Beliefs and Feelings

When Pam opened her heart to Jesus and felt his unconditional love, she and the unworthy part sensed the shame being washed away; the lonely part felt a deep inner connection with Jesus that began to fill the inner void. This acceptance and connection to Jesus diminished the power of the old survival core based on a need for redemption from shame and feelings of loneliness.

The Emergence of a New Core Axis

Since core beliefs and feelings are rooted in core experiences, it is not surprising that Pam's new relationship of acceptance from Jesus gave rise to a new core. Pam now believed she was made worthy through Jesus' sacrifice; she was now connected to God through Jesus (see Figure 3.5). This core emerged as a second axis around which Pam and the two exiles centered. It did not simply replace the original core because the managers and other parts continued to orient themselves around it. Rather, it coexisted alongside the original core.

The difference between the two cores was striking. Pam's experience and new beliefs now paralleled the age-old Christian teaching and experience, known as the Good News (Gospel) of Christ. It centered around God's action in sacrificing His own son to redeem all who receive it (salvation). Pam's original core, however, was based on the conviction that she was unworthy (held as an implicit truth or "gospel" by the parts). Thus, we can identify the original core as the *gospel of the parts,* differing radically from the new core based on the *gospel of Christ* (see Figure 3.5).

FIGURE 3.5. Pam's Internal Organizations: Old and Emerging

	OLD ORGANIZATION (BEFORE CHRIST)		EMERGING ORGANIZATION (AFTER CHRIST)
SURVIVAL COALITION	Managers: Critical part, Pleaser part Firefighters: Hopeless part Exiles: Unworthy part, Lonely part Self	NEW COALITION	Self, self of faith Unworthy part, Lonely part
CORE BELIEFS AND FEELINGS AS SURVIVAL AXIS	Life revolves around survival. I am unworthy. Feelings: Shame, inner void	CHRIST-CENTERED CORE AS AXIS	Life revolves around relationship with Jesus. I am made worthy because of Jesus' sacrifice. I am connected with God through Jesus.
THE GOSPEL OF PARTS	Bad news about the impossibility of redemption.	THE GOSPEL OF JESUS	Good news about redemption freely given.
SURVIVAL STRATEGY	Pleasing others to be found worthy and be connected with others.	CHRIST-CENTERED STRATEGY	Empowered, proactive person using all gifts as mother, spouse, businesswoman, to love God, self, others.

The gospel of Christ is good news about a redemption freely offered by grace to all who would receive it. The gospel of Pam's parts is bad news about the impossibility of redemption. Highlighting the differences between the two beliefs proved useful to Pam later when she was considering which way to lead her two conflicting sets of parts.

Emergence of a New Strategy

A third change resulted from Pam's new relationship with Jesus. As she became free from old survival needs, her self, in partnership with her self of faith, emerged with confidence to lead the way bringing wisdom and compassion to her life's responsibilities. She became proactive in her relationships as mother, spouse, businesswoman, and member of her congregation (Figure 3.5). She wanted to be loving toward God and others as Jesus was to her, based on the heart of the commandments: "To love God with all your heart, soul, mind, and strength and your neighbor as yourself" (Mark 12:30,31).

Two Centers of Organization Within an Individual

Pam had developed alternative mechanisms for the three structures of her personality organization: a new core, a new coalition, and a new strategy. These were forming a new center in her personality that, rather than replacing the original center, coexisted alongside it. The original organization was centered around survival; the new organization around Pam's relationship with God through Jesus Christ. If we picture each organization revolving around its core as an axis like a spinning top, we can observe how totally different the two are in character and content. To underline the difference we can visualize the parts rotating counterclockwise in the old organization but clockwise in the new (see Figure 3.6).

The old organization was centered around the survival core, based on the gospel of the parts (unworthiness, shame, inner void, and the hopeless task of achieving redemption by pleasing others). The new organization is centered around the gospel of Christ (redemption given as a gift).

The self was depowered in the old and felt it was spinning out of control "with parts competing for control." In the new organization, the self is empowered to lead with the Holy Spirit (self of faith). The old organization was characterized by fear, hopelessness, compulsive striving, and depression; the new organization, by hope, grace, and energy. Yet important members of the coalition of parts—namely the critical part and the pleaser part—were still not participating in the joy of the new experience with Jesus. These two managers grew more skeptical and polarized against the new organization. Thus, the seeds were sown for the next stage of Pam's journey.

The Next Stage of Pam's Journey—Internal Conflict

The effect of the emerging new organization on the two managers of the old center was significant. As the relationship with Jesus Christ had an impact on Pam and the two exiles, the two managers not on board became threatened and felt left out. They felt threatened by the emergence of the new coalition of Pam and the two exiles, by the fact that the most deeply held secrets and wounds (the shame of unworthiness and the void of loneliness) were revealed and ministered to. These wounds were the core of the old belief system and survival axis around which their purpose in life depended. They felt their justification for exercising power over the other parts was threatened. Not striving to please people meant for them more rejection and isolation. Hidden was their conviction that if the parts' survival needs were met by Jesus, they would lose their dominant roles and their reason for existence. This put them in a near panic state, since they would be done away with.

Survival Efforts of the Managers—Effect on Pam

The two managers responded by escalating pressure to bring Pam and the other parts back in line. The critical part increased her criticism of Pam's mothering and her relationship with her separated husband. She also criticized Pam's "performance" as a Christian and made Pam think she had to please Jesus, God, and the people of the church. This neutralized the core of the new organization (redemption by grace), turning it back into a gospel of the parts with redemption by performance or "works."

FIGURE 3.6. Two Centers of Organization Within an Individual

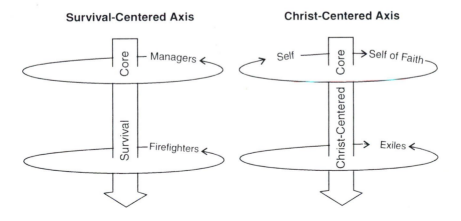

The two managers unknowingly generated within Pam the age-old struggle of Christians striving to live in grace, instead of in "works." The critical part also criticized Pam for not praying and reading the Bible enough and, for not being as loving as she should. These messages had a strong influence on the exiles. The lonely part became frightened of losing her relationship with Jesus, and the unworthy part began to doubt that Jesus had actually established her worth. The hopeless part was frightened and began to worry again that redemption seemed as remote as ever.

The two managers projected their own memories of Pam's critical and rejecting parents onto Jesus. They then imagined Jesus as critical and condemning of them, because they were displeasing him; they became more hardened and closed to a relationship with Jesus for which they secretly yearned. Thus, the conflict between the two internal organizations began to escalate, just as Schwartz describes how polarized parts escalate. Pam's inner polarization differed, however, in that she and the Christ-centered side did not escalate against the survival-centered side by criticizing or labeling it as ungodly.

The effect of this inner conflict over the next four years was significant. It eroded the lonely and worthless parts' sense of being valued by Jesus and connected to him. They became more vulnerable to manager criticisms and increasingly believed they were not measuring up to Jesus' expectations. They came to believe that Jesus, like their parents, was critical and had turned away from them. The transforming power of Pam's relationship with Jesus Christ was eroded, resulting in loss of hope, clarity, and the power for Pam to conduct her life.

As Pam became more discouraged, the two exile parts led by the managers slipped back to their original sense of unworthiness. During the four years that Pam's internal life was regressing, her external life become more challenging. Her daughter, now a preteen, was getting involved at school with peers, which created tension between her and Pam. She was disappointed at her husband's failure in his drug rehabilitation programs and his inability to provide financial support. Those parts that still held the dream of having the family reunited and happy were crushed.

Pam came to me for help. She revealed her transforming relationship with Jesus and strong support from a loving church. Yet much of her new self-confidence and clarity had eroded; she felt hopeless and depressed. She now was engaging in angry outbursts at her daughter and husband. She was confused about what seemed to be the loss of the empowering relationship with Jesus. She felt better off than before she knew Christ, but having tasted some hope and power in her life, she was not content to settle for depression and despair again.

THE INTERNAL STRUGGLE OF CHRISTIANS

Pam's internal conflict is actually a common and perennial occurrence for Christians, especially new Christians. Virgil Vogt, an experienced Chicago pastor, observes that when a person enters a relationship with Jesus, it starts to reorganize the personality. The emergence in Pam of the new internal organization is an illustration of this dynamic. An individual's relationship with Jesus is often transforming because it touches the deepest needs and sets in motion the reorganization to which Vogt referred. In Pam, a new core (self beliefs and experiences) formed, with a new coalition of self and parts, and a new life strategy—the three structures constituting the internal organization. The new organization emerges in varying degrees of tension with the old.

This dilemma is well expressed by the apostle Paul in his lament to the Romans: "I do not understand what I do; for I do not do what I would like to do but instead I do what I hate . . . What an unhappy man I am! . . . This then is my condition: by myself I can serve God's law only with my mind, while my human nature serves the law of sin" (Romans 7:15,24-25).

Paul's transforming encounter with Jesus began the reorganization of his personality. The new organization, centered around Jesus, yearned to do God's will, yet the old organization was struggling for self-centered survival. Paul's disclosure of his inner struggle has given hope to multitudes of Christians who experience a transforming relationship with Jesus, then struggle against being pulled back into the old hopeless position of survival by self-performance.

In the next chapter of Romans, Paul describes the hope of continuing the journey with Jesus Christ. "There is no condemnation now for those who live in union with Christ Jesus. For the law of the spirit which brings us life in union with Christ Jesus, has set me free from the law of sin and death." And again, "If the spirit of God who raised

Jesus Christ from death lives in you, then He who raised Christ from death will also give life to your mortal bodies by the presence of His Spirit in you" (Romans 8:1,2,11).

Paul is referring to the power of the Holy Spirit to help the believer through the internal conflict. The CCIFS model has described this dynamic as the self of faith—the Holy Spirit invited onto the leadership team by the self. The Spirit becomes the source of spiritual help through the confusion of two internal conflicting centers. The believer can stay open to God's "resurrection power," as Paul calls it, to continue the transforming process in the community of faith. Those such as Pam, whose deep wounds and inner shame have only begun to be healed, need clinical help to continue the journey, lest they become too frightened and overwhelmed.

Great need exists for therapists and pastors who can understand the shame and rejection of the wounded exiles, the desperate compulsiveness of the managers, and the tenacity of the internal survival organization. They will know how a healing process, begun with some parts and resisted by others, can be kept on track. From the experience of using IFS therapy to help struggling Christians for more than ten years, I know that IFS therapy is an effective tool for understanding and helping Christians stuck in their healing and their relationship with Jesus. It is my hope that CCIFS therapy can facilitate the work of therapists and pastors in helping wounded and stuck Christians to continue on their spiritual, healing journeys.

CHAPTER SUMMARY

This chapter has introduced the main concepts of CCIFS. It used Pam's case to illustrate that many Christians, in their search for survival and happiness, despair of finding a meaningful and satisfying solution to their deepest problems. They sometimes begin a spiritual journey and encounter in Jesus a transforming and healing new relationship. The spiritual journey does not simply result in a victorious new life, however; instead, the spiritual pilgrim is beset by internal challenges that at times threaten to cause an early and unwanted end to the new journey.

This chapter described new concepts from CCIFS therapy that help us understand this perplexing struggle of faith. It introduced three components of the internal system's organization: the survival core, the survival coalition, and the survival strategy.

1. The *survival core* is comprised of the most formative experiences with resulting self beliefs and feelings.
2. The *survival coalition* is comprised of the parts and usually the self, which are responsible for organizing the internal system for survival by attending to its deepest needs. Core experiences, beliefs, and feelings are carried by key exiles; key managers and firefighters are given the burden of regulating internal relationships and interacting in the external world.
3. The *survival strategy* is the main style of behavior and attitude chosen by the self and parts to carry out these goals.

The core could be seen as a *survival axis* around which the self and parts revolve as a cohesive system to insure survival and well-being. Together, the core, the survival coalition, and the survival strategy constitute an internal *survival organization* held in common by all the parts and the self. The internal conflicts and polarizations among the self and parts occur within the context of this common core and survival strategy.

This chapter described the effects of a spiritual journey and encounter with Jesus Christ on the self, the parts, and survival organization. When this produces a relationship where Jesus' sacrificial love is received, it touches the deepest wounds and self beliefs. More than joy and healing results; a new personality organization is formed alongside the old. A new coalition, a new core, and core strategy all emerge, coexisting with the old. This new coalition begins when the self is appointed by Jesus to lead the system. The self invites the Holy Spirit to join with it to constitute a *leadership team*. And the Holy Spirit becomes a new entity within the personality known as the *self of faith*, which forms a coalition with those parts open to the relationship with Jesus.

The *new core* is comprised of self beliefs, feelings, and experiences with Jesus (including redemption, which establishes the individual's worth because of Jesus' self-sacrifice). The core becomes a *Christ-centered axis* centering the new organization around the relationship with Jesus. And a *new strategy* of engaging the external world through empowered, altruistic attitudes and behaviors begins to emerge.

This chapter used these two coexisting axes in the personality to explain the internal conflict of Christians. Some parts are alienated and threatened by the new core, the new coalition, and the change in survival strategy. They seek ways to undercut the new organization and disable the self. These individuals will need clinical and spiritual help to continue their faith journey. The therapist will assist not only in unburdening the parts in the usual clinical mode, but also with a resolution and inclusion of the struggling parts so they may join the others in the spiritual healing journey.

EXERCISE: SEEKING YOUR OWN INTERNAL ORGANIZATION

Find some time and a quiet place to reflect. If you wish, ask God to help you with self-perspective and clarity. Ask your parts to give you space to reflect. Remind them this is for self-understanding, not criticism; ask them to be available with their self-knowledge as needed.

1. Consider your *survival strategy.* Reflect back over your child-hood as well as adult life. What styles of interaction have you used to interact with the external world. Are these your survival strategies?
2. Consider your *survival core,* your formative experiences with the convictions and feelings accompanying them. Ask your parts to help you recall childhood memories and sensations that illustrate these.
3. Consider your *survival coalition.* Which managers and fire-fighters directed your external relationships? Which ones regulated your internal relationships? Which exiles were they trying to satisfy?
4. How satisfying or frustrating was the outcome of these efforts?
5. Diagram your internal organization with its axis and components (see Figure 3.4).
6. Has your spiritual journey raised up any *new components of your internal organization* such as

__ a new coalition?
__ a new source of spiritual power?
__ a new core (self belief, feelings, or experiences)?
__ new relationship strategies or attitudes?

7. If your spiritual journey has resulted in new organizational components, what effect have they had on your old survival organization?

       __ Its key parts?
       __ Its core?
       __ Its survival strategy?

8. How much tension, if any, has developed between the old organization and the new? Try to diagram the two axes and components as in Figure 3.6. What effect has the tension had on you, your spiritual growth, and your healing?
9. Consider sharing your findings with a trusted friend.

Chapter 4

Christ-Centered IFS Therapy

Do not conform outwardly to the standards of this world, but let
God transform you inwardly by a complete change of your mind

Romans 12:2

Pam was introduced in Chapter 3 as one whose coalition of parts
was commissioned to organize her internal family and find a redeem-
ing person who could heal her shame and inner void. Instead, Pam
opened to Jesus the inner secret of her unworthiness and began to organize her life around a relationship with Him. The survival parts, led
by the managers, were deeply threatened by this new development
and attempted to undercut it, thus Pam was feeling stuck and confused. How is the therapist to help with this complicated internal war-
fare, and where to begin?

This chapter introduces the *techniques* of CCIFS therapy, as Chapter 3 dealt with the *concepts*. In setting forth the full CCIFS model,
the two chapters also serve as a foundation for techniques described
in the remainder of the book. This chapter concludes with a summary
of all procedures utilized in CCIFS therapy (both standard IFS procedures as well as those unique to CCIFS therapy). Finally, an exercise
is offered for the reader.

ASSESSING THE APPROPRIATENESS
OF USING THE CCIFS MODEL

In Pam's case, it was easy to see her desire to integrate clinical
needs with her faith. In my initial phone conversation with her, she
said I was recommended by the pastor of her church. She asked if I

was a Christian counselor. When I said yes, she spoke of her distress and asked if an initial appointment could be set up. In that brief interchange, she provided a clear picture of her clinical needs and her desire to integrate her Christian spirituality with those needs. I was free then to explore with her the use of CCIFS.

In the first session, I noted our common ground of faith in Jesus and asked if she would like to pray for God's blessing and guidance as we began to get to know one another. She said she would like this and seemed delighted that I asked. Thus, at the onset, we were able to set forth our common need for God's guidance.

Identifying the client's interest in spirituality can make several contributions to the collaborative relationship between therapist and client.

1. It begins a spiritual bond based on a common trust in God.
2. It acknowledges that the therapist and client are peers in the eyes of God.
3. Because the therapist is seeking God's wisdom and grace, it helps the client and parts to extend trust to the therapist.
4. It reminds both that the therapist is not God, thus helping the therapist avoid overresponsibility and the client to avoid overdependence.
5. It helps the therapist to see the client through God's eyes, created in His image and filled with gifts and capacities needing help to be released.

These points contribute to the collaborative quality of the therapeutic alliance, one of the foundations for the effectiveness of both IFS and CCIFS.

How should the therapist respond when the client gives no indication in the initial conversation of any spiritual interest? In gathering necessary data, one can ask whether the client has a religious interest or background without imposing any expectations. The alternative is to include a question on the intake form about spiritual interest or religious participation. This then can be followed up by later clarification as appropriate.

Such a religious question can produce several benefits. The client may have spiritual strengths that facilitate the clinical work, as in Pam's case. On the other hand, the client's spiritual condition may be contributing to the problem. The willingness of the therapist to inquire gives the client permission to raise spiritual doubts and fears; there may be anger at God because He does not seem to be helping them in their distress. Clients may feel God is punishing them for their faithlessness. When such questions are brought into the session, therapist and client, using the CCIFS model, can consider which parts are angry at God, which are afraid of God, and why.

The spiritual background inquiry enables the client to disclose other spiritual or existential needs, such as a need for meaning in one's life. Therapist and client can consider how these needs fit with more urgent needs. They can discuss how the therapist may help and what other resources exist, such as pastors and spiritual support groups. It is important for the therapist to stay in "self" and not get hooked by denominational or theological differences. The client will experience relief and hope in eventually understanding the connection between the spiritual distress and their clinical needs. This was clearly the case with Pam. If initial inquiry reveals that the client has no interest in the spiritual, the clinical work can proceed using the IFS model.

INTRODUCING THE CCIFS MODEL

Introducing the CCIFS model to the client begins in the same manner as introducing the IFS model: listening to client problems and feeding back what is said using the language of parts. As the client understands the concept of parts and self, the self's relationship with Jesus and with the self of faith can be introduced. These concepts should be introduced experientially, so that the client can see them in relation to his or her own parts. This keeps the discussion from becoming theoretical and maintains the message that the client can learn to care for and lead his or her own parts.

Pam described her loss of confidence, blaming herself for her inadequacy. She related how confused and distressed she was about the loss of her relationship with Jesus. I reflected her statements to her in parts language: "It sounds as if you have a part that criticizes you pretty strongly, and another part that believes the criticism. Perhaps it actually believes you don't measure up. There must also be another part who works very hard to do what people expect, and perhaps a separate part who feels hopeless about succeeding in pleasing people." Pam said this sounded accurate and was becoming energized.

Using Mapping to Teach the Concepts

I drew a parts map for Pam. This is a diagram illustrating parts in relationship to one another. As I drew on a clipboard, we discussed the possible role of each part, and I then added it to the diagram. It went like this: "The critical part sounds like a manager part who has been given the duty of managing your life. Let's put her in a position of power above the other parts. The part who works hard to please others may also be a manager. Shall we call her the pleaser part?" I added each part to the diagram while describing the roles of managers, fire-fighters, and exiles. As each category came up, I located it on the map (see Figure 4.1).

I continued: "The part that believes the criticism may do so because she carries wounds and negative beliefs for the system. They are *exiles* because they get pushed away from the managers. Let's call her the wounded part." I explained the duty of managers to exile wounded parts and how the exiles must carry the wounds of the internal system.

"The part that feels hopeless about pleasing people may be a firefighter. Let's put her off to the side because she gets called in only when the managers can't control the exiles." Pam responded to the map with considerable interest; she made a copy and indicated she understood the ideas. I went on to explain the self and the spiritual concepts.

Introducing the Self and Spiritual Concepts into the Map

I described Pam's self and the self's capacities, which differentiate the self from her parts and located the self above the parts symbolizing a leadership position (Figure 4.1). I then turned to the spiritual concepts: "From what you described about your relationship with Jesus, you had an encounter with him empowering your life." Many Christians receive the Holy Spirit, who comes to dwell within them to help in leading the parts. I call this the self of faith, because this self invites the Spirit in, and together they form a leadership team with the self making the decisions, and the self of faith helping, supporting, and inspiring.

FIGURE 4.1. A Diagram of Pam's Parts

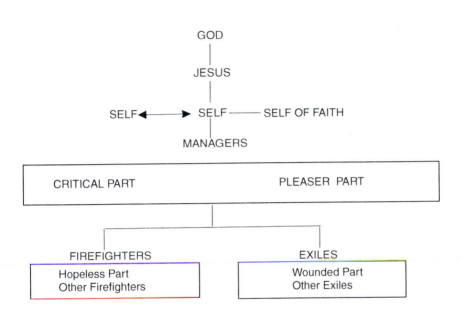

I located her self of faith alongside the self, symbolizing the self's helper role. These concepts fit easily within Pam's spiritual frame of reference, so I described the self's relationship with Jesus and God and located them on the map: "Many Christians, after such an empowering encounter with Jesus, begin to orient their lives around God through Jesus. You may have felt deeply connected to God for the first time. Your self and self of faith begin to center around Jesus and operate with faith and trust in Jesus and God. We can symbolize this with an arrow revolving around Jesus as the axis for your life. Often when our lives begin to be transformed by Jesus, some parts feel threatened. They understand their job to be survival and believe it is not safe to trust in anyone outside their own resources. We may notice this tension within ourselves; we do not blame the parts. We can symbolize this with an arrow revolving around "survival," the parts axis. They are trying to do their job, but it helps us understand why we often slip away from our relationship with Jesus. This introduces the idea that the self, oriented around Jesus, has a different center from the parts oriented around survival. Pam asked a few questions of clarification and added these concepts to her map.

SETTING GOALS

Goal setting can be accomplished easily while mapping, as the client grasps the concepts. For example, as Pam and I talked about the location of her managers (the critical part and the pleaser part), I noted that the self is often pushed to the side by the compulsive managers. One goal, therefore, should be to help Pam unhook from her parts, become elevated again to assume a leadership role, and establish a relationship with each part. For example, the critical and pleaser parts could learn to trust her leadership and thus not be so worried and compulsive. Another goal could be to discover whether the parts are carrying a burden of responsibility from which they can be freed, so as to be at peace with the other parts and help the self lead.

In this discussion of concepts and goals, it is easy for the client to see the self located at the intersection of the internal and the spiritual. This creates an opportunity to set the goal of elevating the self as spiritual authority. In this way the self can restore its relationship with Jesus, with God, and with the self of faith as a teammate.

I went on to describe for Pam the goal of discovering why her relationship with Jesus had slipped away after a few years. Once this was in hand, we would be in a better position to see how to restore it. I noted that the parts could show us why they were upset and fearful about Pam's relationship to Jesus. Our aim would be to help each part, as it became ready, to have its own relationship with Jesus.

As we worked to restore Pam's empowering relationship with Jesus, we would help her learn to unhook from and free the parts. We then could expect to see results in Pam's greater self-confidence to live her own life, to mother her daughter, and to manage the relationship with her separated husband. Pam felt quite hopeful and was ready to begin.

It is important that goals be listed and agreed upon at an early point. This completes the contract for work that the therapist and client will accomplish together and becomes a benchmark against which to evaluate their progress. It is useful to differentiate between external goals, internal goals, and spiritual goals.

- *External goals* relate to the client's external social system. Pam wanted to regain the self-confidence and clarity to manage her life, especially the relationships with her daughter and her husband.
- *Internal goals* are concerned with freeing the self and the parts. Pam and I described her internal goals to be the restoring of her capacity to lead her parts and to unburden them.
- *Spiritual goals* relate to the relationship of the self and parts with the self of faith, Jesus, and God. Pam wanted to understand why she lost her empowering relationship with Jesus and to restore it. We also identified the goal of helping the parts have their own relationship with Jesus.

It is useful to describe for clients the three categories of goals, because it demonstrates that each area is understandable, a distinct way to relate to each area exists, and success with one area contributes to progress in other areas. This description enhances the hope and courage that the self and parts can bring to the therapeutic process. Using the map in describing the goals assists the client and parts in quickly grasping what might otherwise be confusing.

Mapping in the Beginning Stage

The mapping process can contribute to the beginning stages in several ways.

1. It helps the client picture at a glance the elements of the internal system, the self, and the various parts, as well as the spiritual system, the self, self of faith, Jesus, and God. Thus, it gives the self a tool for leadership by providing a new perspective of the internal family, and furthers the process of elevating the self to lead. It locates the self in a position of authority over the parts.
2. The map gives the self a framework with which to picture the self at the intersection between the spiritual and the internal. Thus, the map emphasizes the self as leader and authority for the parts. The self is invited to see the internal system through God's eyes and assume a nurturing role for the parts.

3. The map can be supplemented as therapy proceeds and thus be kept up to date. For example, after unburdening Pam's unworthy part, I made a note on Pam's map. Several months later, the part was engaging in destructive behavior. A glance at the map revealed the previous unburdening process, and it became a simple matter of reminding the part that it had already removed the burden. The part easily removed again to regain her new burden-free role as a little girl. This updating process uses the map as an additional resource for the therapist to keep track of progress with a part, something that could be a prodigious task but is made simple by updating the map.

4. The map helps the therapist to develop the "parts detector." A parts detector is Schwartz's term for the therapist's "radar system" used to detect clients' parts when they jump in and masquerade as the self or try to take over the self. A map gives the therapist a quick scan of each client's parts.

5. The therapist can teach the client to use the map as a tool to keep track of the progress of unburdening parts. Clients thus develop their own "parts detector," so they can listen to their own parts without getting hooked by them.

Pam quickly caught on to the idea of the map and felt encouraged. A major point is to teach the self to look over the parts territory in preparation for respectfully entering the internal system. I told Pam that we needed to test all our theories about her parts by talking to the parts themselves. This caution reminds both therapist and client that the ideas about the client's internal family are only hypotheses until validated by the internal family itself. Together we sensed we had an adequate understanding of her internal system to enter it safely, and when she was ready I would teach her to relate to them. This brought us to the next phase of therapy: working with the parts.

Meeting the Parts and Receiving Them

Pam quickly learned the procedure of letting parts show themselves to her by using the room technique to help her unhook from blending parts. We began talking with the parts that we knew about, the two managers (the critical and pleaser parts), the wounded part (an exile), and the hopeless part (a firefighter). They each had fears about the two of us entering the system.

Pam's meeting with her critical part illustrates the process of working with a protective manager part while using the CCIFS model (similar at this step to the IFS model). The critical part began with persistent criticism of Pam, so I requested that Pam ask the part about this.

Critical Part: You are screwing up too much. You let Samantha [Pam's twelve-year-old daughter] wrap you around her finger. You're such a wimp!!

Pam: I know I wimp out sometimes when she comes on strong, but we plan to find the parts that make me so timid and help them to be freed up and help me to be a better leader.

Critical Part: I'll believe it when I see it. Anyway, you don't want to talk to those timid parts. They're better off hidden; they're trouble.

As the conversation proceeded, we saw the fears that the critical part had (similar to the usual fears of a powerful manager). The wounded part overwhelms Pam with shame and despair; this triggers the hopeless part, which suggests suicide as a solution. The pleaser part, driven by other parts (the sexual part and a lonely part), drives Pam to have an affair to solve the problems of loneliness and shame. And the angry part gets furious and dumps on people, disgracing Pam in the eyes of her friends.

We tried to reassure the critical part by promising that we would help the wounded part not to blend and overwhelm Pam. The critical part was skeptical but continued to listen. Then Pam asked the critical part if it knew about the plan to help Pam be reunited with Jesus and her self of faith so that she could be a better leader. The critical part's response helped us understand another dimension of her fears.

Critical Part: You don't want to mess around with Jesus. You can't trust Him anyway. You asked Him to help your get your life straightened out, but now its worse than ever. He left you just like your dad did. You can't trust Him any more than you could trust your dad.

Pam: What do think would happen to you if I got close to Jesus again?

Critical Part: It would be like before; you listened to him and not to me.

Pam: Yes, I see that you would have felt neglected. I was so excited about Jesus. What if I kept my friendship with you at the same time I was friends with Jesus?

Critical Part: That wouldn't work so forget it.

Pam: Why not? What if you got to be friends with Jesus for yourself?

Critical Part: Naah! Jesus doesn't like me anyway.

Pam: Why not?

Critical Part: I'm too, you know, loud-mouthed, and I don't believe in him anyway. He couldn't like me. He doesn't like anybody who acts nasty like I do sometimes, and I don't believe in him anymore.

Pam: That's the thing about Jesus that is so different. Most people like people because they're nice or they're successful, but Jesus likes us because of who we are and because God made us.

Critical Part: That's hard to believe.

Pam: It's okay that you feel cautious about Jesus. You haven't seen much of Jesus' love. But I can tell you I felt it with Jesus, and it wasn't just for me, it was for all of you parts—you, the sexual part, the wounded part, the angry part—all the parts you'd think He wouldn't love. I think the wounded part felt some of His love—maybe you can check it out for yourself sometime.

Critical Part: I'll think about that.

Pam: Well, remember, you always have a place in our family. Also, is it okay with you if I go to see Jesus again?

Critical Part: What do I care?

Pam: Is it also okay with you if Russ and I talk to the wounded part?

Critical Part: Go ahead. But don't say I didn't warn you!

This conversation with the critical part is an illustration of an early encounter with a manager part. It accomplished several things in the CCIFS model:

1. It taught Pam how to interact with the parts without getting hooked by them. In this conversation, it would have been easy to get in a debate about whether Jesus is trustworthy or not, citing evidence about Jesus dying on the cross. Such debates with parts are seldom useful.
2. It revealed the intimidating style of criticism the part uses, calling Pam a "wimp."
3. It revealed the critical part's fears about Pam and myself entering her family system (the wounded part would overwhelm Pam and trigger the suicidal part). It gave us a chance to reassure the critical part.
4. It revealed how the critical part has projected the abandonment by Pam's father onto Jesus, as well as the critical part's expectation that if Pam were reunited with Jesus, she would ignore the critical part. Jesus would condemn and judge the critical part for her criticisms of Pam. This revelation gave Pam a chance to tell the critical part how Pam discovered that Jesus loves them all, despite their behavior; God made them, and they each had a permanent place in the internal family.
5. It revealed the current attitudes and posture of the critical part: listening and talking, but apparently distrustful. This conversation was an important beginning in the process of developing a respectful and trusting relationship with the critical part.
6. It gave important information to the critical part that Pam herself was changing. When the critical part called Pam a wimp, instead of getting defensive and intimidated (as in the past), Pam stayed in her self and acknowledged the truth of the accusation. She said she had a plan to become more assertive. The critical part knew then that something foundational was changing. Instead of leadership by domination of the strongest part, Pam was

now emerging as a caring leader with a plan that included a respectful relationship with all the parts.

7. It gave the critical part a taste of unconditional acceptance and respect. Pam did not condemn the critical part for her harsh behavior. Rather, Pam not only accepted the part's concern, but invited her to consider a relationship for herself with Jesus. This is the opposite of the condemnation that the part expected.

Pam also asked the critical part if it was okay to talk with the exiled part and with Jesus, as an act of respect for the managerial role of the critical part. This tells her she has a say in the pace of the work. The respect and interest that the critical part feels from Pam is a reflection of the same unconditional love that Pam experiences from Jesus. Pam had "messed up" her life in various ways, but Jesus has accepted her and empowered her to change. So also, the critical part continues to "mess up," depowering Pam instead of empowering her, yet Pam accepts her. Thus begins the process of transformation in her. This acceptance has come through Pam from Jesus (the critical part is too distrustful to receive it from Jesus directly). In the future, the critical part may risk a direct encounter and experience Jesus' love, having experienced it first through Pam. This illustrates a transcendent dimension of Pam's leadership of the parts, being an intermediary between them and Jesus.

It is important that the self gives each of the parts a chance to express fears about the self and therapist entering the system and about the plan for the self's relationship with Jesus. Skeptical parts who are angry at God or Jesus often expect to be condemned as unbelievers. Sexual and violent parts expect to be blamed for their "ungodly" behavior. Burdened exiles are afraid that Jesus will find them unworthy, just as other significant people have. Such parts need to be engaged, listened to, and have their concerns taken seriously. They need reassurance that they too are invited to a new relationship with the self and with Jesus and that they too can change and grow. Such parts also will be alert to whether the therapist condemns or likes them and is competent enough to help them grow. Therapists must be unhooked enough from their own parts so the self is available to feel positive regard toward the client's parts.

Pam and I then talked with the other parts in the survival coalition, the other manager (pleaser part), the two firefighters (hopeless and angry parts), and briefly with the exile (the wounded part). We seemed to be ready for the next step in the healing journey.

MOVING AHEAD

It is important that client and therapist consult about the next step in their work together each time a stage is completed. Sometimes they need to review the effect of the work on the client or to consider questions that have been put aside. It is always useful to stop and appreciate the work they have accomplished together before deciding on the next step. The therapist will have a chance to compliment the client for the courage and leadership shown.

Pam and I then reviewed several possibilities: (1) Should we continue to work with the parts, finding their burdens, and freeing them? or (2) Should we help Pam reconnect with Jesus using a technique called the "mountain exercise"? This is an exercise developed by Schwartz to further unhook the self from parts, so the self can gain perspective on the whole system. In addition to unhooking the self, Pam could also use the procedure to meet Jesus and begin to reconnect with Him. She could also consider if there is something in her daily life triggering her parts, that she would like help with. Pam said she wanted to try the mountain exercise, but first there was a difficult situation that she wanted to talk about.

It is tempting to judge such an external situation to be a diversion from the goal of "parts work." Schwartz observes, however, that such situations are occasions to assist the self in exercising leadership for coping with life, in trying new responses based on a new understanding of the internal family, and in drawing new courage as the internal family permits. "External work" usually assists the internal work and spiritual work. If the client succeeds at new behavior, the parts have more respect for the self's leadership. If, however, the client fails at new behavior, it yields new understanding about which parts are blocking the way. This work can open the door to future unburdening work and spiritual work.

Life Situations Open the Internal Family for Help

Pam described a recent encounter with her separated husband, Ronald, in a way that illustrates how external situations can open the internal system for help. On a bus trip to another city, Ronald stopped by for two days to see their daughter, Samantha. He came unannounced and phoned Pam from the bus station, expecting her to pick him up. He then asked Pam to lend the car to him to take Samantha out to supper and to put him up for the night.

Pam saw this as a continuation of Ronald's demanding, inconsiderate behavior from the past. He sometimes made derogatory comments about her weight or questioned her judgment unfairly about parenting issues. Pam reported that she had always in the past given in to Ronald's demands, swallowed the put-downs, and accepted the intimidation. She said that Ronald was coming back in a few weeks and she would have to go through it all over again. I asked Pam what her parts were saying to her. Pam noted several statements, and together we estimated which parts were involved.

Parts: You wimped out again and let Ronald run all over you (critical part). Tell him to get lost. He doesn't deserve zip from you (angry part). Ronald's attitude is the same as ever, and he acts like he's using drugs again, and Samantha will never have a proper father (hopeless part). You've got to encourage him or he'll stop working on his twelve-step program (pleaser part).

Pam (with an important self-observation): Fear took over my heart, and I knew I had to do something. But I felt unworthy to expect decent treatment from him (wounded part), then I felt hopeless and overpowered (hopeless part). I wanted to find some pot (anesthetizer part) or to go have an affair with someone who would love me (lonely and sexual parts).

Therapist: In a way, this is a horrible situation for you and the parts; but in another way, it's just the kind of situation that can help us see which parts get hooked by Ronald and cause you to get hooked. Then we can help them and help you to lead the way with Ronald. Or you may feel it's better to work on a plan to be more firm with Ronald first.

Pam felt so overwhelmed in the situation that even if she had a plan she wouldn't have been able to carry it out. Instead she decided to do the mountain exercise first. I noted that it is right for her to get grounded in her relationship with Jesus first, so she can be stronger next time in dealing with Ronald and her parts. I realized that any of the three choices (making a plan for dealing with Ronald, working on freeing the parts, or doing the mountain exercise) would help Pam at this time to move toward her goals. How appropriate it was for her to make the decision based on her own judgment and sense of urgency, and how useful for her parts to see me support her judgment!

THE MOUNTAIN EXERCISE
FOR CHRISTIAN CLIENTS

The mountain exercise was developed by Schwartz to help un-hook the self from the parts. With Christian clients, it can be used to help the self reconnect to the self of faith and with Jesus, thus em-powering the self to lead in life situations. This exercise was just what Pam needed at this time, when her parts and her husband were overwhelming her.

The exercise (provided at the end of this chapter) asks the self to gather the parts at the foot of a mountain, calming them so the self can go up the mountain to see Jesus. After Pam settled her parts, I asked if she was ready to ascend with her self of faith. We talked previously about the self of faith as the entity where the Holy Spirit lived in her. Pam said she was ready but needed help finding it. I asked her to step away from her parts and ask God to fill her again with the Holy Spirit. She soon reported that her self of faith was there and ready to go up the mountain. (When clients have not "experienced the Holy Spirit," I refer them to their pastor for this step in their spiritual development. If they indicate they have been prayed for to receive the Holy Spirit but have not ever experienced anything, we make a plan to address this need at a future time.)

Pam proceeded up the mountain with little interference from her parts until she met Jesus at the top of the mountain.

Pam: Jesus is here, but he doesn't have a face.

I considered if there could be any reason that Jesus would show himself to Pam without a face. It seemed inconsistent with His loving character. Several of Pam's parts, however, were threatened by her relationship with Jesus, suggesting the presence of a part.

Therapist: Look around and see if one of the parts has come up.

Pam: Yes, it seems to be the critical part; she's pulling on me.

Therapist: Take her back down the mountain with the other parts and tell her she can watch from there. As soon as you come down, she can tell you anything she is concerned about that happened with Jesus.

Pam soon reported that she had found the critical part and taken her down. When Pam returned to Jesus, she now saw His face, but sensed that He did not like her. This time she found the wounded part up there. After Pam took the wounded part down, I asked her how Jesus felt toward her now.

Pam: I think He likes me.

Therapist: Look close and see. Look into His eyes.

Pam: I can see He loves me.

Therapist: Yes. Anything else?

Pam: He loves me just for who I am, not for how well I do.

Therapist: Yes. What is that like?

Pam: That gives me the feeling I had when I first met him, that I don't have to perform for him or look good.

Therapist: Do you have to do anything at all to keep His love?

Pam: No. Just to stay open to Him. He'll never turn away from me even if I screw up my life again. It's like I've got something solid in me now, and I don't feel shameful and don't feel lonely and empty inside. This is the way it was three years ago with Jesus, and I was able to get myself straightened out.

This sequence illustrates the process of recognizing parts when they come up the mountain to interrupt the self's relationship with Jesus. The critical part interrupted Pam's vision so she could not see Jesus' face, and the wounded part made her feel that Jesus did not like her. After Pam took these parts down, I asked a question to help Pam notice Jesus' attitude toward Her: "How does Jesus feel towards you? Look into His eyes and see." If the client doesn't sense Jesus' love, it is likely other parts are blocking the encounter and must be removed from the mountain. "How does Jesus feel towards you?" becomes a useful diagnostic question.

If the parts finally do permit the self to feel Jesus' love, it is useful to ask: "What is it like to feel His love?" This question helped Pam to grasp the significance of Jesus' love. She realized it would be there for her even if she messed up. This understanding is the opposite of the parts' strategy of pleasing others to compensate for inner unworthiness. Pam now felt that she was worthy in Jesus' eyes and it was "solid," not dependent on her "performance." This is the redemption the whole internal family had sought, not coming from a dependent human relationship, but from God Himself. This awareness is basic to the redemptive process, which will eventually free Pam and all her parts from the endless attempts to please others.

Pam's past experience with Jesus represented the first phase of the mountain exercise: working to have the parts permit the self to encounter Jesus. If they do not allow this, the therapist must get to know them and their fears first and help them. If they do permit the encounter, then the therapist simply assists the self in opening to it and discovering its internal significance. For Pam, Jesus' unconditional acceptance was the foundation of the healing of her unworthiness and of the survival coalition of parts.

The Second Phase of the Mountain Exercise

The second phase of the exercise concerns the application of the relationship with Jesus to the conduct of one's life (the external system). When I sensed Pam was ready, I helped her into this phase by returning to an earlier comment about taking charge of her life again.

Therapist: A minute ago you remembered how you started to straighten out your life three years ago. Now that you're grounded in Jesus again, do you think that you might be able to take charge of your life again?

Pam: Maybe . . . Yes! With Jesus, I could do it like I did before. But what happened before? Why did I lose it?

Therapist: It looks like your self experienced this with Jesus, but your parts didn't, and when things got rough they couldn't trust Jesus or you. But this time we have a better idea of what your parts need so they won't feel so afraid or pushed aside as you lead the way with Jesus. You do seem to be more clear when you're separated from your parts and are here with Jesus.

Pam: Yes, it's great! I'm more confident, not confused.

Therapist: When you're with Jesus, what is your judgment about relating to Ronald?

Pam: I need to be more clear with him about how he treats me. He needs to focus on getting himself healed and not be fussing about how I raise Samantha.

Therapist: We will need to help the parts that look to Him for their needs and accommodate to him, but we can do that. So when you're here with Jesus and not hooked by your parts, you can sense how to relate to Ronald?

Pam: Yes, it's not too hard. I need to set some boundaries with him.

Therapist: How would you do that?

Pam: Maybe I need some guidelines to help me.

Therapist: That sounds useful.

This conversation illustrates Pam's shift from her internal reception of Jesus' unconditional love to its application in her external life. This is the task of the second phase of the mountain exercise. Pam had understood that her first experience with Jesus had empowered her to take charge of her life. This second encounter enables her to take charge of her life again. If the client does not make this connection, the therapist can ask him or her to consider what difference Jesus' love might make in how he or she conducts life.

Pam was already considering the application to her life and how to prevent getting off track and losing her relationship with Jesus as she had before. I acknowledged this as an important concern, assuring her that, in due time, the parts would show us their reasons for getting her off track previously. I suggested we pursue the concept of taking charge of her life again.

Next, I asked Pam about relating to Ronald. She now was able to describe the boundaries clearly: Ronald must focus on his recovery and not judge her parenting skills. She decided to make guidelines for dealing with Ronald. I noted how clear and decisive she was when grounded in Jesus and not overwhelmed by the parts. This helped her see how insightful she was when grounded so she could recognize it more easily in the future. I also wanted Pam's parts (who I assumed were listening intently) to know that I thought Pam's self was quite competent when grounded and not controlled by parts.

The Third and Final Phase

Coming down from the mountain and relating to the parts after the self's encounter with Jesus is the final phase of the mountain exercise. I asked Pam if she was ready to go down and if she needed anything else from Jesus. She said she wanted wisdom to identify further guidelines with Ronald and needed Jesus with her. Jesus said, "Anytime you're ready!" Then Pam gave Jesus a big hug and started down with him. I asked her to consider on her way down if there was anything she wanted to take to the parts or say to them when she came down.

When Pam returned, she told the parts she had felt Jesus' love, and it was not just for her but for them all. Several parts said they did not believe He could love them, because they were bad and nasty. Others said they could not trust Him, that maybe He was like their dad and maybe He was not; it was too early to tell, but they were certain He could not love them. Pam told them she thought Jesus' love was different because He knew we all screwed up, yet loved us anyway. Pam and I recognized that we would need to help each part deal with its own fears about Jesus; but the main point was that they had trusted Pam enough to let her be with Jesus. She thanked them for being patient and letting her go up the mountain. Two parts came to her for a hug, a five-year-old (the wounded part), and a twelve-year-old (the lonely part).

Pam said she felt encouraged that she might be able to take charge of her life again, but she would need help in leading her parts. I said that I was excited about her readiness and about helping her. She asked: Could she go up the mountain to be with Jesus on her own, or did it need to be in a session? I answered that it is possible to do this on one's own, and that this is one of our goals. I noted that in this early stage of getting acquainted with her parts, they would mistrust Jesus and her, and so they might try to block her way. If that happened, I said, we would figure it out; meanwhile, she could use her own judgment about experimenting.

In reflecting on the mountain exercise, Pam and I observed that even the parts antagonistic to Pam's leadership and to Jesus did permit her to have a deep and important encounter with Him early in the parts work, before much trust was established. Perhaps those parts were more worried about Ronald's reemergence and his manipulation than about Pam's leadership and reconnecting with Jesus.

In this final phase of the mountain exercise, the self brings the encounter with Jesus to a close and begins to return to the parts and the external agenda. I asked some questions to help Pam crystallize her insight about the guidelines for Ronald. A final question concerned how she should relate to her parts upon her return from the mountain. She told them of Jesus' love for herself and for them all; together we listened to their expressions of distrust and disbelief. This conversation set up the future work with the parts and crystallized her plan for the guidelines.

The task of the third phase of the mountain exercise is for the self to rejoin the internal family in order to extend the self's experience to the parts and to move to the next stage of the work.

During the exercise, Pam and the parts accomplished several important goals: unhooking from her parts, breaking through barriers of fear with Jesus, renewing her relationship with Him, and experiencing the unconditional quality of Jesus' love. This gave her a foundation for her life that could release the internal family from the search for redemption by pleasing others.

These factors restored Pam's confidence and her ability to manage her life and lead her parts. Pam returned to her parts in a posture of leadership, explaining and listening to them. Although the parts were complaining and fearful, they were looking to her as the transcendent figure standing at the intersection of the internal and the spiritual, the link to God. This change continued the transformation process by changing the parts' focus from pleasing others to fostering their relationship with Pam and her relationship with Jesus. This opened the way for the parts to permit Jesus, with His wisdom and healing powers, to be a part of the next phases, the listing of the guidelines and the unburdening work with the parts who carried the deepest wounds of worthlessness and shame.

Many clients gain a new perspective from the mountain exercise for dealing with the challenges in their lives when they reconnect with Jesus as the ground of their worth. They often gain confidence to conduct their lives. This experience with Jesus early in the work can greatly encourage the self, the parts, and the therapist. Sometimes, however, it is not permitted by the parts.

The managers may attempt to block the self from going up the mountain or impede the self's experience of Jesus' unconditional love. Even in these situations, the exercise provides important information about which parts are distressed and thus directs the spotlight to these parts and their fears. As long as the therapist (with self in charge) can be flexible, the mountain exercise will be a win-win situation for the client. This is true even in the early stages of therapy.

PAM'S GUIDELINES FOR RELATING TO RONALD

Pam needed the perspective and confidence from the mountain exercise to deal with Ronald. Her needy parts had gotten her into this dysfunctional relationship, and they continued to keep her dependent and vulnerable to his manipulations and put-downs. One of her mountain exercise insights was that she needed clear guidelines for dealing with Ronald. His fussing at Pam was a distraction from his recovery program. Thus, if Pam could avoid getting hooked into these manipulations, it would be helpful for Ronald too. She was able to identify several guidelines for future interactions with him:

1. I am not responsible for Ronald's twelve-step program.
2. There will be no visits when Ronald is on drugs of any kind.
3. Put-downs from Ronald are not acceptable.
4. The car cannot be borrowed without one day's advance notice request.

Pam was pleased with her clarity and resolve but unsure about her ability to follow the guidelines. She was also aware that she felt unworthy of Ronald's respect. She continually felt an inner neediness that made it hard to stand her ground when with him. I said that perhaps her younger parts were involved. Did she want to work with them, or should she further prepare for Ronald's impending visit? She said there was time to work with the parts before Ronald returned, and so began a second round of work with Pam's parts. This process illustrates how the external work (making the guidelines) often leads to and propels the internal work (unburdening the parts). Pam and I began by considering her parts map; we focused on a part likely to be the exiled unworthy part. I asked Pam to check with the other parts first, so they could register any concerns.

Hearing the Critical Part's Concerns About Working with an Exile

The critical part came forward to protest: "You shouldn't mess around with the wounded part; it's too wounded and nothing but trouble." I asked Pam to ask the critical part what would happen if we talked with the wounded part. The critical part was convinced that the wounded part would overwhelm Pam. "You are too much of a wimp to stand up to wounded part, let alone Ronald!" the critical part said.

It is tempting to view the critical part as blocking progress and deserving of being put in her place. This seldom is fruitful; the therapist should instead find his or her own part with such a view and help the part to trust the therapist's self to lead. I did have such a part; after helping my part to step back, I was able to work respectfully with Pam's critical part. Pam and I came to see that the critical part's intent was not to put Pam down—but to make her perfect beyond criticism and pleasing to others. We realized that the critical part was the executor of the internal survival strategy, pleasing others to minimize future rejection and abandonment and keeping down the past pain of the exile.

The more we talked, the more we appreciated the heavy burden the critical part carried. Soon she was willing to put away her burden for a time and cautiously to trust Pam and me to help the exile. She appreciated the break from her constant vigilance and the chance to play as a twelve-year-old (her age). She had no interest in Jesus, to be expected of the leader of the survival coalition of parts. With this understanding of critical part, as well as a beginning trust relationship with her, we were free to proceed to the wounded part.

HEALING WITH JESUS:
RETRIEVING AND UNBURDENING
A PART STUCK IN THE PAST

The critical part wanted to monitor the work with the wounded part, so we let her sit on a "balcony" to watch. The work then became not only an effort to help the wounded part, but also a test case for the critical part. Pam was easily able to find the wounded part:

Therapist: Do you see an image of the wounded part?

Pam: I see an old woman with her hair standing on end, and she looks like she is starving.

Therapist: Ask her to show us why she looks that way.

Pam: She said that nobody wants her and she's starving for love.

As we got to know wounded part, we confirmed that she is the part carrying the inner sense of worthlessness. We decided to call her the "unworthy part" to differentiate her from another part carrying the emptiness.

Soon Pam was feeling sick to her stomach. It was the unworthy part putting her pain into Pam. I coached her in helping the unworthy part take her feelings back within herself. Pam then talked with the various parts that were blending with her. One part made her afraid of the unworthy part, another made her angry, and a third part made her dislike the unworthy part. One by one, Pam heard their concerns and reassured them so they were willing to let her talk to the unworthy part.

The unworthy part then showed herself as a four-year-old girl with a ragged dress and a forlorn expression on her face. With some coaching and experimenting, Pam was able to get close to the little girl and hold and comfort her. I told Pam to ask the unworthy part why it was so upsetting for her when Pam related to Ronald. The unworthy part replied she was afraid Ronald (who was her last hope) would reject her and push her away, as others had done. Other parts appeared and showed Pam that if Ronald rejected her, the hopeless part was ready to push suicide as a solution, since Ronald was the last hope for "redemption." I asked Pam to ask the unworthy part whether she had ever experienced this fear of rejection before. She said she had, but it was a long time ago.

Preparing Self and Parts to Revisit a Frightening Scene

The unworthy part had told us her pain was about no one wanting her and feeling starved for love. Pam and I considered if we felt able to go back to such a devastating time. Pam and her parts felt considerable fear about going back, but Pam said she could if Jesus came back with us.

This represents a common dilemma in parts work. We were at the point of going back with the unworthy part and had several clues that her sense of being unwanted stemmed from Pam's mother at an early stage in life. This, we theorized, was the origin of her anxiety about being worthless and her dread of nonbeing. Out of this anguish, the part took on the burden of worthlessness with a survival strategy of pleasing a redeemer person as the only way to gain acceptability. Thus, it was not surprising that Pam and her parts had such fear about going back to what they felt was the edge of nonbeing.

In response to Pam's fears, I asked her if she understood that God's plan was for His love to come through parents so that children would know they are worthy since God made them. But because parents' needy parts and angry parts sometimes get in the way and God's love gets blocked, the children feel neglected and unworthy instead. This is what Pam had experienced as a child. The good news, however, is that God has provided an alternative: His children can experience God's love directly through Jesus. This was what Pam had experienced in her encounters with Jesus. It helped Pam to understand how her encounters with Jesus connected with a very primitive need within her. She saw that our task is to help the unworthy part now to experience God's acceptance and worth through Jesus.

In the next session, we addressed the remaining fears of Pam and her parts about going back to the edge of nonbeing. Pam and her parts were concerned about being swallowed up by nonbeing. Pam and I reviewed the scripture that describes how Jesus, after his resurrection, descended into the place of the dead to free the "captives" (Ephesians 4:8-9). Here Jesus has not only power over death but the power of life (His resurrection) and the power to free the unworthy part from nonbeing, to give her new life that comes from God Himself. Jesus will come with us if we ask Him, and we will be able to go back to the unworthy part's earliest experiences of rejection and nonbeing.

By the next session, Pam and the parts were willing to go back with Jesus and let the unworthy part show us her painful secrets. This illustrates how the possibility of going back into such a terrifying place with Jesus can sometimes provide the margin of safety for the self and the parts. In this case, the possibility that God would bestow directly the love blocked by parents gave hope to the parts suffering from loss of worth and striving for worth by pleasing others.

The idea of Jesus as victor over death descending to give life to those without worth gave hope to Pam's parts who were fearful of being swallowed by the nonbeing of the unworthy part. Pam and I sensed that the path was now clear to return to the past with the unworthy part in the next session.

Going Back with an Exile into the Anguish of the Past

At the next session, I asked Pam if she and her parts felt ready to go back with her unworthy part. I told her that I had checked with my parts, too, and reminded them that we also had gone back into our own anguish with Jesus. He had transformed it, so they now believed He would go back with Pam and her unworthy part. Pam and I agreed to move ahead.

Therapist: When you're ready, why don't you ask Jesus to join us?

(Pause)

Pam: He's here.

Therapist: Ask the unworthy part to take us back, when she's ready, to the first time she experienced the sense of unworthiness.

Pam: We're back; "Unworthy" is very little.

Therapist: Do you have a sense of how old she is?

Pam: Maybe four to five years old . . . she's showing me there is something wrong with her . . . she's bad inside.

Therapist: What makes her think that?

Pam: Mother doesn't want to be with her. She's in a dark place, and Mother is leaving her.

Therapist: What kind of a place is it?

Pam: The big washing machine is there. It's scary.

Therapist: Anything else?

Pam: Mother doesn't want her. She's not good enough.

Therapist: Why does she think that?

Pam: Mother walked away and left her.

Therapist: Does she know where Mother is?

Pam: She's in the house . . . somewhere.

Therapist: Anything else she wants to show us?

Pam: She has to do something or else she won't have anyone.

Therapist: Then what would happen?

Pam: She would disappear.

Therapist: Why would she disappear?

Pam: She wouldn't be connected to anybody.

At this point Pam and I stopped to consider what the unworthy part had shown us.

Mother has left her in a dark place with a washing machine. A basement? Did Mother do it on purpose? Pam thought this was a period when her dad lived away from home and her mother became depressed. Pam felt her mother was most likely overwhelmed by her parts and went into a depression, crying and withdrawing. Pam had sensed the same pattern in her own life when she was twelve years old, when her father divorced her mother. Pam sensed that her mother's depression left her inattentive to the child's needs; her mother may have often wandered off to bed to cry and sleep. The four-year-old showed us how frightened and alone it made her feel. In trying to make sense of her mother's behavior, she came to the best conclusion she could: that Mother didn't want to be with her. Why not? The four-year-old cannot imagine that Mother is bad, therefore she herself must be at fault and unworthy of Mother's attention. Without an emotional connection to anyone, she assumes she will cease to exist. This then is the origin of her dread, the fear of nonbeing. It became apparent to Pam and me why the parts did not want to revisit this dread without Jesus, the Lord of Life!

When we resumed the dialogue with the unworthy part, we asked more questions to allow her to show us how the burden of worthlessness related to the survival pattern of pleasing others.

Therapist: Since the four-year-old feels she will cease to be without being connected to Mother, what will she do?

Pam: She has to find Mother and take care of her.

Therapist: How can she do that?

Pam: She will listen when Mother is upset and hold her hand.

Therapist: How does Mother act when she is upset?

Pam: She sleeps and cries on the bed and forgets things.

Therapist: How does Mother respond when the four-year-old holds her and listens?

Pam: She looks at the four-year-old and smiles some, and sometimes she holds the four-year-old.

Therapist: Does the four-year-old know which parts take care of Mother?

Pam: No, but they're bigger and they push her [the four-year-old] away.

Together we noted that this is where the pleaser part split off from the four-year-old part. The four-year-old carried the burden of worthlessness and was exiled by the pleaser part. This was to avoid interrupting the rescue effort made by the pleaser part to care for Mother, insuring attention from Mother and so continuing the four-year-old's "being" for another day. The pleaser part's caregiving effort then became the daily strategy by which the four-year-old continues her existence. The four-year-old part became a "parentified child" vested with the task of taking care of her mother's emotional needs to ensure some measure of attention and thus her own survival.

This example illustrates why parentified children lose their childhood; all their childhood interests must take second place to the need to please to survive. Pam could now see the connection between her inner dread, her pleaser part's urges, her loss of a childhood, and her mother's fear of the loss of her husband. She wondered if her mother could have had an inner worthlessness from her own mother's coldness and preoccupation with pleasing her own husband (Pam's grandfather). The result seemed to be that Pam was the third generation of women with inner worthlessness, taught to please others to survive. This insight showed Pam that God was not just interested in healing her but in transforming the lineage of brokenness for several generations. Seeing the wounds of several generations also helped explain why her parts were afraid to revisit the dreaded scene and why the transforming power of Jesus was so necessary to reassure the parts that they could tolerate reentering the past.

The Importance of Jesus' Role

As Pam and I were reflecting on the power of this insight about Jesus' role, I realized how important Jesus' role was for me and my parts. I too had experienced such anguish before and remembered that Jesus' transforming power created the margin of safety for me then as well as now. He is there not just for Pam and her parts, but for me and my parts as well.

The results of our ability to reenter Pam's dread with Jesus was substantial; this safe reentry

- enabled us to get to the *bottom* of the anguish, this is the *prerequisite of healing.* As King David said in a psalm, "God requires truth in the inner part" (Psalms 51:6).
- revealed the *memory* of Mother's emotional abandonment that the unworthy part carried with her, forever reinforcing the internal self-judgments and the survival strategy.
- showed clearly the content of the self-judgments, "Mother doesn't want to be with me, I must be bad and unworthy of her attention."
- revealed the dread: "Without being connected to anyone, I will cease to exist."
- revealed the survival strategy that the pleaser part carried out: care for Mother and please her.
- helped Pam to see through adult eyes that Mother's abandonment reflected more on her mother's condition than on Pam's own worth.
- showed the unworthy part and the other parts that Pam, Jesus, and I could enter the dreaded place and not cease to exist ourselves.

These gains opened the door for the next step: for Pam and Jesus to assist the unworthy part in dealing differently with the scene.

THE HEALING OF A MEMORY WITH JESUS

It is not wise to bring resolution before a part has exposed all the horrors and secrets at the bottom of its anguish. Thus, I wanted Pam to ask the unworthy part if she had shown us the worst of the situation and was ready for Pam and Jesus to step into the scene. She answered "Yes," to both questions. Pam and Jesus entered the scene with the unworthy part.

Pam: What do you need and want most?

Unworthy Part: I need Mother to love me and play with me.

Pam: Since Jesus and I are with you, can you tell her.

Unworthy Part: I'll try. [The unworthy part goes to Mother and asks her to play with her]

Unworthy Part: Mother is crying, and she's wounded about Father. She wants someone to hold her hand.

Pam: Where does that leave you? How will you find out if she can love you?

Unworthy Part: [holding Mother's ears and turning Mother's face toward her] I want you to love me. Am I important to you?

Mother: I'm sorry. I don't realize how busy I am. I will try to play with you, but I have a lot to do.

Pam: What do you make of Mother's response?

Unworthy Part: I don't believe she will play with me. It proves I am bad inside like I thought. Maybe if I look cute the way she likes me to and hold her hand when she's sad, she will love me.

This encounter appears to have made things worse, but it has actually clarified Mother's inability to love her daughter and help us focus the dilemma. If the mother's capacity is so limited, where is the source of love and self-worth for the little girl? How can she deal with the situation without becoming a caregiver for her mother?

I decided to suggest a technique that Schwartz developed to help key figures to respond more from the self.

Therapist to Pam: Ask the unworthy part if she would like us to help her mother put aside her upset parts so that she can respond to you better.

Unworthy Part: Yes.

Pam and Jesus go to Mother and ask her to put her upset parts aside so she can respond to her daughter.

Pam: [to unworthy part] Ask Mother again.

Unworthy Part: [holding mother's ears again] I want you to play with me and love me!

Mother: I do love you, but I'm so overwhelmed with feelings I just want to cry a lot. I'm sorry I can't be a better mother.

Pam: [to unworthy part] What do you make of that?

Unworthy Part: I guess she does love me, but she's too sad.

Pam: Can she love you at all?

Unworthy Part: Maybe; she can when she's not too sad.

This encounter becomes the basis for a resolution between the unworthy part and her mother. The unworthy part's assertiveness focuses Mother on the basic question of whether Mother did love her and could attend to her. Jesus and Pam's help enabled Mother to separate from her parts momentarily. Pam and the unworthy part now sense that Mother actually did love Pam but was unable to show her love consistently during that period. The unworthy part then understood that it was Mother who was flawed and not herself.

The unworthy part can now have a new attitude of acceptance toward Mother and her incapacity, which opens the way to receive and appreciate the meager amount that Mother had to give. This is the beginning of a resolution of the broken relationship with Mother. It does not displace the painful memory of Mother's unavailability, but it does put it in a more accurate perspective. It arises from the unworthy part's strength (her assertiveness in confronting Mother) instead of from her inability to get Mother to love her; she can now receive what Mother has to give. The unworthy part's need for unburdening from her worthlessness remains, as well as a need for an adequate source of love and connectedness. The dialogue continues.

Pam: How ready are you to take out the old idea about yourself that you are bad and not good enough for Mother to pay attention to?

Unworthy Part: I would like that.

Had we asked this question of the unworthy part before the encounter with Mother, she would likely have said, "I can't take it out, it's me!" But during the encounter with Jesus, she saw the evidence that it was a reflection of Mother's incapacity and not of her own condition. Pam asked the unworthy part to find the burden.

Unworthy Part: I'm finding a big "blob" that fills my insides.

Pam: How do you feel about yourself when the blob is there?

Unworthy Part: That I'm bad. No wonder Mother doesn't love me!

Pam: Can you take it out by yourself, or do you want help? [The unworthy part needs help. Pam and Jesus help her take the blob out.]

Pam: How do you feel now?

Unworthy Part: Lighter. Nice and warm.

We asked the unworthy part if there was anything left of the blob.

Unworthy Part: No, it's gone. But there is bad skin all over my arms and legs. Jesus is washing it off.

The unworthy part then told us that the bad skin was the shame that accompanied the worthlessness. We asked the unworthy part if there were other burdens she was carrying. She did not think so. Pam and I sensed it was timely to consider her need for a more adequate source of love and affirmation.

Pam: How would you like to be friends with me and with Jesus, especially when Ronald and I are having a fuss and you remember the sad times with Mother?

Unworthy Part: I agree.

Pam: How do you think Jesus and I feel about you?

Unworthy Part: I know that *you* like me, but I'm not sure about Jesus.

Pam: Could you look into His eyes and see if you can tell?

Unworthy Part: He seems to like me.

Pam: Can you open your heart and let some of that love in?

Unworthy Part: Yes, He really does love me. He wants me to stay with Him. He likes to be with me.

Pam: Can you turn to Him and to me when things are scary?

Unworthy Part: Yes, I would like to have someone to turn to. I've always felt so alone.

This appeared to reconnect the unworthy part with Pam and with Jesus. If the unworthy part did not feel Jesus' love for her, we would have checked to see if the old conviction still remained or if other parts were blocking the way.

Unworthy Part: There's no one to care for Mother. I should hold her hand and help her.

Pam: No, that's not your job. Mother is sad and depressed. She'll have to find her own way through. She's a grown-up. Your job is to be a kid and play.

Pam and the unworthy part decided to ask God to send an angel to help Mother find her way. Then the unworthy part would feel free to leave. After Pam and the unworthy part returned to the present, we helped the unworthy part choose a new name ("Cricket") and get reacquainted with the other parts, now without her old role and burden. The other parts had been watching the retrieval process carefully and welcomed Cricket warmly. We told the other parts that since Cricket did not have the unworthiness and shame anymore, it was not necessary for them to worry about pleasing others. Since they all have a place in the internal family, they ought to consider now what they each might like to do. This invitation acknowledges what they are likely feeling: that the system has changed, that none of them will be discarded, and that now a chance exists for them to grow.

Pam and I asked the other parts if they had seen Cricket's new relationship with Jesus. They did and indicated varying responses, from skepticism to strong desire for a similar relationship. Each of them could now consider having her own relationship with Jesus.

The Typical Steps of Unburdening and Recovering a Part

This completed the healing process for the unworthy part. The sequence that unfolded describes the typical steps of unburdening and recovering a part using the CCIFS model. Jesus' presence provided for the self and the internal family enough safety for the part to reenter a dreaded memory and discover its contents. The self and Jesus helped the unworthy part confront Mother, and then aided Mother's self in emerging to acknowledge her incapacity to love adequately. This was evidence for the unworthy part to see that the burden of worthlessness had been put on her by Mother and could now be removed. Pam's self and Jesus then helped the unworthy part to open herself to a new relationship with Jesus; she was "redeemed" by having a new unconditional standing with Jesus. The unworthy part and the other parts no longer needed to search for a redeemer person by pleasing others. Then the unworthy part could release Mother to find her own way with God, with the result that the unworthy part was free to come to live in the present and participate in Pam's present life.

The order of the above steps is one that emerged in the interaction with Pam's self and parts according to their readiness, although movement and order were sometimes propelled by Ronald's visits and other external factors.

This completes the description of the various steps of healing a part with Jesus in CCIFS therapy. The following is a summary of the remaining work with Pam. It illustrates how healing builds on the foundations of the mountain exercise, the working relationship with the critical part, and the retrieval and unburdening of the unworthy part.

Continuing Pam's Therapy

After the unburdening of Cricket, Ronald arrived unannounced on the return trip to his home. He displayed his usual pattern of putting

Pam down, manipulating her for what he wanted, such as borrowing money and the car. Pam felt intimidated as before and gave in to him, unable to hold firm to her guidelines. Pam's critical part criticized her for being a wimp. Pam asked herself if she had regressed back to square one and lost all her hard-earned gains.

As we checked with the parts, we found that Cricket had not been intimidated by Ronald, but that two other parts had surfaced and gotten hooked, the lonely part and the pleaser part. This gave us the opportunity to work with them. These were the parts who sought to fill the internal void and loneliness by seeking Ronald's affirmation and companionship. They took us back to the loss of Pam's father at the time of the divorce and, with Jesus, their memories were healed, as well as their inner void. This void was then filled with Jesus' love.

Even after these healings, when Ronald came around Pam got hooked, but again it was not the healed parts who caused her to get hooked but other parts who had just surfaced. We now could work with them and free them as well. Soon Pam could see that Ronald's visits were not occasions of her failure, as the critical part claimed, but opportunities to test her growth. On each successive visit, Pam found herself more free to manage the relationship with Ronald according to her own wisdom and plan. Soon the critical part herself was unburdened, and even she could see how much Pam had succeeded in maintaining family boundaries without putting Ronald down.

During this time Pam assumed more responsibility for her parts and their needs and growth and began using me only as a consultant. Pam's parts also came to have a new view of her, seeing her not as a wimpy victim easily steamrolled by Ronald, but as a fair yet loving leader.

Pam began relating more to her young teenager, Samantha, in her self instead of from her intimidated parts. Previously, Pam was intimidated by Samantha's nagging and manipulation. Now she was increasingly able to be loving and firm, coaching Samantha lovingly when possible but also being firm when necessary. Pam also began praying every morning for Jesus to give her love and wisdom to lead her parts, to be a good mother for Samantha, and to remain steady with Ronald. And Samantha was developing into a self-confident teen, even able to stand up against her peer group when necessary.

Samantha even told Pam she appreciated how much better Pam listened to her than other parents she observed.

At the last of our periodic reviews, Pam observed that we had fulfilled all her original goals: the internal goals for her self to lead and heal the parts, the spiritual goals to return to the empowered relationship with Jesus and invite her parts to trust Him, and the external goals of managing her life. Pam and her parts had come to the new alignment around Pam and in relationship with Jesus. Each part in the survival organization had been unburdened and had a new relationship of trust with Pam and Jesus. They were finally free from the survival strategy of seeking a redeemer person by pleasing others

God's loving, transforming character was embodied in Pam's self as she led her internal parts and interacted with the external world. Pam herself noticed more of Jesus' traits in her style: patience, love, flexibility with firmness. It seemed that Pam was experiencing the process Paul describes in the foreword to this chapter; not being conformed to the world's standards, but being transformed inwardly by a complete change of mind. This fits with God's reconciling plan for our broken world: embodying His character in people like Pam, and bringing His love and power into their lives (Ephesians 3:19; 4:12-16; and 5:1-2). Since it is a living system, the challenges of Pam's world continue to stimulate her and her parts to rely more on Jesus and to further growth.

Chapter 4 concludes the presentation of the CCIFS model. We end with a summary of the procedures unique to CCIFS therapy, a clinical outline of those CCIFS procedures integrated with IFS therapy (using Schwartz's outline), and an exercise.

SUMMARY OF PROCEDURES UNIQUE TO CCIFS THERAPY

This chapter began by describing the need to determine the appropriateness of using the CCIFS model with a client. It noted the direct and indirect ways that Christian clients express their desire to integrate clinical work with their spirituality and how the therapist may initiate the question if the client does not. Chapter 4 discusses the benefits that can follow from including spirituality. These range from using the client's spiritual strengths for the clinical work on hand to establishing the client and the therapist on common ground before

God. The first opens the way for the healing and transforming power of God, the second assists in developing a collaborative relationship between client and therapist.

This chapter described the use of mapping the self and parts as an effective way to introduce clients to the CCIFS concepts, engage them quickly in a joint venture with the therapist, and exploring and specifying the dynamic quality of the clients' internal family. It presented the mapping process as an effort to hypothesize about the possible managers, firefighters, and exiles oriented around the client's survival axis. It considered the possibility of reuniting the self with the self of faith, and with Jesus, forming a new Christ-centered axis. This can become the source of empowerment for the self, unhooking from the blending parts to lead the way in life, and for God's transforming power to heal the parts and the self.

The chapter emphasized the usefulness of identifying measurable goals around the clients' problems and needs. It noted how combining *internal goals* (the internal system), *external goals* (the client's social system), and *spiritual goals* (relationship with Jesus and God) with the mapping process could give the client an easily understood view of the three areas. This shows the client that the counseling plan is comprehensive enough to include all three dimensions. In turn, the client can acquire a leadership perspective of change that gives hope that important changes can happen. The chapter also noted that including urgent external goals from the social system creates an opening for help to the internal and spiritual systems.

Because of the urgency in her external family, Pam next chose to use the mountain exercise. The chapter described this exercise as the first of several key procedures of CCIFS therapy. Its first phase involved gathering the parts and convincing them to allow the self and self of faith could go up the mountain to see Jesus. If the self is able to go up and meet Jesus, the therapist asks the self to consider how Jesus feels toward him or her. This was used to assess the capacity of the parts to allow the self to experience Jesus' unconditional love. The therapist then helps the self assess the effect on the self and the whole internal system of being loved unconditionally. This love may become the ground for a reorganization of the internal life from being endlessly centered around survival to being centered around the empowering relationship with Jesus.

The second phase of the mountain exercise involved the newly grounded self considering what differences being grounded in Jesus' love makes for the conduct of life. This question can provoke new vision and insights about what structures, boundaries, self-beliefs, or behaviors are now possible.

The third and final phase moved the self from the encounter with Jesus to a consideration of how the self can implement its new role, the management of the parts' need for healing and the leadership of the internal system. The chapter noted possible results of the mountain exercise, one of which is that the parts may begin to see the self in a leadership role at the intersection of spiritual and the physical realities. The self now will have the capacity to lead the internal family from its old never-ending survival orientation to a new empowering orientation built on the relationship with Jesus.

Pam's external family agenda generated an urgency to propel her and her parts into the other dimension of the CCIFS therapy, the healing and freeing of the parts. We saw the process of unburdening a key manager so that parts are secure enough to permit work with one of the central exiles. This illustrated another key procedure of CCIFS, *the recovery of the exiles' buried anguish by reentry into the memory.* Memories may contain such terrifying experiences that the parts and self are too frightened to see their content. In this situation, Jesus' willingness to accompany the self and parts back into the terror may provide the needed margin of safety. The reentry of Pam's exile can now reveal that the trauma had broken relationships and created burdens of worthlessness and shame, which the parts then endlessly carried. The self and parts can now see how the burdens were created by the trauma and are not intrinsic to the internal family.

This knowledge, with the healing power of Jesus, then enabled the *healing and resolution of core memories and relationships,* which reinforced the core beliefs. This led to *unburdening the part* with necessary help from Jesus. This, in turn, led to *helping the part bond with Jesus* in a new empowering relationship, so it could grow without being dragged into the old survival strategy by the other parts. We then saw the last procedure of CCIFS, *the retrieval of the part from the past to the present.* This is similar to the retrieval in IFS therapy, except that spiritual resources and relationships are utilized to complete any needed freeing of the part from past enmeshments.

The chapter illustrated how each subsequent visit from Pam's separated husband caused new parts to surface. This occasioned the healing of each part leading them to their own relationships with Jesus. With Pam as leader empowered by Jesus, and the parts freed of old burdens, the internal system came to a new orientation. Pam could now stay unhooked from her parts and from Ronald. She then developed a respectful but firm relationship with her struggling husband, and a loving, empowering relationship with her daughter, Samantha.

These procedures are tools for moving clients toward the main goal of CCIFS therapy, empowering the self by reuniting self with the self of faith and with Jesus. This in turn releases into the internal system the powers of Jesus for healing, for reorganizing on a new axis, and for developing a new style of relating to people and social systems in clients' lives, one grounded in love and wisdom.

CLINICAL OUTLINE OF CCIFS THERAPY FOR WORKING WITH INDIVIDUALS

What follows is a summary of the clinical techniques described in the chapter. These illustrate the range of techniques available to CCIFS therapy. Yet this summary presents just one of several possible sequences that could be followed.

  I. Client and therapist consider client's spiritual interest and appropriateness of the CCIFS model.

 II. Introducing the CCIFS model to the client

   A. The client describes a problem, therapist feeds back what client says using the language of parts and illustrating with the map.

   B. Therapist introduces basic concepts of the CCIFS model and of the mapping technique.

     1. Everyone has parts, a self, and an internal survival organization. Christians usually also have a self of faith and the beginning of a new internal organization centered around Jesus.

     2. The goals of CCIFS therapy are explained: to elevate the self to leadership with the self of faith, to free the self to stay centered in the love and transforming relationship with Jesus, to free the parts so they can get along and can

come to trust the self and Jesus and so make their contribution to the whole.

    3. Therapist will coach the client in the process; the process can be done safely at a respectful pace.

  C. The therapist asks whether the client is interested in working this way and, if so, negotiates the process.

III. Estimating the territory

  A. The client identifies parts of which he or she is aware. The therapist and client hypothesize about the internal survival organization of parts, the development of the new Christ-centered organization, and the level of conflict between the two.

    1. They consider how to enter the system respectfully.

  B. The therapist and client consider the safety of the client's external context of people or situations and assess ability to proceed with inner work. If needed, they decide to try first to make the external context safer.

IV. Meeting the parts, hearing their concerns, and reassuring them

  A. The therapist helps client to unhook (differentiate) self from blending parts (using room technique) and to talk to parts about their concerns.

  B. Client and therapist consider parts' concerns about going inside safely, especially managers' concerns about working with exiles, and negotiates until parts are assured that:

    1. The self will not be overwhelmed.

    2. Dangerous firefighters will not be released.

    3. The therapist will be able to accept the exiles and remain supportive.

    4. The exile(s) will be able to change.

    5. The external environment is safe enough.

    6. Dangerous secrets can be dealt with safely.

    7. Managers will continue to have a place in the inner family.

  C. The therapist and client consider parts' concerns about the self's relationship with Jesus and negotiate until the parts are assured that:

    1. The parts will not be condemned for their anger at God or their skepticism about the possibility of change.

    2. The parts will not be condemned for sexual, violent, critical, or other "ungodly behavior."

    3. The therapist will be able to accept the "sinful parts" and help them.

    4. Parts have a place in the new relationship with Jesus and are needed and wanted for themselves.

    5. Parts, when they desire, can have their own relationship with Jesus and experience His love.

    6. The therapist can help the client's self remain centered in the transforming relationship with Jesus.

  D. Therapist and client hear from the parts about their roles and relationships.

V. Depolarizing parts as necessary to open the way for unburdening the parts

  A. Client and therapist identify the parts polarized against other parts.

  B. Self meets with each part individually to assess what each part needs to depolarize.

  C. Self helps polarized parts get unhooked by having parts meet each other or having parts meet with Jesus as appropriate.

VI. Identifying the chains (constraints) that bind individual parts

  A. The client's self asks the part in question:

    1. Why does it do what it does?

    2. What is it afraid will happen if it leaves its extreme role?

    3. What burdens does it carry and where is it stuck in the past (i.e. where it got the burden)?

  B. If the part is an exile, the self helps the exile to contain its feelings and not overwhelm the self. If the part cannot contain its feelings, the therapist may work with the part directly. This technique is called direct access and is beyond the scope of this book (see Schwartz, 1997, Chapter 5).

VII. Releasing the chains restraining the parts through unburdening and retrieving the parts from the past

  A. Unburdening a part:

    1. Self asks the part how ready it is to release the task, feeling, or belief (burden). If the part believes the burden is intrinsic to itself, self goes back with part to when the burden was put on. Self consults with part about asking Jesus to come back to help.

    2. When the part is ready, self and Jesus help parts find the burden either in or on it.

    3. Self and Jesus help part remove the burden and dispose of it.

    4. Self checks with other parts to see if they are aware of the change in the part and agree with it.

5. Self may help the part to find a new relationship with Jesus, as desired, and to find a new role in the coalition centered around Jesus, as well as a new name incorporating the part's talents and goals.
6. The part, in the new role, is introduced to the other parts.
B. Retrieving a part from where it is stuck in the past:
  1. Self checks with the managers about any concerns regarding going back to the past.
  2. The therapist helps self check to be sure self is unhooked from the parts and feels ready.
  3. Self consults with parts about asking Jesus to come back to the past with the part.
  4. Part takes self and Jesus back to where it is stuck in the past.
  5. The part shows self and Jesus all that is necessary about the situation until the part is satisfied that the self and Jesus understand the significance of the scene.
  6. Self and Jesus enter scene in a way that the part needed someone to be there originally, helping it to come to a resolution.
  7. Self and part check for any extreme feelings or ideas to be unburdened.
  8. Self helps the part to new relationship with Jesus and helps transform any old beliefs and feelings.
  9. Self helps part to a new role in the Christ-centered coalition and a new name, if so desired.
10. Self helps the part consider when the situation is resolved and when the part is ready to come into the present.
11. The part and self come into the present, and find a safe place for the part in the new coalition.
12. The self introduces the part to other parts and sees that their relationship is respectful.
VIII. Harmonizing the internal family
A. The self continues to assess the needs of the internal family, noticing remaining polarizations and the need for synchronizing new roles so parts fit well together. It notes parts left behind in the survival coalition and helps them. It can convene the internal family with the self of faith and Jesus, as appropriate, for making decisions and problem solving together.

THE MOUNTAIN EXERCISE

1. Relax, lie down if you desire, breathe deeply for a minute or two.
2. Gather all the parts you know at the foot of the mountain. (Refer to your parts diagram, if necessary.)
3. Consider if you would like to take your self of faith with you up the mountain.
4. Talk to the parts about your going on a short trip up the mountain and that you want them to wait for you. If they are worried, tell them they will be able to see you as you go up and that you will only be gone ten minutes or so.
5. When the parts are settled, start up the mountain. Notice what you see and feel as you ascend.
6. If you discover any distractions, emotions, or thoughts as you ascend, note them. This has probably been caused by a part that has come up the mountain. Find it and take it gently but firmly down again with a request for it to trust you and to wait with the other parts. Note results.
7. As you continue up the mountain, continue to notice thoughts or problems and continue to take any parts back down until you reach the top and sense you are in your self.
8. Consider if you would like to look for Jesus or for God. If you do not want to do this, you may want to relate to one of your parts. You can follow the "Get to Know a Part" exercise and worksheet (Chapter 2).
9. If you want to relate to Jesus or to God, either call out to Him or go find Him.
10. When you find Him, note what response you have to being there with Him:

    a. Notice how He feels toward you. Can you receive His affection for you, or are you blocked?
    b. If you can open your heart to take in his love, notice the effect it has on you emotionally and physically and on your self image.
    c. Consider what you want or need from Jesus or from God. Can you ask Him for it?

d. As you get ready to go down the mountain, do you want to take anything from Jesus or from God for yourself to lead the parts? Do you want to take anything for the parts?

11. When you are ready, start down the mountain. As you go, ponder what you want to share with the parts, if anything. Do you want to thank them for waiting? Note how your parts respond.

12. How do you feel toward your parts? About leading your parts?

SECTION III: EQUIPPING CLIENTS WITH LEADERSHIP TOOLS FOR MEETING LIFE SITUATIONS

Equipping all God's people for the work of Christian service

Ephesians 4:12

Section I of this book summarized internal family systems therapy; Section II introduced Christ-centered IFS therapy—the centering of the self and parts around Jesus for healing and empowering. Section III responds to the needs of clients for skills to help them lead their parts in meeting life situations with the new creativity released from the Christ-centered therapy. To equip them for this challenging task, four leadership tools are offered in the following four chapters.

These tools are best taught *during* the therapy process when the client's self needs them to meet tough situations and to integrate the internal gains of therapy. As Schwartz points out, dealing with external circumstances reinforces internal growth. It elevates the self in the eyes of the parts and increases the self's own confidence to lead. The goal of Section III is to assist counselors and clergy with tools to help clients' emerging selves keep pace externally with the internal unburdening of their parts.

Why is it this so important? For some clients, the growth of the self in leadership is a smooth process; for others it is quite challenging. This struggle is illustrated by Pam's experience described in Chapters 3 and 4. After Pam originally turned to Jesus, the inner healing and growth of her self continued for several years. As external and internal stresses mounted, however, the parts regained their control centered around fear, shame, and people pleasing. Even after her self's relationship with Jesus was restored early in treatment and some parts were unburdened, Pam still reverted to old patterns every time her husband returned to town. She became powerless, accommodated to his demands, and then criticized herself for it. This occurred even though she knew her self-worth was secure in Jesus and she did not need to please her husband to maintain her self-worth.

How could this be? One reason is that the self and freed-up parts are only slowly assimilating their new freedom and have little practice in applying it to their life situations. Thus, when confronted with the old stimuli, like the demands of her husband, Pam and her parts are strongly tempted to the old destructive weaknesses.

Secondly, the parts not yet unburdened remain organized around their survival core, so that under pressure they naturally distrust the self's attempt to lead in a new direction. They blend with the self and attempt to steer behavior toward the only possible action (as they see it), the old response. They are afraid that if the new leadership team with its new center is successful, they will be discarded and banished for their opposition. These parts actively oppose or passively undermine the tentative steps of the self to lead toward new responses, so that when stresses come, the old coalition overcomes the efforts of the new self to lead.

What is the solution? The self must interrupt the old sequence of parts, regain its rightful leadership, and find new responses to situations. Of course, this is difficult; yet when the self centered in Jesus is trained and equipped with tools and skills, it can learn and grow into the task. This is what is meant by internal leadership development.

Pam was able to learn, with coaching in leadership tools, how the old coalition operated and what each part needed to trust her to lead. She eventually was able to respond to Ronald's manipulations with assertive effectiveness and later even with grace and compassion.

Teaching Pam to lead her parts included coaching her in the four tools presented in this section. First, she brought her angry parts to a new freedom by using the *forgiveness process* (Chapter 5) to release old resentments stored up against Ronald. Besides "cleaning the slate," she was soon able to "keep the slate clean" by releasing new complaints as they arose from Ronald's continued manipulations. Thus, she was not dragged back into the old posture of a victim.

Pam next developed her "part detectors," the capacity to sense when parts were overwhelming her; she did this by identifying the sequence of reactions of her parts and listing them on a "road map" called the *flowchart* (Chapter 6).

Pam and I then designed a series of steps she could use to get unhooked from the parts when they were overwhelming her. These steps would return her to leadership in the internal family. She listed these steps as a second sequence on the flowchart (Chapter 7). Finally, Pam and I designed a series of steps to assist in developing new responses when under pressure, so she did not revert to the old maladaptive ones. She listed these steps as a third sequence on the flowchart (Chapter 8). The result is that the three tools in Chapters 6, 7, and 8 are mapped in three connecting sequences on the flowchart; the self can use the three sequences separately or link them together according to the situation.

This process of teaching the client new tools in the course of therapy may appear to be a distraction to the unburdening process, but this is not so. The self's growing leadership ability, demonstrated to the parts in tough situations, generates trust in the self. This creates the safety needed for the parts' inner disclosures in the unburdening process. The self can reassure the parts that they will not be judged and discarded in the emerging new order; rather, each will have a place and a contribution to make. Equipping the self to lead in pressing life situations not only helps the internal family find new ways to cope with pressing circumstances, it also compliments and reinforces the unburdening and healing of the parts.

Chapter 5

Cleaning the Slate and Keeping It Clean: The Forgiveness Process

"I would like to wring his neck," my client Nathan proclaimed through clenched teeth. It was his angry part complaining about his boss. This part was frightening the other parts, who then had to use energy to contain the part, lest he overwhelm Nathan's self and carry out the threats against the boss.

Nathan's internal system, lacking a way to resolve problems with people, has assigned to the angry part the role of carrying unresolved issues—now hardened into a lasting grudge against his boss. In some cultures, this resentment is seen as useful energy to propel one toward retaliation and revenge. Jesus, on the other hand, calls us to forgiveness of enemies as well as friends. Because we, our families, and subcultures often lack a way of resolving and forgiving wrongs, the resentment is buried internally and one *appears* to have forgiven. We assign the resentment to an angry part who then is hidden away. This creates an independent, secret power center, not answerable to the self, whose task is to protect the inner family from further wounds. This center reinforces the survival orientation of the parts, by expecting the offender to repent, apologize, and thus heal the wound, reinforcing the helpless victim posture.

This is a harmful and hidden form of dependency. The victim cannot get on with life until the offender "makes it right." On the other hand, the purpose of Jesus' call to forgiveness is to release the victim from the wrongdoer and the wrongdoer from the victim. Released from bondage, the victim can now turn to God, where true freedom lies, and experience healing and new life.

How is this accomplished? The angry parts cannot, nor should they, be simply unburdened as in usual parts work. They point to the offense and say "We didn't deserve this," while other parts are saying the opposite, "We are not worthy of fair treatment; we deserve to be abused and this abuse proves it."

The angry parts' message of self-worth is a truth that must not be lost, even though their revengeful remedies are seldom Godly or constructive. Jesus' life, death, and teachings show us the way to do this. His sacrificial death on the cross is the ground of our forgiveness and our loving relationship with God (Romans 5:8-10). We are invited to forgive others as God forgave us (Matthew 18:21-22), because God is interested in our being free, not bound by resentment toward others.

How is this accomplished without diminishing the angry, resentful parts? First, we must acknowledge the wrongful nature of the abuse. This acknowledgment highlights the truth that we are deserving of love, not abuse. Next the pain carried by our hurt part is owned and brought to God for healing. Then we can be free of the expectation that the perpetrator heals the pain; we can release our resentments and go on with life. Can non-Christians use the process? After the principles are described and discussed, they will also grasp the wisdom of the process and quickly adapt it to their need to break free of resentments.

Our purpose is to describe this process so that therapists and clergy can help clients process resentments and release them, thus freeing the self from the victim stance. The chapter is organized in three sections. The first describes the resentment process used by adult clients who experienced wrongs in childhood. These are difficult to forgive because they occurred when the client was most vulnerable. In the second section we explain how to handle wrongs experienced as adults, from a spouse or employer. These can feel just as painful as childhood wounds, because the vulnerable child part experiences the pain again. Handling these resentments is about "wiping the slate clean." The third section presents a process for handling "current problems," before they become hardened into resentments. These hurts are more easily released if the client acts promptly before the parts repeat the old sequence of wounding, helplessness, and resentment. This is "keeping the slate clean." The chapter concludes with a summary of the steps in the process and an exercise.

For many people, the angry, resentful parts are near enough to the surface that under stress they pop out and wound others. With these people, plenty of evidence can be found of the existence of angry and resentful parts. With such an open display, the therapist and client will check the internal family to see what effect these resentful parts have on the system. For others, such as my client, Gary, resentments are securely hidden; the first step then is to identify the presence of resentments.

STEP 1: IDENTIFYING THE EXISTENCE OF RESENTMENTS

Some resentments are so well hidden that neither the self nor close friends and family know of their existence; yet they can have a profound influence on the internal family. Such was the case with Gary, a handsome thirty-year-old African-American college student who was busy finishing a degree and working on a local church staff. He suffered from depression that left him immobilized and sometimes suicidal with chronic self-hatred, taking the form of despising his appearance and personality. He saw himself as completely unappealing, although he admitted to me that people admired his ability to relate to the teens at church. He also had a circle of good friends, especially girlfriends.

After several months of parts work, we had unburdened several of his powerful managers: a critical part who regularly called him "garbage," a perfectionist part who critiqued everything he did as "not good enough," and a pleaser part who required that he always try to meet others' expectations. Even after unburdening these parts we noticed only minor changes in his insecurity, self-hatred, and depression.

We proceeded to his exile parts. The first took us back to a time when he was thirteen years of age. His father had left the family, and Gary was bewildered and depressed. We went back to that situation with the thirteen-year-old part. Gary and Jesus helped the part confront his dad and find a resolution with him. Gary, Jesus, and the thirteen-year-old then removed a burden of fear and a conviction about his inadequacy, which the part replaced with a sense of being loved by Gary and by Jesus. The thirteen-year-old seemed to be healed, but Gary's self-hatred and depression had not changed noticeably. We asked ourselves: What else is going on?

Another exile part came forward, a seven-year-old, who showed us how Gary's mother had used him to vent her anger at Gary's father, and how it had spilled over onto Gary. "He's a womanizer, a betrayer, and you are just like him; you even look like him," she would scream at Gary. We went back into this argument with Jesus and helped the seven-year-old confront his mother for putting him between herself and his father. We helped him find and cut several "cords" binding him to his mother and unburden his self-blame and inadequacy. Like the thirteen-year-old, the seven-year-old seemed to be healed, but Gary's self-hatred and depression still had not significantly changed.

In the next session, I helped Gary separate from his parts and go up the mountain to be with Jesus (see Chapter 4). Gary had an intimate reunion with Jesus and took in Jesus' love for him as a son of God. Yet in a few days, the experience slipped away and he was feeling as ugly and depressed as before.

Again we asked, "What are we missing?" We turned to the parts for help, and a voice came back, "You don't want to know." After securing permission from the other parts, we spoke to the voice:

Gary: Why don't we want to know?

Voice: God will be very displeased.

Gary: Will you help us understand why?

Voice: God hates people who carry grudges. If he knew, he would turn against us and all would be lost.

We assured the part that God would not turn against him and the internal family as Gary's mother and father had. We said, "God sent Jesus to help us deal with wounds and resentments; that is what Jesus' death on the cross is all about." Thus assured, the part took us directly to the part carrying the grudge, who showed us that the grudge was against his father.

This work with Gary illustrates the first step in the forgiveness process: identifying the existence of resentments. Most resentments are not this well hidden. We can trust, however, that as counselors, when our self is available to the client's internal family with respect and grace, the parts will soon feel safe enough to reveal hidden resentments. Gary and I had no idea how the resentments were related to his self-hatred and depression, but we trusted the parts to show us.

Because of the parts' high level of fear, Gary and I next met with all the parts to reassure them of God's grace. We affirmed that a respectful process would be followed for resolving conflict, which we would help them through. This led us to the next step.

STEP 2: INTRODUCING THE THREE-COLUMN WORKSHEET AND THE MAIN PRINCIPLES

I introduced the process to Gary by describing the three-column worksheet in Figure 5.1.

The left-hand column is used for listing the offender's observable behaviors, such as what was said or done, including facial expressions

FIGURE 5.1 The Three-Column Worksheet

The Behaviors the Person Did That Harmed Me	The Effects of the Behaviors on Me	The Anticipated Effect on Me of Releasing the Resentments

and body language. In the center column, it is important that behaviors be separated from the effects of the behaviors so that the client can hold the wrongdoer accountable for behaviors, yet own the painful effects on self. The client's parts, however, usually expect the wrongdoer to take the hurt away. Unfortunately, this wish reinforces dependency on the wrongdoer. Listing the wounds in column two helps the client and parts own the pain and turn to God instead of the wrongdoer for release and healing. Gary grasped this principle quickly, as do most clients; I often tell them that at this point they are halfway to releasing the bondage from the wrongdoer's actions.

The right-hand column is for listing the effects from releasing the resentments. This can free the client's attitude, feelings, and behavior toward the self and parts, the wrongdoer, others, and even God. The client can now release the resentments whether or not the wrongdoer ever acknowledges them. This independent choice is another step away from the victim stance, and the timing of this decision rests with the client's self in consultation with the parts as to their readiness. After releasing resentments, the client can consider the wisdom of confronting the wrongdoer. I always assure the client at this point that if he or she wants to proceed, I will coach each step.

STEP 3: HELPING THE CLIENT ASSESS THE USEFULNESS AND TIMING OF THE RESENTMENT PROCESS

The description of the worksheet and main principles is usually adequate assurance for the client to proceed with the process. Sometimes there is ambivalence, and it is useful to hear the parts' concerns. Often they need only to be reassured, but at times other steps must be taken before the resentment work.

Gary asked questions and then expressed his excitement about proceeding. We noted that after the resentment process it would be good to return to unburdening the other parts. I asked him to determine if his parts were ready to begin making the list. He felt it was right to start with his father and leave his mother until later. I asked him to make the three columns on paper and to label the column on the left "Dad's behaviors." It is important to be clear about who the focus of concern is, so that when the client brings up grudges about another person, these can be set aside for later work and not confuse the current process.

STEP 4: LISTING THE RESENTMENTS—
THE WORK OF COLUMN 1

I asked Gary to consult his angry part about the most important wrongs his dad did to him.

Gary: The angry part feels that the major thing was Dad's leaving me. He left home when I was thirteen.

Therapist: What was it that was most upsetting about that?

Gary: He didn't tell me about it, explain it to me; he was just missing one morning. I felt like he had ripped my heart out and it was my fault somehow. He had yelled at me a few days before, and I felt like he was angry at me and that's why he left.

Therapist: This sounds like several concerns. We need to list them separately. Let's list the first as his leaving you and his family when you were thirteen. The second is that he didn't explain to you anything about his leaving. The third is that he yelled at you a few days before he left and didn't resolve the tension between you when he left (see Figure 5.2). You also identified some important effects on you. Let's list them in column 2 so we don't forget them. You said you felt like he ripped your heart out. Let's put that opposite "Dad leaving home." It seemed as if it was your fault. Let's put that next to the third point, "his leaving the tension unresolved." Are there any more of Dad's behaviors that related to his leaving home?

Gary: He created a huge fear in me. I thought I'd never see him again.

Therapist: How did that turn out?

Gary: After a few months, he came back to see me and my brother. Then he came every month or so.

Therapist: Let's put the fear in column 2. Should we put it next to his not explaining to you before he left? If he had told you he would visit you each month, you might not have been so frightened.

In this process, the counselor helps the client separate the actual behaviors from the painful incident. It is common for the effects of

FIGURE 5.2. Gary's Resentment Worksheet

Dad's Behaviors That Harmed Me	The Effect of His Behaviors on Me	The Anticipated Effect of Releasing Resentment on Me
Left home when I was 13 and left me behind.	Felt like he ripped my heart out.	Do not have to carry the hidden anger.
Didn't explain anything to me before he left.	Sensed a huge fear that I would never see him again.	Can accept the pain and turn to God with the pain.
Yelled at me a few days before leaving and left the tension between us unresolved.	Believed I was at fault for Dad's leaving.	No longer feel at fault for Dad's leaving.
	Felt responsible for the family as the man of the house.	Free to consider why Dad left and to talk to him.
	Felt I didn't measure up for Dad and others.	Can now see that he loved me.
	Fear of making mistakes and being disliked; had to be perfect.	No need to feel responsible for my mother and brother.
	Forced to choose between loyalty to Mom and loyalty to Dad.	Free to relate to them as adults.
	Forced to be against Dad and be his opposite.	No need to be so perfect or so fearful of making mistakes.
	Must finish college and be a success.	Can get out from the middle between Mom and Dad.
	Couldn't be skinny or look like Dad.	Can see my mother's share of the marriage failure.
	Made a vow to hate Dad and his appearance and hate self for being like Dad.	More free to forgive Dad for his part.
		Open to an adult relationship with Dad.
		Can revoke vow to hate Dad and self.
		Free to consider what gifts Dad gave me.
		Could consider who I am and want to be.

the behaviors to come out during the process, such as the feeling that "he ripped my heart out." This is an important expression by one of the wounded parts. It is necessary that it be acknowledged, but it should be identified as an *effect* of Dad's behaviors and differentiated from Dad's *behaviors*. This sorting process is critical because it re-establishes the boundaries between Gary and his father. Once established, the offender can be held responsible for the column 1 behaviors while the client can be asked to own the pain (column 2). After listing the feelings as soon as they come out, it is useful to return to column 1 often, until the angry parts feel the list of resentments is complete. This facilitates the final goal of "wiping the slate clean."

A second kind of sorting accompanies listing the grudges: that of differentiating the wrongful from appropriate and well-intentioned behaviors. Most clients do this naturally, because the parts carry a yearning for justice and do not want to wrongfully accuse. Occasionally, clients need help to see if the resentment is with the parent's reasonable spanking or yelling at the child for running in the street, or if the yelling involved shaming and undue threatening: "You stupid kid" or "If you ever do that again, I'll. . . ," or if the spanking is more like a beating. The exact shaming or threatening words and behavior should be listed as though it were a court of law.

This provides for an important dimensions of column 1 work, adjudicating the offender's behavior, the means of holding the offender accountable. As noted earlier, the child, when originally wronged, needed to have a "judge" or protector figure interrupt the offender and say "Stop, this is wrong." The parts then would not have felt the doubt and self-blame making them unworthy of respectful and loving treatment. Angry parts usually carry the sense of injustice. The column 1 process of identifying the offender's behaviors as unjust accomplishes a missing step; it releases these parts, who then feel satisfied that justice is done. They also feel satisfied because, as in Gary's case, they are given a voice after being hidden for years and dominated by the manager parts and self-blame parts.

Angry parts are usually frustrated at not being able to do their task of protesting the undeserved treatment. Thus, they get sidetracked into revenge fantasies; however, when allowed to participate in adjudicating the wrongs and when appreciated for upholding self-worth, they will be ready to join the self and other parts in releasing the resentments. Because the parts are so actively engaged in this process, the client can be offered "homework assignments," such as completing columns 1 and 2 between sessions. As the angry parts are brought out of hiding and given a respected role in the process, they are less frightening to the self and other parts, thus providing for internal reconciliation between polarized groups of parts. This opens the way for the next step: listening to the hurt parts. Angry parts are now able to be less fierce and overprotective of the hurt parts. The manager parts are not so worried about containing the frightening anger parts and can listen to the self's assurances about "owning the pain."

In Gary's case, although the resentment process was proceeding effectively and Gary and his parts were feeling hopeful, we still had minimal clarity about the cause of Gary's self-hatred. We hoped this could become clear as we worked on column 2.

STEP 5: LISTING THE EFFECTS OF OFFENDING BEHAVIORS—COLUMN 2 WORK

Since Gary's hurt parts had spoken out during the column 1 work (we listed these hurts in column 2), we reviewed these first. We then asked the hurt parts to show any additional effects of the behaviors of Gary's dad. The managers felt the process was safe and permitted Gary's hurt parts to show us their painful memories. We added these to the column 2 list (see Figure 5.2):

"I felt responsible for the family as the "man of the house.""

"I felt I didn't measure up for Dad nor for others."

"I felt fearful of making mistakes and being disliked. I had to be perfect."

"I was forced to choose between loyalty to Mom and loyalty to Dad."

As Gary's parts showed the anguishing dilemma of choosing between parents, the truth dawned on him that he was forced to choose *against* his dad, an important step to understanding his dislike of his dad and his own self-hatred. The parts then showed Gary that he needed to be the opposite of his dad in every way. This explained his urge to finish college (his father had not been able to finish), his prohibition against being skinny (his dad was), and looking in any way like his dad (face, hair, skin color). We asked the parts how they could comply with these prohibitions. They slowly revealed that since they could not change Gary's appearance they did the next best thing; they made a vow to hate Dad and his appearance and to hate Gary and his appearance for looking and being like his dad.

This revelation encouraged Gary in being able to understand for the first time the dynamic of self-hatred and father hatred. He quickly realized that his mom was equally at fault, but he had put total blame on his father. We noted the need for a separate resentment process for his mother. This opened the door to releasing his resentments toward his father.

Several parts were worried about Gary's vow of self-hatred, thinking it to be a permanent pact even taking precedence over his relationship with God. I explained that Gary and his parts could renounce this vow and unburden the part carrying it. We agreed to consider this and the release of all resentments at the conclusion of the forgiveness process. Gary and his parts were excited at this and ready to proceed to work on column 3.

This case was chosen because it illustrates the deeply hidden, powerful dynamics sometimes involved with resentment. Once the angry parts are satisfied by adjudicating their resentments (column 1) and have differentiated between the wrongdoer's behaviors and their wounds (column 2), a safe zone is created permitting them to reveal hidden anguish and coping strategies, such as Gary's self-hatred vow.

If more safety is needed, counselor and parts can talk to individual exiles about not overwhelming the self with their pain. They will need to be reminded that disclosure is for releasing resentments, which will in turn open the door to further healing at the right time. The exiles, thus reassured, usually are satisfied to know that their time is coming. (Generally, when not enough safety exists for working with the exiles' wounds directly, a structured resentment process can be an intermediate step freeing up angry parts, acknowledging exiles' wounds, and elevating the role of self; this can create enough safety to proceed later to the exiles.)

STEP 6: LISTING ANTICIPATED EFFECTS
OF RELEASING RESENTMENTS—
COLUMN 3 WORK

Gary and his parts were hopeful after the revelations of column 2, and ready to proceed to column 3. I clarified by asking, "When you are ready to release resentments, what effect do you think it would have on you?" Step by step, Gary considered columns 1 and 2; slowly he saw the new possibilities. We listed them at the appropriate places on the worksheet as follows:

- No need to carry the hidden anger, could accept the pain, and turn to God for healing.
- Free from feeling at fault for Dad's leaving, could consider why he left and talk to Dad about it as appropriate.
- Free to see that Dad loved me.
- No need to be responsible for Mom and brother, free to relate to them as adults.
- Do not have to be perfect or fearful of making mistakes.
- Can get out of the middle between Mom and Dad.
- Free to recognize Mom's share of the marriage breakdown, more free to forgive Dad for his share, more open to an adult relationship with Dad.

In the column 3 process, the self progressively steps away from the locked-in perspective of the angry and hurt parts and sees the situation from a new perspective. Gary realized he had taken his mother's view and turned against his father and himself. The more he realized this, the more his heart softened toward his father and himself. The effect was to make it possible for him to consider revoking "the vow." This opened the door to considering the personality and genetic gifts his dad had given him. Gary saw clearly for the first time who he (himself) was and wanted to be. Gary and I then added these items to the column 3 list and were ready to move to the next step.

This completes the explanation of the work of the three columns. Note that each column progressively elevates the self and frees the parts. In the first column, the self listens to angry parts, adjudicating resentments a step toward freeing the angry parts. In the second column, it listens to the hurt parts, which assists in freeing them. In the third column, the self, with new separation from the parts, takes a fresh look at the situation(s), the cost of maintaining the old victim posture, and the possibilities for growth and healing that might result from releasing grudges and, in Gary's case, the vow as well. The self and parts began a dynamic journey with one another. Now a need exists for an assessment of how far they have come; the next step is designed to provide this assessment.

STEP 7: HELPING THE CLIENT ASSESS READINESS TO RELEASE RESENTMENTS

I asked Gary to consider his readiness to release his many resentments. He said he was already feeling more free and was seeing both his dad and mom in a new light. He then checked with his parts regarding their readiness and received a surprising answer: they were ready to release the resentments, but did not feel safe enough to release the vow. Because each step forward frees the internal system more, we decided to proceed with the parts readiness and come back later to the vow. Had the parts not been ready, we would have sought out the particular parts not ready and worked with them.

STEP 8: DESIGNING A RITUAL FOR RELEASING RESENTMENTS

I then asked Gary to consider a simple ritual for releasing his resentments. I explained that a ritual is useful as a signal of freedom from dependency and enmeshment with the wrongdoer. For a Christian, it also signals a new step with God. The self comes to God confessing the long-held resentment as a preoccupation keeping self from God. The self asks forgiveness, hands over the resentments, and listens for new directions from God.

I also noted that a ritual is especially useful for the parts because they think concretely. I reminded Gary about the Old Testament ritual of burning a sacrificial animal on an altar; the smell of the burnt offering was pleasing to God. He could borrow this ritual and burn the list of resentments. The parts see and feel the flames, smell the smoke, and hear the words of confession and release. These actions represent for them evidence of a decisive act that releases the angry parts from carrying resentments and the hurt parts from being the sole carriers of the pain. The ritual signals these steps. Then, the various parts can change their posture simultaneously.

Gary decided to use the burning ritual. When he had finished praying and the flames had died down, he said that during the prayer and burning, something released inside and the parts told him they were now ready to release the vow. He wrote the vow on a sheet of paper, confessed to God, renounced it, asked God to show him the truth regarding his dad, his self, and his body, and burned it. After the vow was burned, Gary said that God wanted to show him new things regarding his dad and himself. This brought us directly into the next step.

STEP 9: ASSIMILATING THE EFFECTS
OF RELEASING

Working with the effects of releasing resentments begins with distinguishing in column 3 between what is happening now (and needs facilitation immediately) and tasks that can be scheduled after the completion of the resentment process.

Gary was now free to acknowledge that his dad had kept a place in his heart for him and that he loved his dad. This led him to reconsider his dad's traits that he had formerly hated. I asked Gary to name the traits he was considering. He listed his dad's intelligence, his passion, and his caring for others. Had his dad given any of these to Gary, I asked? Gary noted several: a love for learning and for teaching others, the joy of performing music and a love of rhythm, the enjoyment of fishing and the outdoors, and his way of relating to others with humor, respect, and caring.

I asked Gary how he felt about himself now, considering that he possessed a number of these traits. He said that it looked like God had given these traits to his dad and then to himself through his dad, so he should thank God and his dad for them. Since God gave these traits to him as a sign of His love, he was free to enjoy them and to appreciate himself. He acknowledged that he used most of these same traits with the teens and in his college classes.

I asked if he felt differently about his body now. He said he felt free to be part of the men in his father's family, who had tall, lean, healthy bodies; he could appreciate the body they had given him. As Gary completed this process of identifying new attitudes about himself and his dad, we noted that this seemed to be the resolution of Gary's self-hatred. We rejoiced together and thanked God.

We next directed our attention to other effects of this resolution: Gary no longer felt the need to carry the hidden anger, nor to be perfect; he was less fearful of making mistakes. We then acknowledged the need to finish the agenda with his father before going on to other tasks (healing the parts, dealing with his mom's hurtful behaviors), which could be scheduled later. This illustrates how Step 9 identifies those processes already occurring and brings them to completion, while setting aside what can be dealt with later. In Gary's case, this permitted the resolution of his father hatred and his self-hatred, which then provided strength for the final step, the encounter with the wrongdoer. Because this is often frightening, it is tempting to put even the consideration of it aside, causing the opportunity to be lost.

STEP 10: CONSIDERING THE WISDOM OF ENCOUNTERING THE OFFENDER

This step has three parts; first, assessing possible benefits and dangers of a confrontation with the wrongdoer; second, planning for the successful outcome of this conversation; finally, executing the plan.

The goal of the forgiveness process is the release of the self from its resentment and the forgiveness of the offender. Since the self can be released with or without encountering the offender, the client should consider whether benefits can come from an encounter. Gary noted several advantages that could result from talking with his dad:

- He could validate his memory of the events.
- He could inquire about his dad's point of view.
- He could ask questions to fill in gaps in his knowledge (how the marriage tensions affected his dad, why he left, what he felt about leaving his family).
- He could tell his dad how angry he had been toward him and how God helped him to release the blame and begin healing the wounds.
- He could tell his dad how he discovered traits that he respected in his dad and that he now understood how his dad had nurtured the same traits in himself.

Gary decided to talk to his father about the past events. Several of his parts, however, were afraid that his dad would get defensive and not be able to listen. The hurt parts might feel revictimized, and Gary's angry parts might jump out at his dad. Gary and I reminded his parts that it is important to find out if his dad could listen; the parts could always elect to watch from a safe place. The hurt parts and angry parts were willing to try this. Gary was concerned that the conversation would not go well. He decided to ask his dad to come to my office so that I could facilitate.

Gary's dad accepted the invitation. In the session, I set the stage by explaining that Gary had discovered some wounds in their relationship that he wanted to share if Ted (his dad) was interested; I was there to help them listen to each other. Ted said he would try to listen, so Gary began with the safest topics: his memories of events and dates. Ted added useful information that Gary as a child could not have. Ted sensed that Gary was not trying to blame him and relaxed a bit.

Gary said that he had been hurt and resentful but had processed this with God in the counseling setting. He now wanted to share his understanding with his dad. Gary described the effects of Ted's departure. Ted acknowledged Gary's pain and said he too felt pain and guilt about the events; although he believed in God, he had never come to a sense of forgiveness about the events. Perhaps this conversation could help resolve it. Gary and Ted continued to have a productive conversation, each discovering missing pieces from the other's perspective. At the conclusion, they said wanted more conversation and felt safe enough with each other to meet on their own.

This illustrates the three processes of Step 10. First, Gary assessed the possible benefits and dangers before deciding to talk with his father. Next, helping the parts as needed, he and I planned for a safe process. Finally, he carried out the plan by inviting his dad to the conversation.

Often the offender, given such an opportunity, will own his or her part of the wrongs, understand the pain caused, and even apologize. The victim discovers why the wrongdoer acted as he or she did, and the groundwork is provided for a renewed relationship between them. This is the process Jesus invites us to (Matthew 18). The depth of the new relationship is determined by what is possible and desired between the two and may involve a slow rebuilding of mutual interest and trust.

Yet there are reasons reconciliation can get blocked. Most commonly, the offender's denial and defensive parts block the way to full discussion of the past. Or the victim's angry parts creep in and use the occasion to blame and punish the wrongdoer. This reinforces the wrongdoer's need for denial and defense; the two find themselves back in the old cycle of blame and shame. However, even this can be a reality check for the victim, revealing the limits of what is possible. It is also an opportunity for the victim to apologize for contributing behavior as appropriate and, having released self and the offender, to go on with life. This completes the description of the most difficult resentment process, that involving childhood wounds.

THE FORGIVENESS PROCESS WITH WRONGS EXPERIENCED AS ADULTS

The resentment process described above works as well with adult wounds with a few important modifications.

Kirsten, an American woman, had left her husband, Bihari, in India after thirty years of experiencing his unfaithfulness, manipulation, and verbal abuse. She came to me feeling wounded and diminished as a person. Many clients, experiencing similar wrongs as adults, are surprised to find these wounds just as painful as childhood ones, even though they believe themselves less vulnerable than children. Why is this so, and how can the resentment process be modified to help them deal with their adult wounds and resentments?

The bad news is that as adults our needy and wounded parts can hook us into wounding relationships with an employer, a friend, or a spouse, which repeat the very kind of abuse we experienced as children (making us feel reabused, resentful, and powerless). The good news is that in centering our lives around Jesus instead of our needy parts, we can release our resentments and step into a new freedom in relating to others more autonomously. We will use the story of Kirsten to describe how to use the resentment process for processing adult resentments. (The steps noted in brackets or by headings refer to the ten steps used previously for the childhood forgiveness process.)

Kirsten's Story

As Kirsten described Bihari's verbal abuse and unfaithfulness, we soon discovered her compliant and needy parts. These parts had originally drawn her into the relationship with Bihari and then kept her there despite his continuing abuse. In therapy, we brought several of her manager parts and wounded parts to Jesus for unburdening and healing. Then, angry and resentful parts were permitted to come forward from their place of confinement. The angry parts alerted us to the need for the resentment process by revealing the resentments built up over the years. Having *clarified the existence of the resentments and the need for the resentment process* (Step 1), I *described the worksheet and the resentment process* (Step 2). I noted that releasing resentments would enable Kirsten to step out of the old dependent victim position with Bihari and consider new possibilities in the future. It was clear that for Kirsten *this was the right time to deal with resentments* (Step 3). Although the first three steps are the same as in the childhood resentments process, the next steps require some adaptation.

Step 4: Listing the Resentments (Column 1)

Those with adult resentments find it easier to list their issues than those with childhood wounds because adult memories are more accessible and clear. Kirsten had clear memories of Bihari's wounding behaviors even from the earliest incidents thirty years previously; thus, she was able to complete the column 1 list quickly. Her angry parts soon felt satisfied as we sorted and identified Bihari's wrongful behaviors. During this sorting, Kirsten realized that she herself contributed to the abusive relationship by swallowing the put-downs, by not speaking up for herself forcefully, and by responding sometimes with anger to punish Bihari. This illustrates a second difference from processing childhood resentments. Because adults have more choices and power than children, they often participate in the ongoing wrongs, either actively responding in kind or passively accommodating and enabling. For adults it is important to acknowledge this.

The more the angry parts are satisfied by hearing their concerns adjudicated as "wrongs," the more ready they are to allow the self to see how some of the parts contributed to the ongoing abusive relationship. This is important in two ways: first, it softens the angry parts from their resentful and self-righteous posture opening the way for release of resentments; and second, it alerts the self to the need for new responses and new internal growth.

As self insight increases, it is useful to have clients make a separate list of their own role in the continuing abuse. As Kirsten did this, she quickly saw the need to take responsibility for her periodic angry responses and withdrawal from interaction. The list is then set aside as we return to the main task of identifying all the problems. Because adult memories are clear, the client can make a comprehensive list of the resentments between sessions and bring it in for sorting and processing with the therapist.

Step 5: Listing the Effects of the Offending Behaviors (Column 2)

Kirsten and I then asked her hurt parts to show the wounds they received in the relationship with Bihari. As we listed these, Kirsten realized that these were the same wounds as she received in childhood in her family of origin. She then saw clearly how her own family had withheld respect because she was female; it even taught her to accommodate to family males who treated her as second class. This prepared her to relive the same experience in her marriage. This illustrates an exciting feature of the resentment process with adult wrongs. Kirsten could see why she got hooked in and stayed in the abusive relationship. She realized that it was appropriate to hold Bihari responsible for his abusive behavior; yet she had to heal and change her behavior if it was going to be different in the future. She understood that she could leave Bihari to seek happiness with another man, but without an internal transformation she would end up in another abusive relationship. This realization reinforced Kirsten's self and her parts in the growing determination to release resentments and move forward with her own inner healing. Kirsten and her parts became increasingly willing to acknowledge the wounds instead of pushing them away as she completed the column 2 list.

Step 6: Listing the Effects of Releasing Resentments (Column 3)

Now that she understood how her own inner dynamics contributed to the abusive relationship with Bihari, Kirsten realized the way out was not in looking to Bihari or other men for affirmation but to the unconditional love of Jesus. She added this to her column 3 list and realized that this freedom made it possible to consider what God wanted with her marriage.

The next two steps, *assessing readiness to release* (Step 7) and *designing a ritual and release* (Step 8), are the same as with childhood resentments. Kirsten finished the three columns and checked with her parts. They were ready to release the grudges and go forward with the healing. She also wanted to confess to God her part in the marriage breakdown, ask for forgiveness, and, at the right time, acknowledge this to Bihari.

Kirsten then designed a satisfying ritual of release for herself. She wrote on paper a word or two to represent each resentment. She then tore them off one by one and threw them into a nearby stream to be carried away by the current while releasing them to God in prayer. She felt this brought closure for her.

Considering how to assimilate new growth (Step 9) works the same as with childhood wounds. Kirsten and I reviewed the column 3 list of anticipated effects. She identified those who could be immediately incorporated into her life and those who should come later. Before any conversation with Bihari, she wanted to learn how to be more assertive when she felt Bihari or others were pushing her around. In following sessions she identified her accommodating part and her fearful part as the parts which cause her to "wimp out" instead of stand up for herself. We helped her devise a new sequence of responses to perceived wrongs and worked with her parts until they were ready to let her lead the way in the new patterns. (These new sequences will be described in the next chapters.)

Over the next weeks, Kirsten practiced her new responses until she grew more confident. Next we *considered the usefulness and timing of a conversation* with Bihari about her resentments (Step 10). As she considered what might be accomplished and the dangers involved, Kirsten recognized that the main agenda (releasing her resentments) had already been accomplished; she was not dependent on Bihari's participation in a conversation. She realized that a conversation could be useful in bringing resolution between them and even greater understanding. She could report that she had released her resentments and asked forgiveness for her participation whether Bihari owned his wrongs or not. Kirsten now had a greater dependence on God and was free to accept whatever outcome might result. Bihari had been asking to visit from India to persuade her to return with him. She was cautious about his ability to manipulate her, so she decided to invite Bihari to my office, so I could facilitate the conversation. He accepted her plan and upon arrival in our city came with Kirsten to my office.

Kirsten identified in a straightforward way Bihari's hurtful behaviors and acknowledged her part in the breakdown of the relationship. Bihari in turn admitted the damage that his affairs had caused but did not grasp his diminishment of Kirsten, choosing to see it as her oversensitivity. Kirsten was not very surprised by this; she accepted it as a realistic example of Bihari's unchanging attitude toward her. She felt energized by her new ability to express her concerns to Bihari and accept his responses without feeling helpless or trapped by his minimization of her concerns. She even felt confident enough to have several conversations with Bihari on her own; in the end, she concluded little hope existed of a relationship based on mutuality and respect.

Many couples, however, can come to a new understanding after such a process and rebuild the foundation of their relationship. When one party releases resentments, the self is available to the partner in a new way. The partner's self is then energized (especially when the love of God is present) to enter a mutual appraisal of what went wrong and to consider the possibility of a fresh start. This is certainly what Jesus expressed: "If your brother sins against you, go to him and show him his fault. If he listens, you have won your brother back" (Matthew 18:15).

KEEPING THE SLATE CLEAN: A SHORTHAND VICTIMLESS PROCESS FOR CURRENT SITUATIONS

This unit presents a shorthand version of the resentment process for clients who have recently experienced being wronged and have not found a way to resolve it. Typically, such a client's hurt parts begin to feel victimized and powerless, activating the angry parts. The manager parts then try to control and quiet both groups, resulting in a frozen inability to respond assertively. This further triggers the angry parts who try to break through the managers' control with angry behavior, making the situation worse. However, if the managers can stifle the angry reaction, the angry parts must carry the unresolved wound as resentment. Other firefighters come in to clean up the mess with their remedy of choice: withdrawal, drugs, sex, depression, etc. The goal here is to help clients interrupt the sequence *before* their parts feel victimized and hopeless in the old maladaptive spiral. Then the self is free to respond creatively; thus the internal family, even though wronged, is not a victim.

The principles of this process are the same as the process above, with the exception that the parts have not yet hardened into powerlessness and resentment. Since the sequence has been caught in such an early stage, we can proceed directly to the main steps; identifying the wrongs, owning the wounds, releasing the resentments for new responses to the offender. If the self can be quickly empowered to lead the parts to a more proactive solution, not only will a better resolution result, but the self may learn a new paradigm for future situations.

The victimless wrong. Just as the act of forgiveness reflects Jesus' forgiveness and love from the cross, so too does forgiving a wrongdoer *before* experiencing any powerlessness and victimization. Jesus demonstrated this on the cross. Having released his life to God as he was facing death ("not my will but your will be done" Luke 22:42), and rather than be intimidated and victimized, Jesus was empowered to forgive: "Father forgive them for they know not what they do" (Luke 23:34).

Pastor Vogt of Reba Place Church calls this the "victimless wrong" and observes that Jesus decides to forgive even while the crime itself is still in progress, and he invites us to forgive in the same manner. Jesus recognizes that we are tempted to feel victimized and powerless by the wrongs done to us (people taking our property or committing physical violence against us). He instead invites us to return to God, the source of our security and self-esteem. We are then not victimized but free; we can choose to forgive quickly and respond creatively (Matthew 5:40-41).

Dan's Incident

My client Dan served on the staff of a residential unit for handicapped adults. His fellow staff member, Johnathan, age fifty-five, was intimidating to Dan, only twenty-five. Once Johnathan was away and due back at 10:00 p.m., at which time Dan would be free to leave. Late in the evening, Johnathan called to inform Dan he would be late but offered no reason. Dan said he had a commitment, so he needed to leave at 10:00 p.m. as scheduled. Johnathan responded he would not be back before 11:30 p.m. Dan felt stuck and forced to comply, but insisted Johnathan return no later than 11:30 p.m. Johnathan finally returned at 12:30 a.m. Dan was upset and asked Johnathan why he was so late. Instead of giving an explanation, Johnathan sidestepped the issue, saying, "You've never done anything for me. Just go home now you should be ashamed for getting upset." Dan departed feeling frustrated, used, and hurt. The next day, Dan tried to talk with Johnathan about the incident, but Johnathan again sidestepped it, teasing Dan for being in such a hurry to get home.

Often our clients find themselves in such situations with friends, spouses, associates, or supervisors. They and their parts feel and react as they had experienced in the past, wounded, stuck, and abused. Their angry parts soon protest the unfair treatment and take the internal family into an explosion of anger or into the old victim posture of resentment and withdrawal.

I told Dan a simple process could release his parts, so that his self can find new ways to deal with the situation. He was interested, so I described the three-column worksheet and the principles of separating wrongful behaviors done to him from the hurts experienced. I noted the principle that he could hold Johnathan responsible for his behavior, while owning the pain himself and turning to God with it. Releasing the resentments would free him to respond in more creative ways. Dan wanted to proceed; after a short conversation with his angry and hurt parts, he identified Johnathan's most hurtful behaviors (column 1):

- Johnathan did not ask Dan if he could stay later; he just assumed it.
- He did not keep to the agreed-upon later time.
- He did not apologize or give any explanation for either offense.
- Instead, he teased and blamed Dan.

We then consulted the hurt parts and listed the effects in column 2:

- He felt used and belittled.
- It was painful because his parents did not listen to his needs either, yet imposed their choices without consulting him, thus his hurt parts were feeling reabused.

This demonstrates how, before the resentments form, the hurt parts can quickly show why a situation is so painful for them. Often this is satisfying enough for them to permit the self to release the anger, especially when plans are made to revisit the hurt parts later for healing.

Dan and I next considered the effect of releasing the anger (column 3). Dan's angry part protested strongly that Johnathan should be "made to pay" rather than be forgiven. We thanked the angry part for doing his job of alerting Dan to the wrongs. We noted that we had confirmed his judgment and listed the wrongs, but that it was the job of the self and God to discern how to respond. The angry part said he had to protect the hurt parts and see that their wounds were cared for by getting revenge or at least an apology from Johnathan. We said that caring for the hurt parts was the job of the self and that we would take the hurt parts to Jesus for healing at the right time.

This conversation demonstrates how the shorthand forgiveness process quickly brings the principal parts forward and clarifies the roles the self wants them to take, as the self considers new possible responses to the situation. This is a form of boundary making for the parts, in this case the angry part. The self thanks the angry part for alerting the self, reinforcing him for doing the desired task. The self also corrects him for his impulse to vengeance by reminding him of the self's job to discern the best responses and to care for the hurt parts. Because the old sequence has been interrupted *before* the offenses multiply, and because the hurt and angry parts have not been exiled but invited to participate, they can more easily accept their clarified roles and let the self carry out its leadership role.

Next, Dan listed possible results from releasing the grudges with Johnathan (column 3):

1. He could release the anger and not become immobilized by stewing about it for days.
2. He could see Johnathan's teasing and blaming as a smoke screen and not get hooked by it.
3. He was free to consider why Johnathan was insensitive and manipulative at times and not take it so personally.
4. He could consider if a constructive way to resolve the situation existed without being dependent on Johnathan to be reasonable.

Dan was surprised at the new energy and ideas emerging as we made the list. As the self and offended parts move through the process, they feel less like a hopeless victim. They can see why the other person behaved so and feel hopeful for a respectful resolution.

Dan said he and his parts were ready to forgive Johnathan. I asked him to read the resentments and say out loud that he was releasing them to God. After doing this, he felt relief and a new hopefulness. I asked him to reconsider the items in column 3. He pondered a moment and then proclaimed, "I get it now—Johnathan is stuck somehow and can't deal with this. That made me feel stuck. Now I see it wasn't a big deal, but I was taking it personally; now I've released him, and I know what to do next."

Dan's Resolution

In the following session, Dan related that he consulted with his supervisor for advice. The supervisor pointed to a solution for the problem. There was someone on call for such situations of noncoverage, so Dan was not left holding the bag when Johnathan was late. Dan asked Johnathan if they could talk to the supervisor together to resolve the situation, but Johnathan refused. Dan then simply told Johnathan that he did not like it when he came back late because it interfered with his evening plans. He had forgiven him and wished he would not do it again; he considered the matter closed. Dan reported feeling truly settled about this and ready to go on. I congratulated him and together we considered the new steps that helped the situation to such a resolution (many recommended by Jesus).

- He had not responded in anger or withdrawn.
- He went to Johnathan seeking to resolve it. (Matthew 18:15-17)
- He forgave, even though Johnathan had made fun of his concerns and twice refused to discuss it. (Matthew 18:21-22)
- He returned to God, his source of security and esteem.
- He chose to forgive before his parts became victimized and stuck.
- He released his wrongdoer from the expectation that he would even discuss the issue.
- He told his concern to his wrongdoer without anger and said that he forgave him, closing the matter. (Ephesians 4:15)

As we reviewed the steps, Dan considered the possibility of using this new sequence again when the occasion arose, instead of getting frozen in resentment. We did not know how these new responses would affect his relationship with Johnathan; one year later, Dan reported that Johnathan had never returned late again nor had he teased Dan. The relationship was clearly more respectful. Clients regularly report that after using the victimless process, they feel less hooked by wrongs and often find new ways of resolving tensions.

This concludes the description of the three variations of the resentment and forgiveness process. A summary follows, listing the steps of the resentment process. An exercise concludes the chapter.

CHAPTER SUMMARY

This chapter has described the resentment-forgiveness process for helping clients "wipe the slate clean" of past resentments and "keep it clean" of present offenses. The process is an extension of the freeing strategies Jesus taught and demonstrated through his life and death. It allows one to break free from the dependency on a wrongdoer that resentment creates to restore one's security in God and to release the wrongdoer, opening a way for reconciliation.

The chapter described the steps in the process and the dynamic which the three-column worksheet generates. Instead of isolating angry parts, the process engages them for identifying and adjudicating the offender's wrongful behavior. It separates these behaviors from their effects by listing the behaviors in one column and the effects in another. It thus reestablishes the boundary between self and the wrongdoer. The wrongdoer can then be held accountable for behavior, and the self can own the pain and other effects of the behavior.

The resulting clarity elevates the self to leadership of the parts. The angry parts, after the adjudication step, feel that the right of the self to fair treatment has been upheld. They permit the hurt parts to disclose their wounds, which are validated by the listing of the effects in column 2. With the assurance of God's healing, the self and parts can own the pain and release the expectation that the wrongdoer must do the healing. The angry parts and the hurt parts have no further need to hang onto the resentment.

The self is now free to consider the resulting changes in attitude, feelings, and behaviors from releasing the resentments (column 3). In consultation with the parts, it can choose to release resentments whether or not the offender acknowledges wrongdoing or acknowledges the wounds. The self, freed by its independent decision to release, can confront the wrongdoer and expect benefits for both parties.

This chapter used the first case to describe an adult with resentments from wrongs experienced as a child and the second case to show resentments experienced as an adult. Both studies described the process of "wiping the slate clean" of past resentments. A third study showed the use of the resentment process to release anger at a *current* wrongdoer *before* the parts experience victimization and wounding. This results in a "victimless crime," freeing the self to consider many creative and respectful responses to the wrongdoer. This is the process of "keeping the slate clean."

CLINICAL OUTLINE
OF THE FORGIVENESS PROCESS

1. Identifying the existence of resentments.
2. Introducing the three-column worksheet and the main principles.
3. Helping the client assess the usefulness and timing of the process.
4. Listing the resentments: the work of column 1.
5. Listing the effects of the offending behaviors: the work of column 2.
6. Listing the anticipated effects of releasing the resentments: the work of column 3.
7. Helping the client assess the readiness to release.
8. Designing a ritual and releasing the resentments.
9. Assimilating the effects of releasing.
10. Considering the wisdom of encountering the offender.

EXERCISE: WIPING YOUR OWN SLATE CLEAN

Consider any stored up anger or resentments you may have. Set aside thirty minutes with paper and pencil and make a three-column worksheet for yourself.

1. Begin with a few minutes of relaxing and deep breathing.
2. If you want, ask God to give you courage, and insight about yourself and your parts.
3. When ready, ask your parts to show you a glimpse of any unresolved offense and the offender. If they show you more than one situation and one offender, select one for this exercise. Write it in column 1. Write any feelings in column 2.
4. Now that you have a resentment to work on, consider whether it is too big for this private exercise. If you sense the need for a simpler concern, you can thank the parts, acknowledge their concern, and ask them to show you a simpler or more current situation. For example, it could be what someone did to you in the past week. Write the new situation in the first column and appraise its appropriateness for this exercise.
5. When you have an appropriate situation, tell your parts you want to use this exercise to learn more about the process. If they have reservations, listen to them, evaluate their concerns, and respond, either proceeding after reassuring the parts, selecting a different situation, or terminating the exercise for the present.
6. When you and your parts are ready, proceed to the task of column 1, identifying the offender's behavior(s). If the parts have shown only feelings but not the situation itself, ask them to show the behavior that caused the feelings. Try to identify the behaviors as specifically as possible: content of statements, voice level and tone, body posture, and actions.
7. Go to column 2. Ask your hurt parts to show the effect each behavior had on you. List these until each of the parts has been heard.
8. Ask your parts to show whether they have resentment toward the wrongdoer. This may be accompanied by a sense of holding a grudge or by a stuck feeling. The feeling of hurt alone doesn't prove that you are holding a grudge. If unsure, consider if you and your parts can affirm the following statement: "I was hurt but I am not holding it against this person any longer. I have released it." If you have released it, you may choose to continue the exercise for the sake of learning, or you may select another situation where you are holding a grudge and repeat Steps 3 through 8.

9. Proceed to column 3. List the effects that releasing the resentment might have on you. This may free you and your parts internally to consider the reasons the offender acted as he or she did, freeing you to consider changes in your relationship with the offender or freeing you to behave differently with others and with God.

10. Assess how ready you and your parts are to release the grudge(s). It is important to separate from your parts for this assessment, remembering this is an "executive decision" made by the self in consultation with the parts. If you are ready to release, then go on to the next step. If the parts are blending, ask them to separate from you and to show their concerns respectfully so that you can consider them and respond appropriately. If the parts will not separate, consider this evidence that they are not ready to release. If the parts are satisfied and you are ready to release the grudges, go to the next step.

11. Consider designing a simple ritual of releasing. This may include a witness or prayer partner. When ready, release the resentments in a concrete way, such as a written or verbal declaration. In this way, you and the parts hear it and witness it.

12. Review your column 3 list and consider how to assimilate the items there into your life. Do you want to share any of these steps with a friend?

13. Consider encountering the wrongdoer. What could be gained? Would it be a mutually respectful encounter? If you feel doubtful, consider if your parts or the wrongdoer's parts have a hidden agenda. You may want to seek counsel from God and others.

Chapter 6

Spotting the Parts' Downward Spiral: The First Sequence of the Flowchart

Take every thought captive and make it obey Christ

2 Corinthians 10:5

With the words above, the apostle Paul urges Christians to be self-observant, identifying thoughts (and the parts accompanying the thoughts) that lead away from their newfound freedom in Christ. We as therapists can observe both in ourselves and our clients how easily the challenges of life trigger the parts' old survival responses. Like a chain reaction, the parts quickly overwhelm the self with old responses of inadequacy, powerlessness, people pleasing, and anger, creating the destructive "downward spiral."

KIRSTEN'S SITUATION

Kirsten found herself overwhelmed by the parts as she struggled with her adult children's reactions to her divorce. In Chapter 5 we saw how Kirsten's needy, compliant parts overwhelmed her for thirty years. The resulting demeaning relationship with her husband Bihari maintained her belief that as a "second-class person" she did not deserve anything better than his unfaithfulness and belittling. But Kirsten's new relationship with Jesus now grounded her worth in God's love. After several powerful parts were unburdened, she abandoned her long-standing resentment again Bihari and saw clearly no possibility of a relationship with him as an equal partner. For the first time feeling worthy of respectful relationships, Kirsten proceeded in consultation with her church to terminate the marriage.

When confronted by the anger of her adult children at the termination of the marriage, Kirsten was again overwhelmed by her parts and dragged by them into the old "second-class," confused, compliant, and hurt posture. Disappointed and full of self-doubt, she wondered if anything had really changed after the so-called healing of her parts and grounding in Jesus.

At such times our clients feel confused and discouraged. Does a setback mean the healing and the empowering of the self was shallow and will the internal family regress under pressure to an earlier victim state? No! Rather, a setback reveals only that challenging situations can, in spite of profound healing, produce the old chain reactions of the past. Kirsten discovered this in a distressing way. Healing the parts and empowering the self with God are but one among all the steps in the transforming process. If the client is not to remain dependent on the counselor for help in every situation, the self in stress must develop the skills to regularly unhook from the parts to find new responses to tough new situations.

This chapter introduces the first of three sequences for aiding the self in meeting these challenges. Here we focus on helping the self find and interrupt the part's old downward spiral of responses. This process is based on the discovery that instantaneous knee-jerk reactions of parts to powerful stimuli are understandable. The parts react and trigger one another in an old pattern, overwhelming the self and initiating the old maladaptive survival behaviors, which throw the internal family into a downward spiral.

We will see how the counselor can help the client discover these old sequence(s) that parts generate in response to stimuli. We will ask: How do the affected parts perceive stimuli? What feelings do they have? What do they say and do to other parts and the self to produce behaviors they believe will rescue the internal family from the perceived threat? When the client can see the answers to these questions clearly, the whole sequence begins to make sense. It can then be listed in the first column of the Christ-centered flowchart (see Figure 6.1); this helps the self more quickly spot the downward spiral when the next situation arises. The client can use the flowchart as a road map, both before and during the situation, even when feeling overwhelmed by the parts.

FIGURE 6.1. Christ-Centered Flowchart

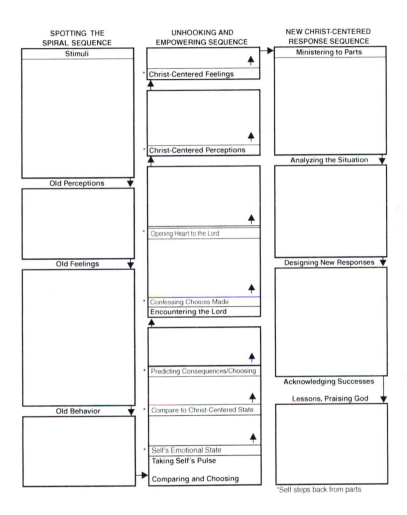

This chapter focuses on the downward spiral of the parts; it anchors the next chapter in which we see the self unhooking from the blending parts and returning to a leadership position. These two sequences then undergird a third, in which the self discovers new responses to the situation. The goal of the flowchart is, as Paul directs, to take each part's thoughts (leading into self-destructive patterns) and lead them back to freedom in Christ under the leadership of the self. Each chapter concludes in a summary, a clinical outline, and an exercise.

The chapter is organized around the therapist's steps to assist the client in developing and using this first sequence of the flowchart: describing the sequence, showing the client how to discover the parts' downward spiral, listing this on the flowchart, aiding the client in testing the understanding in a live situation, and, finally, debriefing to find the parts' hidden core responses. Each of these steps is presented with their substeps (subheadings).

OBSERVING THE CLIENT'S NEED FOR LEADERSHIP TOOLS

"You left me out of the picture, Mother, while you decided the fate of our family. You're treating me like a child," cried Kirsten's daughter, Elizabeth, in a heated phone conversation. Now a professional living in a different city, Elizabeth reacted strongly to her mother's decision to divorce her father. As I listened to Kirsten's responses, I began to realize her need for the tools to lead her parts.

Noting if the Client's Parts Are Getting Hooked

I listened to Kirsten's confusion and withdrawal into helplessness and resentment. Having helped her unburden several of her parts carrying shame and helplessness, I recognized her parts triggering one another and overwhelming her. Kirsten was discouraged by how easily they could revert back to the old helpless posture and drag her with them. After months of freeing her parts and watching her self emerge as leader, I expected we could quickly help her parts return to their new unburdened state so her self could lead in meeting new challenges. However, we would need to interrupt the healing process for a short time.

Considering the Value of Interrupting the Parts' Healing Process to Equip the Self with Leadership Tools

Usually we help the self heal individual parts one by one. Kirsten instead needed to reestablish leadership so she could respond to the present challenge. I decided to tell her about the flowchart, so that we could decide together if she should use it. Parts long organized around a survival axis will, even though unburdened, be pulled back into earlier beliefs, feelings, and reactions. They then overwhelm the self and lead the internal family back into the old maladaptive responses, leaving the self defeated and discouraged. It is important, then, to invest time in helping the self lead the parts in dealing with the challenges. Initially distressing for clients, these situations can become occasions for the self to learn to lead under pressure. This can greatly facilitate the unburdening work with the individual parts.

Showing How Parts Get Hooked Under Pressure and Generate a Downward Spiral

I explained to Kirsten how common it is for parts to revert back to old patterns under pressure and overwhelm the self. Most people become discouraged believing they have not done well or conclude that the parts really were not unburdened.

Neither belief is true. Once unburdened, parts *can* quickly be restored to their new freed-up state. I noted that Kirsten is learning to lead her parts and was right on course. I described the flowchart as a leadership tool to help her understand how parts get triggered so quickly. I offered to describe how the flowchart works; she could decide if it was timely to use it now. Whether or not the client proceeds with the flowchart, this offer creates several opportunities.

1. Describing a struggle in flowchart categories puts it in a learning, faith context; it reinterprets a defeat as an opportunity for growth. This normalizes the experience, so the client can see that everyone must learn to lead the parts.
2. The flowchart descriptions reaffirm the counselor's faith in the self's capacity to lead the parts; they give hope that the self can learn.
3. The clients gains information about how parts regress under pressure and how once healed they can be quickly empowered again.
4. In considering the flowchart option, the discussion reengages the self's decision-making capacity.

DESCRIBING THE FLOWCHART AND HELPING
THE CLIENT TO ASSESS THE TIME FOR ITS USE

It is useful to begin with an overview of how the three columns, as individual tools, fit together. I gave Kirsten a blank flowchart and described the left-hand column (see Figure 6.1).

- The *downward spiral* is designed to spot the parts as they trigger one another in their old survival sequence. They perceive the stimulus as a threat to be survived. Their response usually overwhelms the self and creates a damaging downward spiral.
- The four blocks in the column are connected by downward arrows. The column shows that the downward sequence is not just a single fast chain reaction but an understandable sequence of parts that can be interrupted by the self at any point.
- The *unhooking sequence* (center column) is accessed through the old behavior block at the bottom of the first column; it offers a way out of the old destructive behavior. The arrows lead upward to the Christ-centered feelings at the top of the center column.
- The goal of this second tool is to help the self unhook from the parts even when the self is overwhelmed and to empower for leading in the situation.
- The Christ-centered feelings block at the top of the center column has an arrow exiting to the right-hand column, *Christ-centered responses*. The purpose of this third tool is to assist the self in ministering to the parts and to try out new responses. The arrows lead down the column to the last block, which invites the self to review and learn from the results of each new response.

I asked Kirsten if my explanation of the flowchart made sense. She affirmed that it did and might clarify the confusing encounter with her daughter Elizabeth.

Client Decides on the Use of the Flowchart

Kirsten felt encouraged and decided it would be worthwhile to interrupt the individual work with the parts for a time. The client quickly grasps the flowchart and feels hopeful of growing as a leader.

There is relief that the old sequences are not inevitable, that there is a systematic way of unhooking from parts when overwhelmed. Counselor and client can then consider the trade-off between helping the self lead in the situation versus continuing to heal the individual parts. Parts frightened by the tough situation will often urge the self to grow and learn to lead better. At other times, the need instead is to free individual parts before helping the self grow.

Kirsten and her parts felt that the situation with her children was so distressing that leadership needs should be the next priority. She reassured several manager parts that they would still have a place when she emerged as the leader; she notified several wounded parts that we would return to them as soon as the intensity of the situation allowed.

Client and Therapist Decide Which Flowchart Tool to Use

It is possible to separate the three columns of the flowchart and use each as an individual tool. For example, Kirsten could start with Christ-centered response sequences (third column) if she felt new responses were most urgent or with the unhooking sequence (second column) if releasing the self from blending parts was more needed. She could return to other sequences later as needed.

Clients usually learn the function of the three tools quickly and discern where to begin with the flowchart. Like many clients, Kirsten decided to start with the first sequence, feeling she needed all the help she could get. The chapter now proceeds to this, the survival sequence—the downward spiral.

DEVELOPING A ROUGH DRAFT OF THE PARTS' SURVIVAL SEQUENCE

It is useful for client and therapist to develop an approximation of how the parts think and feel. Calling this a "rough draft" confers freedom to explore the situation without the pressure to get it exactly right. In beginning the rough draft, the client selects a recent distressing incident that triggered the parts in a destructive sequence. Because Kirsten was deeply distressed at the phone call from her daughter Elizabeth, we chose this as the stimuli and added it to our copy of the flowchart in the stimuli block (see Figure 6.2). It is useful for the client to fill out the parts sequence to get familiar with the process (using a pencil to facilitate changes).

FIGURE 6.2. Kirsten's Parts Spiral Listed in Her Flowchart

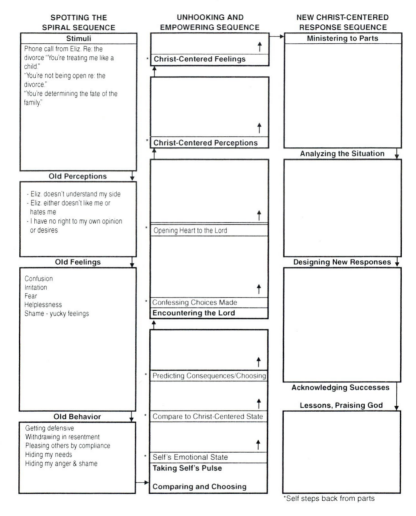

Therapist Describes the Purpose of the Rough Draft

The therapist can say: "The rough draft is an overview of how the whole sequence flows, the distress your parts experience, and why they trigger one another off. With it you can spot the sequence for yourself as it's happening. Does this make sense?"

Spotting the sequence and understanding the parts' distress is important to enhance the self's skill and elicit its compassion. The rough draft will also highlight the destructiveness of the sequence. The self must not turn against parts or join with other parts that hate the distressed parts. Giving a blank flowchart to clients reinforces the message that they can work at spotting and understanding themselves.

Client Isolates the Stimuli

The client can quickly grasp the idea of an event triggering parts' reactions but often needs help in isolating the precise stimuli from the variety of other stimuli involved.

Therapist: Let's start on the stimuli block. What was it about the phone call that was difficult?

Kirsten: It was something that Elizabeth said about my treating her like a child [pause] oh, yes, I wasn't keeping her informed about the divorce, and I was determining the fate of the family myself.

Therapist: She's feeling left out and saying you did it?

Kirsten: Yes. I did tell each of my children I was becoming more clear about the divorce—I didn't know how much to tell them. I didn't want to dump my complaints about Bihari on them.

Therapist: It seems you used your best judgment. We can come back to this if you want, but at this point let's list Elizabeth's statements in the stimuli block under "phone call from Elizabeth about the divorce":

- "You're treating me like a child"
- "You're not being open about the divorce"
- "You're determining the fate of the family"

Is this close enough for now?

Here Kirsten identified the content of the phone call. Later, she will notice Elizabeth's complaining, whiny tone of voice in triggering her parts. The client thus experiences how, by careful discrimination, she can isolate the precise stimuli triggering her parts.

Client Identifies His or Her Own Response(s) to the Stimuli

The client first notices his or her overt responses, like an angry statement. Withdrawal behavior, however, is more covert and often not noticed without help. It may be driven by a hidden feeling, such as shame, that the parts hold at a semiconscious level to keep it out of self-awareness. Thus, it is useful to invite the client to begin by describing apparent reactions.

Kirsten: I don't know exactly what my reactions were. I was just so confused that I didn't know what to say, and I was starting to get irritated, so I was afraid of getting angry at her.

Therapist: It sounds like you put your finger on three feelings: confusion, irritation, and fear. Is that right?

Kirsten: Yes. I was also feeling helpless too.

Therapist: Let's list these in the old feelings block (see Figure 6.2). (I noted to myself the apparent polarization of the two parts: irritation at Elizabeth on one hand, perhaps from an angry part, and fear that the angry part would attack Elizabeth. This polarization may have caused some of the confusion.)

Therapist: What happened next?

Kirsten: I told her that these were decisions I had to make for myself—I think I was angry or defensive when I said it. Then I said I had to go and ended the conversation. We agreed that we would have another phone call next weekend.

Therapist: These sound like behaviors. Let's put these in the old behaviors block (see Figure 6.2). What should we write down?

Kirsten: I guess I got defensive and then withdrew, feeling angry and resentful.

Therapist: Yes. Anything else?

Kirsten: I usually either give in or withdraw. I'm finally learning to stand up to my husband; you'd think I would be able to stand up to my kids.

Therapist: What do you make of that?

Kirsten: I think I was confused so I withdrew, feeling resentful that Elizabeth didn't understand my side of it.

Therapist Helps Client Identify the More Hidden Responses

Previously Kirsten noticed not only her withdrawn behavior but also one of her part's hidden perceptions: "Elizabeth doesn't understand me." I decided to pursue this to help Kirsten with the more hidden responses. Such perceptions, often held at a semiconscious level, require extra help:

Therapist: I'm interested in your sense that Elizabeth didn't understand your side of it. Could you focus on that for a moment and see what that's about?

Kirsten: I don't have any idea.

Therapist: What else did you say to yourself? About her or yourself?

Kirsten: [Pause] Oh, my gosh—I just now am realizing it. I actually felt that Elizabeth didn't like me, that she hated me. I know it sounds crazy.

Therapist: No, it makes sense if we remember it's how the parts think. Let's put that on the chart. It sounds like a perception rather than a feeling, so let's put it in the perception block (see Figure 6.2).

Kirsten is beginning to spot the parts' hidden responses. I selected one of her comments that pointed toward a perception and asked her to consider it further. Since the parts' perceptions are often in the form of self statements, I used Schwartz's question, "What did you say to yourself?" If more help is needed, the therapist can ask if parts are present who will help the self understand what they believed about the situation. Or the self can be invited to return to the scene through active imagination, so that parts can show how it was for them.

This step is similar to the usual parts work, except that here the focus is on getting an approximation of the parts' perceptions and feelings so the self can see an overview of the sequence. This shift in focus explains why I didn't pick up on Kirsten's important observation that her behavior toward Elizabeth was the same as her old responses to Bihari. Nor did I pursue other insights such as self-hatred. Though important, these observations could sidetrack the rough-draft process and will be pursued later.

Kirsten began to smile after realizing that Elizabeth's confrontative statements made a part of her conclude that Elizabeth disliked her. She commented that the sequence was starting to make sense.

Client Considers the Whole Sequence

After hidden pieces of the sequence are discovered, it is useful to pause so the client can notice the whole sequence—how it begins, flows, and results in behavior often unintended. After Kirsten discovered the parts' perception that Elizabeth did not like her, she grasped the whole sequence. Her comments illustrate this:

Kirsten: Now I see how Elizabeth reacted to me out of her own feelings and how my parts assumed that this proved she didn't like me. It's not surprising that my other parts reacted defensively, made me confused, and got me to withdraw.

Therapist: Yes, you've got it. That's the value of seeing the whole sequence—you see why the parts react so strongly. This is the role of the self—you have stepped away enough to see the whole reaction pattern. How does it feel?

Kirsten: It's such a relief to make sense of it. I don't feel the confusion. I'm clearheaded.

Therapist: Yes, that's the beginning of the unhooking process; you see how the stimuli triggers the parts, resulting in the defensive responses. Now you're not only using your "parts detector," you're using your "sequence detector." That's your new leadership tool. Now that you've tried it out, you can use it again when you're in a tough situation.

Kirsten: Yes, then maybe I can make better judgments about how to respond.

Finding the missing pieces shows the self the whole pattern, which in turn helps the self step away from the blending parts and gain the perspective needed for new responses. It is important to pause so the client can note what it feels like. Often the parts report a sense of satisfaction at being understood rather than blamed by the self. The therapist then labels the new skill as the "sequence detector" and urges its use again in tense situations.

Client Checks the Completeness and Accuracy of the Sequences

Once the self has a view of the whole sequence, it is useful to ask the client to review the four blocks and consider additions or if the entries are accurate. Any additions or corrections are added to the appropriate blocks.

Client Prepares to Test the Rough Draft in a Situation

The therapist and client can now consider if the client is ready to test the rough draft in a real situation. Clients often have specific questions about the anticipated encounter. Kirsten was concerned that she had not used good judgment in not telling Elizabeth her reasons for the divorce. Because she was now separated from the parts, her self was available to consider the question. After a few minutes' conversation, she understood how to balance her own needs as a spouse and her children's needs for information and reassurance.

Kirsten wanted to clarify the goal of testing the rough draft. I explained that the purpose was to see if this is actually what the parts do when they get hooked. I also noted the value of observing if the rough draft actually helps the self to stay unhooked from the sequence.

I said that Kirsten could debrief on her own after the encounter, and we could review her findings in our next sessions. I reminded her not to expect perfection, but to experiment and learn. After this field test of the rough draft, the debriefing session provides a rich source of learning about the parts under pressure and the self's capacity to stay unhooked. Kirsten's anticipated encounter with Elizabeth was a safe enough situation for her to try out the rough draft, and she felt ready for the experiment.

Other clients may face more dangerous situations for which they need specific coping strategies. Such circumstances may not allow time for the usual step-by-step teaching of the three sequences. More coaching may be necessary, such as selecting and teaching a few strategic skills from the survival sequence, the unhooking sequence, or the new responses sequence. This approach is a shift for the client from learning to use the flowchart to preparing to meet a specific situation.

In debriefing after the situation, the therapist and client will use the flowchart as a framework for analyzing the results. Kirsten's situation illustrates the typical step-by-step pace of the three sequences, with the client gaining mastery of each step before going on to the next.

TESTING THE ROUGH DRAFT IN A LIVE SITUATION

During the next week, Kirsten had a phone conversation in which Elizabeth asked why Kirsten wanted the divorce. Having heard from her father that he had apologized for his wrongdoing, Elizabeth did not understand why Kirsten could not accept his apologies and rebuild the relationship. Kirsten again avoided the question and quickly concluded the conversation; however, she succeeded in telling Elizabeth that she loved her and would always be her mother and care about her.

Client and Therapist Debrief the Encounter While Looking for New Insights and New Skills

At the next session, Kirsten stated she had not done any better than in previous conversations with Elizabeth; she felt confused, then avoided the main issue and withdrew. She even said she felt worse during the conversation than prior times but somehow *now* felt stronger. We agreed to pursue this by recalling the last encounter with Elizabeth:

Kirsten: The confusion was still there—and something else—very strong. I think its [pause] guilt or shame.

Therapist: Do you want to see what that's about?

Kirsten: It has to do with not having a right to my own opinions or decisions.

Therapist: Is that more of a feeling or a belief?

Kirsten: It's a belief, but there is a feeling that goes with it. It feels yucky—shame, I think.

Therapist: Good job of noticing those. We can add them to the flowchart (see Figure 6.2). Is there more on those or do you want to consider why you're feeling stronger?

Kirsten: Let's go on. I think I'm feeling stronger because somehow I stepped back from the yucky feeling, and I wasn't as overwhelmed by it. I had the parts sequence in front of me so I could notice the feeling more while it was happening. Also I prayed and journaled about the feeling after the conversation; that's when I got in touch with the old belief that I didn't have a right to my own opinion. But I didn't identify the shame until just now.

This conversation illustrates the first phase of the debriefing and underlines several features of the process thus far.

1. *Client and therapist collect data about the parts' survival sequence.* New observations are added to the flowchart to be tested in the next situation. The accuracy and completeness of the chart is enhanced by each trial. The parts can see that the self understands their concerns, which provides a foundation for the next sequences, the unhooking and leading of the parts in new responses.

2. *The role of the client changes.* Instead of the therapist being the expert, now the client is the expert, since it is the client's reactions that are under investigation. The client enters the situation without the therapist, works hard, reflects on the results, and debriefs later with the therapist. This reflects a change from being a victim of parts

to an explorer of an internal frontier. Not only is new data discovered about hidden convictions, but the self's authority with the parts is enhanced. In this instance, Kirsten discovered that she does not yet have authority to change the outcome but has the power to step back, observe, and understand.

3. *The client may be energized from the shift in role.* Kirsten invested several hours outside of therapy reflecting on her conversations with Elizabeth. She saw that the old conviction of having no right to her own opinions was driving her defensive behavior. She learned to use the flowchart during conversations and noted how her parts reacted in sequence. Instead of the first powerless conversation, she now actively engaged in research, observing and reporting the latest results to the therapist. This explains her sense of feeling stronger. This new hope and energy is a common experience at this phase. And for Kirsten, such experiential learning with a coach who believed in her was a totally new experience.

4. *The therapist's role shifts.* The therapist has broadened the clinical, coaching task to include training the client in a new skill. The therapist, an officebound "cheerleader" with the client "in the field," depends on the client for new field data that is then used in debriefing. The therapist notes not only the data but also the growing skill of the client's self at stepping back and observing the parts.

LIFTING THE VEIL: CONNECTING PARTS' PRESENT BEHAVIOR TO HIDDEN CORE RESPONSES

After the debriefing, when the client's self is more differentiated from the parts, it is good to urge the client to consider the connection between the behavior of the parts and hidden core features: feelings, beliefs, experiences, and strategies of the survival axis (see Chapter 3). In Kirsten's case, I noted her excitement at the new discoveries and skills and considered it a good moment for this task.

Therapist: You made some important discoveries that we've added to the flowchart—like discovering that some of your parts thought that Elizabeth doesn't like you or hates you. This may illustrate a core belief—that someone important didn't like you or hated you as you were growing up. There may be other core features that could help us understand why the parts respond so strongly. Would you like to take some time to investigate these?

Kirsten: Yes, that makes sense [looking at the chart]. In the old perception block, the sense that Elizabeth doesn't like me connects with the sense that I have no right to my own opinion or desires, and then I feel shame and get defensive and withdraw.

Therapist: Let's add those to the chart—"no right to my opinion" in the old perception block and "shame" in the feeling block. Who was it that the parts thought didn't like you?

Kirsten: That's the message my mom and dad gave me—that they didn't really like me and that I didn't have a right to my opinion or needs. I remember a few times when I was upset about something—they would laugh at me instead of taking me seriously. Other times, they would just send me away or get angry at me.

Therapist: How does that connect to the parts' perceptions on the phone call with Elizabeth?

Kirsten: It's the same feeling. When Elizabeth is upset with me, the parts think it's like Mom and Dad dismissing me or laughing at me and therefore Elizabeth doesn't like me either. I have no rights as a person, even though I know Elizabeth loves me.

Therapist: Your parents laughing at you and the sense of their not liking you, and not having a right to your opinion, these seem to be core perceptions.

This illustrates the process of *lifting the veil*. Once Kirsten's noticed that her parts were responsible for the perception that Elizabeth does not like her, the process had begun. She was able to connect current perceptions to the core experience of being laughed at or sent away in anger when she expressed her distress or needs. The memory of this scene reveals the *original* trigger event. The parts interpreted the parents' responses as dislike, which told Kirsten she had no rights. She easily connects this core experience to Elizabeth's present anger and now understands why her parts perceive Elizabeth's anger as dislike with accompanying loss of rights.

Kirsten and I continued to pursue other core reactions. She confirmed the feeling of shame, the next link in the sequence, as a core feeling associated with not having rights. Next Kirsten considered core behaviors:

Kirsten: I know one major response is withdrawal—that's what I did with Elizabeth—but there's another urge there too [pause]; it's to please others. Yes, that's it. I had to please Mother, figure out what she wanted, and do it. I also had to hide the shame and anger in order to present a nice face to Mother and not have any needs of my own.

Here Kirsten has discovered the last piece of the puzzle, the core behaviors constituting the parts' survival strategies: taking a compliant posture toward her mother by hiding her needs, her shame, and her anger. Since we had not previously identified all these core features, the debriefing process was important in capturing insights that Kirsten was receiving both in the field and the debriefing.

Where core features have already been identified and parts healed before the challenges present themselves, the process of connecting core features to the parts' response may proceed more quickly. For Kirsten, the situation intruded before the core features were known and provided the data for lifting the veil. Later, when we returned to the unburdening of the parts, we enjoyed the benefit of these discoveries from the flowchart process.

Kirsten had by then accomplished the task of this step, to lift the veil and reveal the hidden core responses. She then understood how the core features constitute an axis around which the parts have tried to organize life to survive the original threat and its pain. She saw how this survival orientation determines the sequence of responses to a threatening event through perceptions, feelings, posture, or behavior, with the resulting downward spiral. Client and therapist will continue to observe if the parts meet all high-stress situations with the same pattern or whether they have alternate patterns for different situations.

APPRAISING THE SIGNIFICANCE
OF THE CORE RESPONSES

Having lifted the veil and seen a field-tested view of the parts' core responses, clients can now consider its effect on their lives. This conversation with Kirsten illustrates the process:

Therapist: You've discovered an important core sequence by analyzing how your parts responded to Elizabeth's feelings and questions. What do you make of it?

Kirsten: It's pretty sobering. Even with my children who I know love me, I still feel they don't like me and I don't have any rights. Then I feel shame, get defensive, and accommodate or withdraw.

Therapist: That's a very good summary. Would you like to consider how that sequence affects your life?

Kirsten: It gets in the way of my relationship with Elizabeth for one—we could have a more adult relationship and enjoy each other, but on my side, as soon as anything comes up between us, I go into this old thought pattern that my parents taught me and feel I don't deserve to be respected and have equal standing in the relationship. It's the way I let Bihari treat me for thirty years, thinking I didn't deserve any better. It's pretty neurotic.

Therapist: You're saying that this pattern your parts learned as a way of survival in your childhood has gotten carried on in your life as a self-perpetuating problem?

Kirsten: Yes, especially with family members and friends. I don't do it when I'm in a professional role.

The Self Sees That the Core Responses Are Self-Perpetuating and Destructive, and Begins to Consider Changing

Kirsten has used the survival sequence of the flowchart to step back from her parts and see the continuing effects of the whole sequence on her life. She observes how even with a daughter who loves her, her parts cause her to perceive and react as though she is still a child being shamed by her parents. She sees the old self-perpetuating, destructive pattern blocking the way to respectful and loving relationships. Understanding this, she begins to imagine changing the old pattern and finding a new one. The self is ready to become a change agent for the internal family.

As with all change, the internal family next polarizes; the parts seeking change oppose the old coalition that wants to maintain the status quo. Each side attempts to recruit the self in an effort to prevail over the other. The self can be recruited into thinking, for example, that since the old parts cause the problem, they should be eliminated. This terrifies them, and they try again to overwhelm the self and its change advocates.

To avoid aligning with either side, the self needs: (1) a nonblaming understanding of the core parts' effort to continue the old sequence, creating compassion in the self and a desire to help them change; and (2) a plan for change that is nonpunitive and nonpolarizing.

A Nonblaming Understanding of How the Core Parts Perpetuate the Problem

The therapist must be alert to the variety of parts for or against change. In this way, he or she can assist the self in avoiding taking sides, as is illustrated in the following dialogue.

Kirsten: I see how bad this pattern is. I want to get rid of it. I don't know if I can change it, since I've been doing it all my life. Part of me wants to get rid of those parts that keep me hooked. I'm sick of feeling like a second-class person.

Therapist: It sounds like there are some parts there who would like to get rid of the core parts. It's important that you don't get hooked by them into wanting to get rid of these parts. Why don't you consider why they keep reverting to the old responses?

Kirsten: I guess when I'm in a situation like where Elizabeth is angry at me, it feels the same as Mom and Dad laughing at me, and then I think that Elizabeth hates me, too.

Therapist: That's probably right. So why do you think they keep doing it?

Kirsten: Well, I suppose they're stuck; they get hooked by the situation.

Therapist: Yes, I think that's it. The scene with Elizabeth creates what is called a flashback state for them where they reexperience the original trauma. So when Elizabeth gets angry at you, it feels for them like they're actually back there being abused by Mother and Dad.

Kirsten: Yes, that's what it feels like for me.

Therapist: The point is that they can't help it—they need help to get unhooked from the past, and that's part of the plan.

Kirsten: I know that sometimes I'd like to get rid of them.

Therapist: Yes, these are probably the parts who want the change.

Kirsten: So how do I not get hooked by either group and lead the way?

Therapist: This first column of the flowchart shows the parts' sequence when it gets activated; that's the first step in getting unhooked. The next section explains the unhooking sequence so you can complete unhooking. For now, you can be alert to the temptation to get rid of some parts and can remind yourself and those parts that we're here to see that no one gets rid of them.

Kirsten: I think I can do that.

We see here the use of the flashback concept in helping the self to avoid blaming core parts and getting embroiled in parts polarization. Schwartz's idea of the parts "living in the past" is another way of describing this. By observing and understanding, the self steps back from the parts and maintains compassion for them. The self also needs to retain the hope of change and not fall into the parts' desperation. A plan of change helps the self to accomplish this.

A Respectful Plan of Helping the Parts Change

At this point, Kirsten has seen the need to avoid getting hooked by the polarized parts. As is common with many clients, Kirsten then asked about how she could help the parts change. I reminded her of the healing and unburdening plan that we had originally begun. Now I helped her see how the flowchart fit in with the unburdening of the parts.

Therapist: The next stage of the flowchart will help you unhook from the parts in the heat of the situation, so they can feel safe enough for you to find better responses. When the situation with Elizabeth and your other children gets settled enough, we can then go back to the healing and unburdening, so that each part can grow and be assured of a place in the family.

We then checked with both groups of parts, to see if they were listening to the new understanding of the core parts' responses and the plan for healing. They heard and were calm enough to let Kirsten proceed with the flowchart. She expressed eagerness to go to the next section of the flowchart, the unhooking sequence.

Kirsten's self-destructive survival responses illustrate a covert pattern of internalizing self-blame and pleasing, often hard to detect. The opposite pattern of compulsive overt behaviors (angry outbursts, sexual behavior, substance abuse), while more apparent, indicates similar hidden survival sequences needing to be brought to light so the self can see the core axis and lead the way to change. The same process of making a rough draft and finding the core responses is used.

This first column of the flowchart, the survival sequence, is a tool for observing how situations trigger a flashback state with accompanying destructive core perceptions, feelings, and behaviors. Seeing this from a nonblaming perspective mobilizes the self's compassion to help the parts change. With this respectful plan in mind, the self can avoid getting hooked by one group of parts or the other and assume a role of leader-change agent. The self can reassure the parts that each has a place and an invitation to grow; the self's increasing sense of skills mastery creates new hope and energy.

Many clients like Kirsten use time between sessions to process encounters using the survival sequence, taking walks, journaling, or praying. Sometimes they write out sequences in the flowchart format to analyze old responses to see how the self got hooked by the parts. Later, they are encouraged by their growing skills of unhooking and finding new responses, of calming parts, holding them, comforting them, even singing to them in the shower—in all manner of creative ways.

Clinical sessions are used then for debriefing, reporting, and analyzing the discoveries and lessons of recent encounters. Each growth step contributes to a growing self-discovery and proactive lifestyle, quite different from a previous "helpless victim" or angry posture.

This empowering provides the energy and fresh perspective for the next challenge: to be able to unhook from the parts under pressure and to interrupt the old destructive sequences using the unhooking sequence.

CHAPTER SUMMARY

This chapter introduced the parts' "survival sequence," the first of three sequences in the flowchart. Although each is useful separately, together they constitute a way for the self to identify the parts' destructive survival responses, to separate from the parts and to lead into new responses in tough life situations.

The survival sequence is seen as a tool for helping the self when overwhelmed by the parts' powerful core beliefs, feelings, and defensive behaviors. The chapter used Kirsten's story to illustrate the teaching of clients to develop and use this tool. The therapist showed Kirsten how to make a recent troublesome encounter with her daughter the basis for understanding the sequence of responses directed by the parts' survival pattern. With the therapist's help, Kirsten identified the old perceptions, feelings, and behaviors of the parts.

Kirsten tested this in the next encounter with her daughter. She was able to analyze the results and report to the therapist, so that the draft could be corrected by field experience. Coached by the therapist, Kirsten was able to lift the veil hiding the core responses in each category—the perceptions, feelings, and behaviors originating from early childhood experiences of mistreatment. Kristen could then understand the parts' destructive sequence with a nonblaming concept, the flashback state, the parts experience of the present encounter as a reliving of childhood mistreatment. Kirsten saw clearly how the parts' behavior perpetuated the destructive cycle in her present relationships.

The chapter concluded with a wiser Kirsten, now more freed of the parts' domination by seeing the whole parts' sequence. Because of her process, she felt energized to understand and change subsequent encounters.

CLINICAL OUTLINE: SPOTTING THE DOWNWARD SPIRAL OF PARTS

The following is a listing of procedures for coaching a client in developing and using the survival sequence tool (the first sequence of the flowchart):

I. Therapist observes client's need for leadership tools to deal with challenging situations. Client describes the distress felt. Therapist notes if parts are overwhelming the self and considers the value of interrupting the healing to teach the self leadership tools.

II. Therapist describes the flowchart and assists client in deciding whether to interrupt the healing of the individual parts to learn tools to deal with the situation.

   A. Therapist describes the three leadership tools in the flowchart.

      1. The *downward spiral* identifies the parts' old sequence of reactions, perceptions, feelings, and behaviors that result in a destructive spiral.

      2. The *unhooking sequence* empowers the self by returning it to spiritual grounding and to leadership of the internal family.

      3. *Christ-centered responses* help the self discover and implement new responses to future challenging situations.

   B. If client chooses to develop the flowchart, together they decide which of the three tools to use. They make plans to return to healing of individual parts as soon as the client feels confident about the pressing situation.

III. Therapist helps client construct a rough draft of the parts' survival sequence.

   A. Client selects a recent distressing incident that triggered the parts in a destructive sequence.

B. Therapist describes the rough draft as an approximation of the survival pattern for the purpose of viewing the parts sequence and assessing its consequences.

C. Client isolates the stimuli that triggered the parts and identifies apparent (conscious) responses to the stimuli, usually behaviors and feelings. Therapist helps client enter the responses on the flowchart.

D. Therapist assists client in identifying the parts' perceptions, which are typically held at a semiconscious level and more difficult to observe. (Schwartz's question, "What did you say to yourself about the interaction?" can help in identifying hidden perceptions.)

E. Client considers the whole sequence and any destructive consequences.

F. Client and therapist review the goal of the tool: developing the client's "sequence detector," the skill to spot the parts' sequences.

IV. Client tests the rough draft in a live situation.

A. Client observes how the parts react in the situation and how much space the parts give the self to lead.

B. Client and therapist debrief the encounter, looking for new insights and skills while incorporating any changes onto the flowchart. Therapist reinforces as appropriate the new autonomy of the self and emerging skills.

V. Therapist helps client lift the veil, revealing the parts' core beliefs and responses.

A. Therapist helps client connect the parts' responses to hidden core beliefs and responses to see the hidden survival axis around which the parts have organized the client's life and responses.

B. The client continues the discovery process in subsequent situations to see if the parts use different strategies in different situations.

VI. Therapist helps client identify the consequences of the core responses.

A. Therapist and client consider any self-destructive and self-perpetuating quality of the parts' sequence and the need to interrupt it.

B. Client needs a respectful healing plan and a nonblaming understanding of why parts remain hooked into the self-destructive pattern. Therapist offers the "flashback state" concept

where parts experience the present situation as past trauma, overwhelming the self and perpetuating the destructive pattern.
   C. Therapist and client review the healing plan:
      1. All parts have a role in the new style.
      2. The survival sequence is a tool for the self to see the parts' need for help in getting out of the destructive pattern.
      3. The unhooking sequence and the Christ-centered response sequence can be learned by the self to lead in new responses.
      4. After the situation is resolved, therapist and client return to the unburdening to finish freeing the parts.

THE "ROUGH DRAFT" EXERCISE: SEEKING YOUR SURVIVAL SEQUENCE

The goal here is to make a rough draft of your own survival sequence. Create a chart on paper (using Figure 6.1 as a model) by drawing four blocks in a vertical column with arrows. Have blank paper handy as a worksheet.

   1. Use your favorite way to relax—lying down, deep breathing, etc.
   2. If you wish, ask God to help you with insight and compassion for yourself and your parts.
   3. Select a recent incident that triggered reactions in you that you wish to explore. Note it in the stimulus block with a phrase. Use a pencil so you can erase and change entries as needed.
   4. Let yourself drift back to the scene.
   5. Notice any discomfort you experience. Note your reactions on the worksheet with a word or phrase for each. Do not make these entries on your chart yet.
   6. Recall your behaviors. List these with the words spoken, the changes in your voice, expression, or posture. List the most important behaviors in the old behaviors block.
   7. Identify your feelings and list them on the worksheet. Enter the most important feelings on the flowchart.
   8. Consider how you perceived the situation, what you believed about what the other person was doing or saying. Ask "What

did I say to myself during the incident about the other person or about myself?" List these on the worksheet and enter in the old perceptions block.

9. Try to isolate the precise feature(s) in the incident that triggered your response. Add this to the stimuli block.

10. Reread the whole sequence from top to bottom. Make corrections or additions as needed.

11. Having stepped back from your parts, consider the effect your parts' sequence has had on the outcome of the situation. What effect has the sequence had on other situations in your life? Note this on the worksheet.

12. See if you can lift the veil to discern some of your parts' core beliefs, feelings, and behaviors. Add these to your flowchart.

13. Do you perceive a survival axis around which your parts try to organize their efforts and your life? Note this in the old behavior block. Has there been opposition to your efforts to organize your life around your values or around a transcendent relationship such as with Jesus or God?

14. How much do your parts hook you into their core realities? How has this affected you life? Have there been positive as well as destructive effects? How have you coped with the negative effects?

15. How interested are you in learning to unhook from your parts' sequences and in leading the way into new behaviors? Note this on the worksheet.

16. Do you have a nonblaming way of understanding why your parts react as they do? State it briefly on your worksheet.

17. Are you interested in proceeding to the unhooking sequence, or are there other steps you need to take first?

Chapter 7

Unhooking and Empowering:
The Second Sequence of the Flowchart

Your Father in heaven knows you need all these things (food, clothing). Instead of worrying be concerned with His Kingdom and what He requires and He will provide you with all these things.

Matthew 6:32-33

Jesus observed (in Matthew's Gospel) that we are too caught up in social and material worries and invites his followers to center on a relationship with God, trusting Him for their needs and seeing His plan for their life. Today, Jesus again invites us to a God-centered state where we will have confidence to meet the challenges of life. This living by faith is the remedy for an overwhelmed state.

When the parts overwhelm the self with their old perceptions, feelings, and behaviors, the self and parts feel and act like the powerless victims of the original wounding experience(s). While the first sequence of the flowchart addresses this condition, the second sequence introduces a way for the self to unhook from the parts and the overwhelmed state so that it can return to an empowered state to lead.

This chapter will continue the case of Kirsten to illustrate this process. After being confronted by her adult daughter Elizabeth in the two phone encounters described in the previous chapter, Kirsten felt overwhelmed. The first sequence enabled Kirsten to identify how her parts, triggered by Elizabeth's anger, experienced the situation as childhood abuse. Although overwhelmed and unable to act, Kirsten did perceive her overwhelmed state as a sequence of parts reacting to Elizabeth's anger. This insight enabled her to see that she could respond in a different, more proactive way. Proactive responses require two further steps. The first is to unhook and empower—the focus of this chapter. The next is to design and apply these proactive responses—discussed in the next chapter.

Although most clients progress from column 1 through columns 2 and 3, if the situation requires, I can begin with 2 or 3, and then return to the first column as needed. Here, the second tool of the flowchart provides a foundation for the third, which is the development of new Christ-centered responses.

TAKING THE SELF'S PULSE— COMPARING AND CHOOSING: THE CROSSROADS OF THE FLOWCHART

The "pulse block" of the unhooking sequence (see Figure 7.1) is a crossroads, the point at which the self is invited to separate from the blending parts and to lead in a different path. Three tasks must be accomplished: taking the self's pulse, comparing the self's emotional and spiritual state to the Christ-centered state, and choosing which road to travel. Each task corresponds to a step on the flowchart.

First, the client completes a self-assessment tool, which emphasizes the symptoms that can emerge under pressure. These may be physical (for example, headaches), emotional (anxiety), or behavioral (angry outbursts). The client is urged to pay attention to these reactions as the means used by the parts in overwhelming the self. Once these are clearly seen, the self can take the necessary steps toward regaining leadership.

Introducing the Client to the Emotional State Block

Once Kirsten could see her emotional state (in the second phone conversation with Elizabeth) as confused and helpless, her need for a way to unhook from the powerful parts became clear. I directed her attention to the arrow leading from the old behavior block (see Figure 7.1, bottom of first column) to the pulse block (bottom of the second column). The arrow points from the survival sequence to the unhooking sequence, thus inviting her to unhook from the parts as a way out of the overwhelmed state.

FIGURE 7.1. Taking the Self's Pulse—Comparing and Choosing

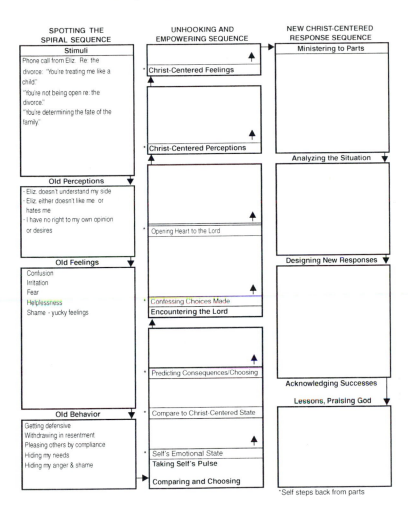

The first step in differentiating from parts is to *take the self's pulse* to determine the extent of hooking into the destructive cycle in progress. The emotional state block is the tool to assist her in this task.

I asked Kirsten to review her first column and identify her most observable feelings, sensations, and behaviors. She selected confusion and powerlessness. I then invited her to relax and recall difficult moments on the phone with Elizabeth (the stimuli) and to confirm if these reactions were prominent, noticing especially the physical reactions. These are assessed by the question from Hakomi therapy: Where are they located in your body?

Kirsten: I feel the confusion and powerlessness; they make me withdraw.

Therapist: Good observation. Anything else?

Kirsten: No, I don't think so.

Therapist: Where are the confusion and powerlessness in your body?

Kirsten: The confusion is in my head but there's something else too; it's like a knot.

Therapist: Anything else about the knot?

Kirsten: It's heavy. It's a knot of heaviness.

Therapist: Can you sense what it's about or get it to tell you?

Kirsten: Yes, it's . . . oh my, it's that I'm bad. It's the yucky feeling and that's why I have no right to my own opinion and that's why I am powerless to act. That's why I have to please others and I am not valued but I get used instead. Then I feel angry about it.

The Hakomi technique of locating the emotion in the body has helped Kirsten track the confusion and powerlessness back to the yucky feeling (the shame) that underlies the powerlessness and has given her a very useful sensation as an alert when the parts are taking over.

We then listed in the pulse block under the self's emotional state (see Figure 7.2) the confusion in her head, the knot of heaviness in her chest; the feeling of being bad and the sense of having no right to act.

Therapist: Are these feelings part of the flashback state you were describing before?

Kirsten: Yes, this is what it felt like when Mother would laugh at me and ignore my concerns. No wonder I feel powerless and shameful and want to hide when Elizabeth gets angry at me.

FIGURE 7.2. Kirsten's Unhooking and Empowering Sequence—First Draft

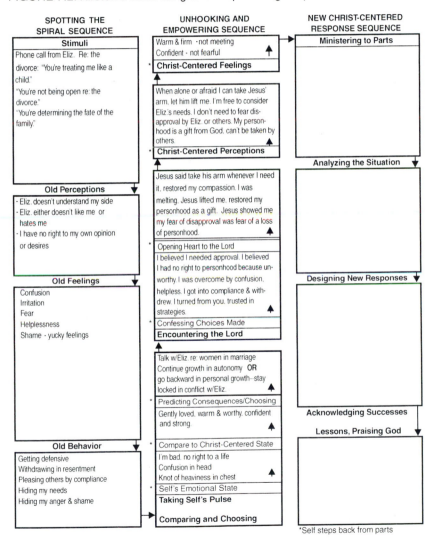

*Self steps back from parts

Therapist: Is this list enough to help you take your emotional pulse in the heat of the moment?

Kirsten: I think so. I notice the confusion in my head first, then the knot in my chest, the yucky feeling and the sense of being bad.

Note the steps used in creating the self-assessment tool. Revisiting the scene in active imagination and using the Hakomi question helped Kirsten connect shame with the heaviness in her chest and how the sense of being bad is the reason for her powerlessness (having no right to a life). We thus reinforce a sense that reactions are understandable and do not have to determine her life. Disclosing hidden reactions also alerts client and therapist to the presence of parts carrying wounds concealed under the reactions. These wounded parts are not attended to at this time but are noted for work after the situation is resolved.

For Kirsten, this revelation of hidden shame and self-hatred was an indication of hidden incest experiences. These were pursued and healed later in the treatment process.

Instructing the Client on the Use of the Emotional State Block

Most clients understand the concept of using the tool to alert them to the blending parts; however, they often are not skilled at the behavioral steps involved. It is useful for them to review their understanding of the steps, looking for missing steps or confusion. The process of using the tool includes the following:

- *Before* entering the situation the self prepares by reviewing anticipated reactions listed in the emotional state block.
- Self attempts to spot reactions, especially physical, before and during the situation.
- Self tries to step back from parts as soon as possible (the flowchart shows an asterisk to the left of the blocks to remind the self.
- Self considers the extent that the blending parts are affecting the ability to respond.

- Self attempts to connect the intensity of the parts' reactions to previous trauma and to note when experiencing a flashback state.

The client should be clear about the goal of this block in unhooking and empowering self. The emotional state block, in giving the self its first sense of blending, begins the process whereby self systematically moves from an overwhelmed state toward an empowered leadership state, making it an agent of growth for the internal family.

Comparing the Self's State to the Empowered State (the Need for Choice)

It is difficult for the self to grasp how weak it is when overwhelmed by the parts. It is even more difficult to envision an empowered state at that time, one separate from parts and moving toward empowerment. Some of Kirsten's parts, during the phone calls with Elizabeth were throwing her into a flashback state of past shame and powerlessness, while others were judging her for not being a good mother to Elizabeth.

In describing the power of the parts to overwhelm the self, Schwartz notes how burdened parts attempt to feel better by dumping their distress onto the self and staying enmeshed with the self. The core coalition of parts is often afraid of losing its influence and even of being eliminated by the self's empowering. These dynamics create powerful impulses for the parts to blend with the self. The self has the formidable task of unhooking from these parts when activated. It needs not only a source of empowering to unhook but also a vision of proactive posture. It is important that the source of both be independent of the enmeshed internal system; this provides the needed autonomy for the self to lead the parts. The therapist then can help the self appropriate the needed vision and power for the new posture.

For many, this source of transformation is God or a "high power." For Christians, it is God through Jesus. The empowering comes from centering around a relationship with Jesus, under God, assisted by the Holy Spirit embodied in the self of faith (see Chapter 3). This relationship becomes the source for both the vision of the new posture as well as the power to appropriate it. The next block on the flowchart, the Christ-centered state, helps the self experience this state and note its characteristics. It provides evidence that taking a proactive posture in the situation is actually possible. This creates hope for the self to lead forward in the face of many parts who are convinced that a life of powerlessness is predetermined.

Identifying the Christ-Centered State

This step provides content for the empowered state as a reference for the overwhelmed self. To find this content, the self must identify the perceptions, feelings, and behaviors experienced when it is free of the parts and encounters Jesus with his unconditional love. Yet many Christians, although committed believers with varying degrees of biblical, doctrinal, and theological knowledge, have never experienced a parts-free encounter with Jesus, God, or the Holy Spirit, or sensed its transforming effect on them. This is easily remedied by inviting the self to separate from parts for a time. Even a brief encounter, free of parts, provides the evidence needed to complete the Christ-centered state block.

Kirsten's case illustrates this. Because she had a long-standing faith in Jesus, I simply asked her to recall when she felt close to Jesus or to God. At a loss, she said she had a strong commitment to Jesus but did not feel close to him or to God. Although she went to worship regularly and entered into the singing and prayer, that did not help her feel close to God.

I asked her to recall a time when we invited Jesus to help unburden her unworthy part. She remembered that she and Jesus had removed the burden, that the part felt Jesus' love and did not need to "measure up for people" anymore because its worth came now from Him. But she felt this did not have any affect on her own closeness to Jesus. I asked Kirsten if she wanted actually to encounter Jesus. She said she did, but some parts were afraid. I said we could talk to them to see if they were willing to let her have such an encounter.

Kirsten, like many Christians, was able to draw close to Jesus at times of distress, but her frightened and skeptical parts always managed to keep her from a real encounter with him. Consequently, she had little sense of what a Christ-centered state could be like.

Inviting the Client to an Encounter with Jesus

Schwartz's mountain exercise is helpful for clients in settling their parts so that the self can have a parts-free encounter with Jesus (see Chapter 4). I urged Kirsten to settle her parts at the foot of the mountain in the usual manner. When she arrived at the mountaintop, she heard a chorus of parts say, "It's not possible to talk with Jesus." Kirsten immediately heard another voice, which she took to be her self of faith, respond, "Try it and see."

After Kirsten succeeded in separating the parts from her self, I noticed tears running down her cheeks. "Jesus is bending down to pick me up," she said. "He wants to love me, but I can't receive it." I helped her bargain with the worried parts, who finally agreed to sit out for "sixty seconds" while Kirsten related to Jesus. In this brief time, Kirsten opened her heart to Jesus: "I feel his love. He actually loves me; His love isn't frightening, it's warm and gentle. I even feel a bit of confidence and strength."

The parts could not tolerate more of this gentle love, having only experienced force and shame previously. In that brief moment, however, Kirsten experienced enough of the Christ-centered state to identify its characteristics: feeling gently loved, warm, worthy, as well as strong and confident. We listed these in the Christ-centered block (see Figure 7.2). These words would remind her when feeling the confusion, the heavy knot in her chest; she could remember the warmth and worthiness experienced with Jesus.

This brief encounter with Jesus was strong enough to give Kirsten the information needed to fill in the Christ-centered state block. The therapist must be prepared to help the self in this process. As noted in Chapter 4, the question "How does Jesus feel toward you?" is useful in opening one's heart to Jesus and in finding parts that are blocking the encounter. The self may need help settling the parts or negotiating with them for a brief time for the encounter. The therapist then asks, What is it like for you?

In this way, the self can note the effects of the encounter—in Kirsten's case, the warmth, which she will compare to the knot in her chest and confusion in her head. Later, the self will use this evidence to remember the alternative to the wretched powerless state: that it has the capacity to choose. The credibility of the choice comes from the self experiencing it in the encounter with Jesus. The choice now strengthens hope and elevates the self as the agent of change for the internal family.

Upon our completion of the Christ-centered block, Kirsten's face lit up; she said, "It's amazing to think that I might not have to always feel overwhelmed; I could have a new lease on life." This exclamation illustrates one result of the comparison between the two states: the highlighting of the oppressive nature of the old state and the possibilities of the new state. The mere realization of a choice is a step out of the victim posture. The self is energized and pessimistic parts with their claims that change is impossible are quieted.

Predicting the Consequences of the Two Paths and Choosing

The final step of the pulse block is predicting the consequences of pursuing the parts' survival sequence or the Christ-centered path and choosing between them. The self must make an informed choice. When written into the pulse block, the predictions become another tool to help the self make choices in the heat of the situation.

The self must face the consequences of the choice. It seems evident that the old survival sequence leads to a destructive outcome and the Christ-centered choice a positive outcome. Yet since parts operate from their survival base, they will minimize or deny the destructive consequences of the survival sequence. The self then will remain on the fence, rationalizing that the old responses are not so destructive.

For Kirsten, the survival route would further damage the relationship with Elizabeth by sidestepping Elizabeth's real questions about the effect of the divorce on the family. Kirsten's parts, driven by fear of Elizabeth's anger, minimized the results of Kirsten's withdrawal. They minimized Elizabeth's need (because of her engagement) to deal with the equally important question of whether a woman can be an equal partner in marriage, the very area in which Kirsten was experiencing a breakthrough. Kirsten could have helped Elizabeth by sharing her experience and insights; instead, her parts overwhelmed her with the victim perception of helplessness.

The predicting block highlights both the need and the possibility of a change. The self is not stuck; it has a choice. The more concrete the consequences are, the more useful the tool can be. The self, emerging from an overwhelmed state, can cut through the parts' denial and make a choice with the therapist's help. Although the parts see the choice as huge, it is a series of small steps. Instead of choosing a totally new response to the situation, the self is turning to Jesus for empowerment to view the situation in a new light.

Helping the Client Complete the Predicting Block

Clients need assistance in seeing that consequences are predictable and good grounds for making choices. They need help in making their predictions as concrete as possible.

Therapist: The predicting block asks you again to step back from your parts and consider the consequences of going with the parts' survival responses compared to turning to Jesus for new responses. Consider the results of following the parts' pattern. Try to be as specific as possible.

Kirsten: Well, if I pursue the current route with Elizabeth, I guess it would damage our relationship further.

Therapist: Yes, that makes sense. Now see if you can be more concrete. Look at the emotional state block and the old behavior block and see how your parts get you to feel and behave.

Kirsten: [Looking at flow chart] For me, it's confusion and fear, then I hesitate and withdraw. I'm sure Elizabeth thinks I'm sidestepping her questions and so is angry at me.

Therapist: Okay. So what would happen if you stayed with this strategy?

Kirsten: I suppose we would get locked into this. Her angry at me, me afraid of her.

Therapist: Then what?

Kirsten: We would probably become more distant. She would eventually stop trying to hear my side and just take her father's side against me.

Therapist: That sounds pretty realistic. Now consider how pursuing the parts' plan would affect you aside from your relationship with Elizabeth.

Kirsten: I guess my growth would get sidetracked. I faced the issue in my marriage; so instead of carrying it forward into my relationship with Elizabeth, I'd be going backward.

Kirsten decided to put two phrases in the block (see Figure 7.2), one relating to her relationship with Elizabeth ("staying locked in conflict with Elizabeth") and the other about her self ("going backward in personal growth").

Next, I asked Kirsten what might result if she turned to Jesus and proceeded with Christ-centered leadership. She said she would break free of generations of subservient women by extending her hard-won growth into the relationship with Elizabeth. She added the phrase "continue growth in autonomy" to the block. Kirsten considered how strategic her choice could be for Elizabeth as she approached her own marriage. She noted that as the next in several generations of dependent women, it was important for Elizabeth to face before her marriage the issue of a woman's role with her husband. Empowered by a relationship with Jesus, Kirsten felt she would find a way to share her emerging autonomy without blaming Bihari or entangling Elizabeth in parental issues. Kirsten became hopeful as she considered this and decided to add the phrase "talking with Elizabeth regarding women's roles in marriage," sensing it would remind her of the expected results and help her to choose.

We see here the process of helping clients to realize they have a choice; they can predict the consequences and select appropriate key phrases for the flowchart. Kirsten was quite clear that she was choosing the second option (turning to Jesus), to lead her parts. She was not sure, however, that she could actually pull it off. I reminded her that the pulse block, like the unhooking sequence, was to break down what seemed like a giant step into more manageable steps. With each step, she would see what she could accomplish and where more help was needed. She said she was ready to try the new tool in her next phone call with Elizabeth.

Kirsten Tests Her Pulse Block

At our next session, Kirsten reported on this phone call. She felt that she was overwhelmed by parts again and was no more free to respond than previously, becoming defensive and cutting short the call. Yet in debriefing the conversation and comparing it to the words in the pulse block, we noticed instead that she made progress in spite of the outcome.

First, she sensed the knot in her chest, using the emotional state block. She then stepped back enough to observe that the parts were starting to "blend" with her. She connected the knot with a growing sense of being bad, having no rights, and feeling powerless. She also connected the responses with Elizabeth's angry blame, a useful sharpening of the stimuli that initially triggered the parts' reactions. Next, she remembered the Christ-centered state of warmth and confidence, which revealed how strongly the parts were blending and how she had lost touch with the love experienced from Jesus.

Kirsten remembered the predicted negative results of talking with Elizabeth when following the parts spiral. She thought of new possibilities of relating to Elizabeth (when in a Christ-centered state), although she could not yet achieve them. She was determined to explore empowerment with Jesus (predicting and choosing blocks) and surprised to discover some hope along with the usual discouragement and self-criticism. She was understanding events *during* the process and feeling less overwhelmed.

Kirsten also noted that she had stepped away from the parts enough to do the steps in the block, which led to understanding and seeing that she had a choice. She saw that although she was not yet able to change the behavioral outcome, she could turn to Jesus for empowerment to start the process. She had accomplished the two goals of the testing process: testing the contents of the pulse block to see if they are accurate enough to be useful in the tension of the situation and stepping back from the parts to accomplish the steps in the block. Together, these contributed to her sense of hope.

We considered that parts judge the self on an all-or-nothing basis; because her *behaviors* with Elizabeth did not change, they judged her a failure. The focus of the field test was not final behavioral goals, however, but the intermediate goals of reinforcing her spiritual growth and skill foundation—later to result in new behavior with Elizabeth.

Kirsten now felt that having done the steps once she could do them again. She was ready to go on to the next block. I congratulated her on a successful testing of the block and on her mastery of the skills. We checked with her parts to see if they noticed that she had accomplished the goals of the block and was ready to go on. They acknowledged her success; some were even hopeful, although others were skeptical that she could lead them to anything new. We recognized this and asked them to withhold judgment, affirming that she could continue to learn and grow in leadership skill. They reluctantly agreed.

This debriefing process emphasized many of Kirsten's accomplishments that the critical parts would have overshadowed by their perception of failure. Kirsten had separated from the parts, tested the tool, and tested herself. She also sharpened the stimuli by noting the role of Elizabeth's anger in triggering the parts and connecting it to her parents' angry blaming of her as a child. Kirsten saw how these parts get hooked into a flashback state and thus are more likely to overwhelm her.

The debriefing revealed that even as parts are hooked, Kirsten's self is learning to unhook in the presence of the stimuli and the hooked parts. In working through the steps of the block, the self is seeing the need to lead stuck parts in a new direction, as well as how difficult and yet important it is to separate from the parts. This experience, along with the experience of success at separating, reinforced the self's growing determination to separate and act independently of the parts. This is the opposite of the self being overwhelmed by the parts. Growing self-autonomy is the foundational goal of the pulse block. This independence and determination is needed if the self is to break through the discomfort and resistance of parts to the next block (encountering the Lord).

Debriefing is necessary for the self to identify success in the face of the skepticism and criticism of the parts. Field testing the block is set up as a win-win process. Either the client wins by accomplishing the steps or by gaining information needed to accomplish the steps. As therapists, we must have our own selves available for the debriefing process, lest our parts get hooked into the client's self-criticism and discouragement. Otherwise, we fail to help them see their successes so they can move forward.

ENCOUNTERING THE LORD BLOCK

The client now recognizes how powerfully the parts can draw the self into their distressed state and senses the need for a way back to an empowering relationship with Jesus. How can the self, overwhelmed by survival reactions and drawn into destructive responses, now turn back? In this first task, the self is invited to return to Jesus using the biblical model of repenting through confession. The self identifies the ways it has turned away and acknowledges them, while seeking a restored relationship through forgiveness. This step is labeled "confessing choices made" (Figure 7.2).

Now restored to relationship, how does the self receive the needed empowering, a step it has previously been unable to take? This second task, identifying the self's inner defenses against opening to Jesus and receiving his unconditional love, is labeled "opening the heart to the Lord" (Figure 7.2).

Confessing Choices Made

Having been drawn away from Jesus by the parts' survival reactions, the self now considers which of these reactions should be acknowledged in returning to the relationship. The client lists the most important of these in the confessing block and considers his or her readiness for the encounter with Jesus. Client and therapist may note ways that the parts' survival reactions have harmed others as well. Some clients in unhooking and empowering become strong enough to identify wrongs previously denied and can feel remorse for them. It is important to list these wrongs separately, so the client can discern with the therapist how repentance for these wrongs fits with encountering the Lord. If a need exists to confess the wrongs and seek forgiveness, should this happen before or after the client encounters the Lord? How does this fit with lowering the defensive barrier of the heart to receive Jesus' forgiveness and love? Often listing the wrongs is the needed step for lowering the barriers to Jesus' unconditional love and forgiveness. Client and therapist can then discern the next steps. It is best to finish the empowering sequence and flowchart in dealing with the situation and then to proceed to confession and restitution to those wronged by the client. Like Kirsten, many clients simply note the ways their reactions have contributed to the breakdown of relationships and these are dealt with through new responses to the situation at hand.

Kirsten and the Confessing Step

Kirsten worked through the pulse block following the disappointing phone call to Elizabeth and recognized her parts' power to disable her efforts to respond differently. Now she felt even more determined to pursue the route of empowering with Jesus. This determination became a key factor in her eventual recovery. I directed her attention to the "confessing step" and asked if she had ever had an experience of repentance and forgiveness with God. She said "No," but did understand the concept of forgiveness through Jesus' death on the cross. She and several parts were uncertain, however, about whether Jesus would forgive or condemn her.

I observed how common her uncertainty was. Many Christians even with little biblical knowledge or experience with God are aware that when they are stuck in old victim behaviors harmful to self and others, they are not being true to self or to God. Many do not understand God's forgiveness through Jesus and simply need to be informed, after which they are ready to take the next steps with Jesus.

Many others who understand God's forgiveness remain stuck in fear that He will condemn them, reinforcing their view of self as losers and sinners. It is tempting to try to convince them with biblical arguments. However, when working with parts, attempts at persuasion are seldom productive and run counter to the goal of self-empowerment. Instead, the Christ-centered IFS model helps the self in staying separated from the parts and endows the self with a transcendent capacity to find the way. The therapist invites the self to the next step and assures the parts, so they will not block the way to growth.

For Kirsten, the next step was to consider which of the survival reactions (listed in the self's emotional state block) was most disempowering. She took a minute to separate from her parts and then began to consider the extent to which she had allowed the parts' spiral to overwhelm and take her away from Jesus. She saw her responsibility in the downward spiral and the value of acknowledging this to Jesus. This is the process of ownership of one's actions. Without ownership, only blaming of self and others exists. With it, the possibility of sorrow and contrition exists, which can result in lowering the defenses around the heart. The self, through this confession process, thus prepares the way for opening the heart to Jesus.

Kirsten considered the power of her emotional reactions to separate her from Jesus. She selected the important ones, naming them as though addressing Jesus:

- "I turned from you, Lord, and trusted in old strategies."
- "Instead of responding to Elizabeth with love and wisdom, I used compliance and withdrew."
- "Instead of feeling worthy and confident as when I'm with you, I let myself be overcome by confusion and helplessness."
- "I believed I had no right to a life or to my own judgments."
- "I believed I needed approval from others to act."

Kirsten observed that each of these survival responses had become a habit in a victim way of life, a way to compensate for her lack of worth. Living the old core for fifty years, she kept her heart closed to Jesus' love and power, although she understood herself to be a Christian. Seeing the effects of this old orientation and tasting anew Jesus' unconditional love, she felt ready to risk opening herself to him.

Listing the features of the old survival core showed Kirsten's self how the old core beliefs and behaviors kept her from her deepest desires to be loved for herself and empowered as a person. She now realized that in turning from the old core to Jesus she could receive the foundation of a new posture.

Kirsten's parts, however, continued to be anguished about her decision. They correctly observed that she was giving up the old hope of achieving their dreams and needs through her own efforts. This was quite frightening to them; some parts were sure that their worst fears of being judged, shamed, and controlled by Jesus would come true. One by one Kirsten reassured her parts until they were ready to grant her the needed space for her encounter with Jesus while they huddled nervously and watched.

Kirsten's self had now accomplished the first task of the encountering the Lord block—finding a way to turn back to the Lord. Now separated from her parts, she acknowledged the destructive behaviors and beliefs interrupting her relationship with the Lord and repented. Her heart was set on facing the Lord and seeking His mercy and empowerment. For most clients, this repentant attitude lowers the barriers of the heart that past self-sufficiency has erected. The self is now ready to open the heart to Jesus.

Many clients realize they are the ones who kept Jesus and his transforming love out. Jesus quietly waited, not forcing his way in. Now that the self opens its heart, the resources of grace can freely enter: forgiveness, unconditional love, wisdom, and courage. The self receives these from God as a birthright freely given, not something withheld until earned as in the family of origin.

The Confession Process with Clients Who Have Been Shamed

A few clients see the owning of responsibility and confession of sins as further shaming and become stuck at this point. They may have been introduced to personal responsibility by a shaming authority figure at too young an age. It is best to slow the confession process for them, to help the self and fearful parts in evaluating the steps of confessing and opening the heart to the Lord. It is important to identify any "shaming" as abuse, even in a religious context. This will identify an important source of wounding and allow self and therapist to acknowledge the appropriateness of the managers' cautions. It also permits a dialogue with self and managers about the process of turning away from survival responses to an empowering relationship with Jesus. They can explore the question of whether this is another shaming process or only the self's choice to turn from a destructive path to a hopeful relationship with a loving and forgiving God. It is useful to note the difference between "toxic shame" coming from a shaming authority figure (as discussed by John Bradshaw*) and the "healthy shame" the client feels in perceiving past destructive choices.

Healthy shame is illustrated in Jesus' parable of the prodigal son (Luke 15:11-32) who demanded his inheritance money and then squandered it in reckless living. He eventually comes to his senses and says to himself: "All my father's hired workers have more than they can eat, and here I am about to starve! I will get up and go to my father and say 'Father I have sinned against God and you. I am no longer fit to be called your son; treat me as one of your hired workers'" (Luke 15: 17-19). The son saw the destructiveness of his path and felt remorseful. This healthy shame resulted in a humility that opens the closed heart. There is nothing now to block the father's love; the son returns, not demanding a restoration of his birthright, but hoping only to be treated as a hired servant.

What was the father's attitude during the son's folly? Did he judge and condemn his son or shame and pursue him, treating him like a child? No, the father waited and kept his heart open. And when he

---

*Bradshaw, J. (1988). *Healing the Shame That Binds You.* Deerfield Beach, Florida: Health Communications, Inc.

saw the son returning, he ran and embraced him with a heart "full of compassion," kissed him and organized a feast to celebrate the return of his lost son. The son is received not as a servant but restored to the full standing of his birthright.

Jesus' story illustrates the son's painful experience in coming to the place of repenting and taking down the barrier in his heart to the father. It also shows the posture of the father, waiting for the son to return, keeping his heart open, and allowing the son to choose if and when to return. This posture is underlined by another biblical image, that of Jesus waiting for us to open our hearts to him: "Behold, I stand at the door and knock, if anyone hears my voice and opens the door I will come in and fellowship with him" (Revelation 3:20).

Often the self and parts need to be assured that God will not forcefully violate their boundaries, even when they are on a path of self-destruction. Instead, he knocks at the door and waits with open heart. If they respond, He is free to give them all the grace and power needed, their inheritance as His children.

After such a decision, clients' parts may still be unable to imagine a God who does not shame or control. However, if the self with its capacity for transcendence sees the importance of testing this possibility, then self and therapist can attend to the needs of any remaining stuck parts until their cautions are satisfied.

Some parts, put off by the religious language, can be made more comfortable with words like "acknowledging" instead of "confessing." Others who relate more easily to God than Jesus, can reframe the flowchart as God centered. The important point is for the self to find a way to separate from the parts, and open the door to an empowering relationship with God.

Opening the Heart to the Lord

In the confession block, the therapist helped the self with a solution to the first task, finding a way to the Lord through taking stock of the failings of the survival plan and realizing the need for repentance. The way is now clear for the self's second task, to receive needed empowering through opening the heart to Jesus and assimilating his grace; this will lead to a new posture toward the situation.

The therapist will need to follow the process carefully and be ready to help the self in staying unhooked from the parts. The mountain exercise is a useful aid for maintaining a needed separation for the self.

Fearful, skeptical, and angry parts must be acknowledged and given the assurance and safety needed to allow the self to take this step. The therapist's own parts must be silent so the client and Jesus will have the needed space to interact.

Kirsten's Encounter with the Lord

Having listened to her parts and responded to their fears, Kirsten gathered them at the foot of the mountain to settle them. She reminded them that they had already seen the good results of going to the mountain (in the pulse block). She pointed out the urgent need for a new way to relate to Elizabeth. Eventually even the fearful and skeptical parts were settled and she was able to go up the mountain without much interruption.

Kirsten: I see Jesus; he's waiting for me [pause]. Now I'm in front of him. I'm so weak I can't stand. I'm nearly melting into the ground. I don't have any being of my own [pause].

Therapist: Anything else you want to show him?

Kirsten: He's reaching out to me—I'm taking his hand. Some kind of life is coming from him into me. My body is firming up and taking shape—it's his life inside of me.

Therapist: What's happening now?

Kirsten: I have my own life now—it's from God. It's the being God gave me when I was born. Mother nearly drained it all out of me. Now Jesus has restored it and filled it out. It's from God and comes through Jesus [pause].

Therapist: What's it like to have that life in you?

Kirsten: I feel my strength again and my confidence. I'm a being, a person; I don't need to get approval from anybody to be a person with opinions and a life. I just am. God made me and God loves me.

Therapist: Anything else?

Kirsten: Jesus is saying I don't need to fear. I think I understand. I was always afraid of others' criticism or anger. Now I see—I always thought that people's disapproval would take away my personhood—like Mother tried to do. So Jesus is showing me that my being comes from God so I don't need to fear people's anger or disapproval (pause).

Therapist: What else?

Kirsten: I need to be able to relate to Elizabeth differently.

Therapist: Do you want to ask Jesus about it?

Kirsten: [pause] He's showing me that my parts think Elizabeth is like Mother when she's angry and critical of me—so she will take away my personhood too. Jesus is showing me that I don't have to fear Elizabeth either because my personhood doesn't depend on her moods.

Therapist: Are you interested in why Elizabeth is angry and critical of you?

Kirsten: She is upset about the divorce. She's wondering what will happen to our family and can't understand the change in me. I can understand why she's upset now that I'm not afraid of her.

Therapist: Where's Jesus now?

Kirsten: He's sitting here with me now. I'm holding onto His arm.

Therapist: How does he feel toward you?

Kirsten: He loves me for myself. I can feel it. He likes being with me. Now He's telling me that whenever I need strength I can just take His arm and He'll be with me.

Therapist: How is that for you?

Kirsten: I've felt alone all my life; now I don't ever have to be alone . . . He'll be with me and will help me find the way through.

Therapist: Is there anything else you need or want from Jesus?

At this point, Kirsten was ready to come down the mountain. She hugged Jesus and thanked Him, assured that she could come to Him whenever she needed to. Next, she talked to the parts who had been carefully watching. Some were amazed and hopeful. Others were afraid and skeptical. She reassured the fearful parts that they were not going to be discarded or overlooked and asked the skeptical parts if they would wait and see how she could do now as a leader. They were temporarily reassured, but we were alerted that they would need reassurance before Kirsten changed her responses to Elizabeth. I noted that the "ministering to the parts" block in the third sequence could be such an occasion.

Kirsten and I also noticed that the skeptical and fearful parts, which before had only agreed to a one-minute encounter, had tolerated a much longer time. We mentioned this to them and commended them and all the parts. Had there been parts that continued to block the way, it would have been necessary to seek them out, hear their fears, and find a way to help them before proceeding.

Debriefing the Encounter with the Lord

The first step in this debriefing is to help the client understand the significance of the encounter. Once understood, the client can easily select the central features for listing on the flowchart to assist the self in returning to an empowering relationship with Jesus in the future.

I asked Kirsten to recall the important features of her encounter and consider its effects on her. With help, she quickly saw that her melting (loss of personhood) resulted from her family "draining" the personhood originally given her by God. Jesus lifting and filling her had restored this as a birthright. She no longer needed to fear others' disapproval (including Elizabeth's) as she had in the past. Kirsten noticed that with fear of Elizabeth gone, her compassion for her was restored. Finally, she connected Jesus' invitation to take his arm whenever needed as a resolution of her aloneness, restoring her confidence to find a way with Elizabeth and with her life.

Recapping the experience, Kirsten selected the features that stood out and described them, another step in the assimilation process. She decided on the following (which we added to the flowchart; Figure 7.2):

- Jesus showed that my fear of disapproval was fear of loss of personhood.
- I was melting; Jesus lifted me up and restored my personhood as a gift.
- He restored my compassion to Elizabeth.
- Jesus said to take His arm whenever I needed it.

Kirsten's self is coming into empowerment. This feels uncomfortable because her past experience said that she had no right to a life of her own, that she must forever depend on others' approval. Finding this clarity (in the confessing block) she is able to approach Jesus with that previously hidden truth. And Jesus is free to respond to her deepest shame and need.

Kirsten's experience of melting was a disclosure in body language by her most primitive parts, too young to use words or visual memories but in the presence of Jesus able to communicate vividly through bodily movement. This is the "truth in the inward parts" that David refers to in the book of Psalms (51:6 KJV). With the hidden shame revealed, the power of life can flow into her as a gift from God not dependent on others. For Kirsten, a lifelong victim of engulfment, first by her mother and family of origin and then by her husband of thirty years, receiving her personhood from God releases a new life of autonomy. Released of fear of her daughter, she will discover a new way to relate. As with most who have been swallowed up by others, Kirsten also experienced profound neglect and isolation. These too are being resolved by Jesus' ongoing presence with her and his availability for her needs.

Kirsten's task now is to assimilate her new status, to overcome old fears, and to discover new responses to each situation. The next two blocks will help her first with new perceptions about herself in each situation, and second with new feelings as she stays grounded in her birthright with God.

CHRIST-CENTERED PERCEPTIONS

The task of this block is to identify new beliefs and perceptions of self and others resulting from the encounter with Jesus. These are listed to extend the new perceptions into future situations. The therapist may believe that because the parts allowed the self to encounter the Lord and saw the self's empowerment they will not interrupt the constructing of the perceptions block or the feelings block. Some parts, however, feel threatened by the self's new status, and the therapist must be prepared to help the self notice any threatened parts before proceeding. The therapist begins by inviting the self to build the perceptions tool by reviewing the old perceptions block (first sequence) to compare it to the opening the heart block and to consider emerging perceptions for the future.

Kirsten's Experience

As Kirsten considered her old perceptions, she was surprised to note that she now viewed each one differently.

Kirsten: Now I'm not threatened by Elizabeth's not understanding my side, I see that I haven't shared my views with her yet so of course she can't understand. I need to do that soon. I'm not threatened by her anger now. I can understand why she's angry. I know she doesn't hate me, she's just angry. It doesn't affect my personhood; that's given by God.

Therapist: What else?

Kirsten: Since I'm not afraid of disapproval anymore by Elizabeth, or anyone else for that matter, I'm free to be compassionate to others. Before, when I was confronted with anger, my parts would overwhelm me with their fear. Now I can take Jesus' arm when I'm overwhelmed and let Him lift me up. Then I'm not alone and I don't need to give my self away and let myself be used out of fear.

Kirsten and I then summarized her perceptions and listed them on the flowchart.

- My personhood is a gift from God and cannot be taken away by others.
- I don't need to fear disapproval by Elizabeth or others.
- I'm free to consider Elizabeth's needs.
- When I'm alone or afraid, I can take Jesus' arm and let Him lift me up.

We discussed using the perceptions block. Kirsten thought she could use it for a quick reminder of the new grounding of her self worth in Jesus and the importance of taking Jesus' arm when she felt afraid or alone. She also sensed she could notice when she lost her compassion for Elizabeth. This would alert her to the fact that her parts were becoming afraid.

Kirsten now understood how to use the block and was ready to go to the Christ-centered feelings block. Like many clients, she has duplications between the perceptions block and the opening heart block. It usually is not important to edit the blocks at this point. It is important for the block to remind the client that the grounding in Jesus provides the self with a fresh outlook.

CHRIST-CENTERED FEELINGS

The transition from building the new perceptions block to building the new feelings block is a natural one in that the new perceptions give rise to new feelings. The therapist must not become complacent, however, because the parts may feel threatened by the feelings block, even though they were not activated previously by the perceptions block.

The client identifies the new feelings resulting from the encounter with Jesus and from the new perceptions. As with other blocks, the client selects the most important for listing in the block. This block then is an additional tool for the self to take the pulse and notice not only when the self is free of parts blending but also when it feels empowered. The self can then take an "empowered pulse" by comparing its present feelings to the feeling state described in the block.

Identifying the new feelings is also important, because they can easily be forgotten due to the efforts of worried or skeptical parts distracting the self from the new emotional state. When identified, the feeling state becomes evidence for self and parts that the self is indeed changing. This reinforces hope.

Kirsten's Process

After describing the goal of the block to Kirsten, I invited her to reread the old feelings block and the opening the heart block; I asked her to try remembering the feelings experienced in the encounter with Jesus.

Kirsten: The most powerful feeling was the sense of melting. The melting was a deeper feeling than the fear or the yuckiness I usually feel.

Therapist: Say more about the melting.

Kirsten: It was the thing I had been running from all my life. I had organized my life to avoid it but here it was and then I knew that it was the loss of my personhood.

Here Kirsten has identified the significance of the melting as the core experience of her internal family.

Kirsten: The next thing I felt was Jesus' hand. It was so gentle and loving and then I felt myself fill up and become firm. It was like I had boundaries now and what was inside the boundaries was me. That probably sounds strange. I had known in my head that I had my own boundaries, but they felt like a sieve. This was the first time I had a sensation of my own definite boundaries as a person.

Therapist: It makes sense to me. Any other feelings along with the sense of boundaries?

Kirsten: Oh yes [remembering]. I felt warm inside myself, warm and firm, a kind of warm energy, and I think that's when I started feeling this confidence.

Therapist: What was the confidence like?

Kirsten: Like I could do things I couldn't do before; stand up to people when I needed to.

Therapist: How is that for you?

Kirsten: I don't know yet; exciting, I think. My parts are terrified that I will do it.

Therapist: Any other feelings?

Kirsten: No, I didn't feel the fear like I usually do, just the warmth and firmness and confidence.

Therapist: Could you notice if those new feelings are present or absent when you are about to talk with Elizabeth or Bihari?

Kirsten: I think I could. They're distinct and seem like the opposite of the old feelings of fear and powerlessness and yuckiness.

Therapist: When you're ready, consider how you would like to phrase these feelings in the flowchart.

Kirsten settled on two phrases that reflected the new feelings, contrasted them with the old feelings, and added them to the flowchart:

> Warm / Firm—Not Melting
> Confident—Not Fearful

This completed the building of the feelings block.

Observations on the Process

The dialogue illustrates the process of helping a client reconnect with feelings resulting from the encounter with Jesus. Because some feelings may be particularly frightening to parts, they will try to arrange for the feelings to get overlooked, hence the need for help. Once recovered, the new feelings are evidence for the self as well as for skeptical and hopeless parts that something real happened in the encounter. In Kirsten's case, as with many clients, the change is spiritual and ontological—the recovery of personhood as grounded in

God—not always meaningful to frightened parts. Change in feelings, such as from melting and fearfulness to warmth and confidence, is considerably more convincing. This may be persuasive evidence for the parts to give the self more space to try new responses to the situation.

Noting the new feelings in the block then helps remind self and parts of the changes, as the self prepares new responses. The block then serves as an updated pulse block enabling the self to take an "empowered pulse" revealing when the self is not only free of the overwhelmed state but also in the empowered state. In Kirsten's case, this means not just being free of the melting, fearful, powerless feelings but also experiencing the warmth and confidence associated with her grounded state of personhood from God.

This completed the building of the new feelings block as well as the completion of the unhooking and empowering sequence. The next phone call from Elizabeth was due in a few days and would give Kirsten a chance for her empowered self to step forward. I cautioned Kirsten not to expect too much of herself since we had not discussed the new response sequence. I urged her only to notice what effect her new freedom has in her conversation.

Kirsten's Field Test

At the beginning of the next session, Kirsten described a recent phone call with Elizabeth. Bihari had presented himself to Elizabeth in a positive light, so she angrily demanded that Kirsten forgive him and give him another chance. Kirsten was pleased to say that this time she did not terminate the conversation to run from Elizabeth's anger. She acknowledged Elizabeth's emotions instead and understood that Kirsten wanted to sort out her own feelings so that she could speak respectfully of Bihari and not embroil Elizabeth in the conflict. Elizabeth appeared to accept this grudgingly.

Therapist: What made you feel that Elizabeth accepted what you said?

Kirsten: Her tone of voice changed considerably.

Therapist: How so?

Kirsten: From a loud, sharp, aggressive edge to a quieter tone—like she was understanding and ready to listen.

Therapist: How did you feel about that?

Kirsten: Hopeful; like for the first time I felt hopeful that maybe we could find our way through this.

Therapist: How do you account for her change?

Kirsten: I think she sensed I wasn't backing away from her concern *but trying to listen.*

Therapist: How do you explain your change in response?

Kirsten: I did not feel intimidated this time like before. I took my pulse before I called, and I didn't feel afraid, but I didn't feel confident either. I asked the parts to give me space and found my way back to Jesus until I felt my empowered state, more confident and warm. Then I called her. When Elizabeth got angry and critical, I noticed I didn't have the urge to run and didn't feel like I was melting—that was different!

Therapist: What happened when you found your way to Jesus?

Kirsten: I reached out, took His arm and felt close to Him. I felt my personhood was in place.

Therapist: What about your parts?

Kirsten: I had asked them for space, and I guess they gave it to me to go to Jesus and then to talk with Elizabeth.

Therapist: Anything else?

Kirsten: Even though I wasn't intimidated, I still didn't know what to say about my side of the issue. But I could see that I needed to sort out how much to tell her—so I told her that.

Therapist: How wonderful! You saw your own need to think it out and told her you would get back to her. That satisfied your need and her need?

Kirsten: Yes, she accepted that. We came to some agreement together for the first time in this matter. I'm so relieved.

Therapist: Do you notice anything else about yourself?

Kirsten: For the first time, I was able to think clearly in the face of anger, and I wasn't ashamed to speak up about my own needs while responding to hers.

Therapist: That sounds like someone with personhood. Congratulations to you and your parts. You did an excellent job of leading and your parts did a good job of trusting you and giving you space to lead. I also noticed that you have found a quick and streamlined way of using the sequence. I don't know how aware you were of it, but it would be easy to identify your streamlined route on the flowchart so you could use it again when you need it.

Kirsten: Yes, I would like that. Confronting criticism or anger is the hardest for me. I'm not quite sure I could do this with Elizabeth again, let alone with other people. It all happened pretty fast.

The Streamlined Flowchart

Kirsten and I spent a few minutes listing the steps she had taken and noting the route on her flowchart as follows:

Step 1

First sequence—stimuli block: As Kirsten anticipated the phone call, she noticed that what triggered fear was not the content of what Elizabeth said but that she was critical and angry. Kirsten added a summary phrase to the block and underlined it: "Elizabeth or others being critical or angry at me" (see Figure 7.3).

FIGURE 7.3. Kirsten's Unhooking and Empowering Sequence—Streamlined

SPOTTING THE SPIRAL SEQUENCE	UNHOOKING AND EMPOWERING SEQUENCE	NEW CHRIST-CENTERED RESPONSE SEQUENCE
Stimuli Phone call from Eliz. Re: the divorce: "You're treating me like a Child." "You're not being open re: the Divorce." "You're determining the fate of the family." Eliz. and others being critical or angry at me.	Warm & firm - not meeting Confident - not fearful **Christ-Centered Feelings** When alone or afraid I can take Jesus' arm, let him lift me. I'm free to consider Eliz.'s needs. I don't need to fear disapproval by Eliz. or others. My personhood is a gift from God, can't be taken by others. **Christ-Centered Perceptions**	**Ministering to Parts**
Old Perceptions · Eliz. doesn't understand my side · Eliz. either doesn't like me or hates me · I have no right to my own opinion or desires	Jesus said take his arm whenever I need it, restored my compassion. I was melting. Jesus lifted me, restored my personhood as a gift. Jesus showed me my fear of disapproval was fear of a loss of personhood. * Opening Heart to the Lord	**Analyzing the Situation**
Old Feelings Confusion √ Irritation √ Fear √ Helplessness √ Shame - yucky feelings	I believed I needed approval. I believed I had no right to personhood because unworthy. I was overcome by confusion, helpless. I got into compliance & withdrew. I turned from you, trusted in strategies. * Confessing Choices Made **Encountering the Lord** Talk w/Eliz. re: women in marriage Continue growth in autonomy OR go backward in personal growth--stay locked in conflict w/Eliz. * Predicting Consequences/Choosing Gently loved, warm & worthy, confident and strong * Compare to Christ-Centered State	**Designing New Responses** **Acknowledging Successes** **Lessons, Praising God**
Old Behavior Getting defensive Withdrawing in resentment Pleasing others by compliance Hiding my needs Hiding my anger & shame	I'm bad, no right to a life Confusion in head Knot of heaviness in chest * Self's Emotional State **Taking Self's Pulse** **Comparing and Choosing**	

*Self steps back from parts

Step 2

Forewarned, Kirsten stepped back from her parts immediately and decided to bypass their old perceptions, feelings, and behaviors by going directly to the Christ-centered feelings block. She used the block to take her empowered pulse and assess whether she was both unhooked and empowered. She represented this step with an arrow from the stimuli block to the Christ-centered feelings block. We noted it was a significant accomplishment not to get hooked into the downward spiral of column 1 and saw that she was far less over-whelmed than previously.

Step 3

Seeing she was not yet empowered, Kirsten went to the opening heart block, asking her parts to give her space to return to Jesus for empowering. We drew an arrow from the Christ-centered feelings block to the opening heart block. She had used each statement and so drew a line under each. (She did not need the confessing choices block since she was not drawn into the downward spiral.)

Step 4

Grounded in Jesus again after taking His arm, she followed the usual arrow from the opening heart block to the Christ-centered per-ceptions block, where she again stepped back from her parts to take on the new perspective of statements one and two. "I don't need to fear disapproval since my personhood is a gift from God" (underlin-ing statements one and two on the flowchart).

Step 5

When she felt she had assimilated the new perspective, she followed the arrow to the Christ-centered feelings to take her empowered pulse again, observing that she now felt more in self and empowered. She made the phone call to Elizabeth.

Kirsten was encouraged after discovering a streamlined sequence. She now saw clearly the steps used, so she was confident she could use them again. She was able to picture in graphic form how she mas-tered the steps of the first two columns and reduced the number from ten to five. She also remembered to step back from the parts at each point.

Some clients, after mastering several steps and designing a stream-lined flowchart, experiment by listing their steps on a card so they can carry it with them into the situation for prompting as needed. It is use-ful to encourage clients to adapt their flowchart, incorporating the skills into daily living, finding quicker routes, bypassing old behav-iors, taking their pulse, and unhooking from parts. The continually adapted flowchart then not only focuses on mastering the tasks at hand but helps clients notice where they are stuck and where they are succeeding. This becomes a self-measuring and self-motivating process.

Debriefing at the End of the Second Sequence

Debriefing after the second sequence is important because it is the first chance to assess the self's ability to utilize the first two sequences. Has the self been able to sense when the parts are overwhelming it and to unhook and turn to Jesus for empowering? Has its empowerment made a difference in responding to the situation? Because of the win-win nature of debriefing, the client and therapist can be objective and recognize when self is incapable of these steps. The self wins either by mastering the new steps, or by discovering what has not yet been learned and the steps needed to learn it. Because critical and hopeless parts often focus on what the self has *not* been able to accomplish yet, the client will need help in coming to an objective view. The therapist can point out accomplishments (Kirsten's remaining with the conversation in the face of Elizabeth's anger) and resulting evidence of success (Elizabeth's change of tone as well as her words).

The therapist can ask if the client understands how he or she achieved the new behavior and can assist in listing the steps taken. When the client can list the steps and see their effects, the process becomes repeatable because he or she now knows how to achieve the desired result. This ability to predict results generates the confidence it can be done again. The therapist can also help the client notice when he or she has found a more direct route to the empowered state and in marking it so it can be used again (as with Kirsten's streamlined flowchart).

Finally, client and therapist can note the significance of the client's new skills. For Kirsten, the ability to break out of the old survival state into an empowered one generated hope and confidence. Her ability to accomplish the new sequence validated the content of the flowchart (e.g., fear in the face of anger was due to a fear of her personhood being lost, that the remedy was to seek personhood from Jesus and not from people). Her empowerment with Jesus validated the theory about the problem and the solution.

As self and parts review the evidence of self's progress, some fundamental conclusions often emerge: e.g., the self, when empowered, has the capacity to respond assertively and lovingly to the situation and to continue to grow in competence at unhooking and empowering. The client slowly replaces the victim attitude with a win-win one, and expects in every new encounter to win by succeeding or by falling short and learning from it. Often the client grows closer to God, sensing that in new responses God will show His wisdom about life choices. These new attitudes equip the self to lead the parts while being more respectful of them and their needs. The client sees that the parts, when respected, will follow the self's lead and allow the space for empowering and leading. Finally, the client will even sense that the therapist can soon become dispensable when the self has learned the tools of autonomy.

It is important for client and therapist to acknowledge what the parts have contributed with their gifts and skills and their willingness to give space to the self when needed. Acknowledging this reinforces those parts who paid a price to trust the self in the face of their fears.

CHAPTER SUMMARY

This chapter describes the unhooking and empowering sequence, the second sequence in the flowchart. When in the first sequence the parts overwhelm the self by their powerful survival reactions, the self now has a way to unhook from them and to become empowered to lead. The case of Kirsten was continued to illustrate the steps taken developing the sequence with the client and coaching him or her in mastering it.

The taking self's pulse block, the first of four in the sequence, is seen as the crossroad of the flowchart because it invites the self to choose between the parts' destructive sequence and a new empowered path. The chapter describes the step of taking the pulse as an assessment tool in which the self compares its current state to that of being centered in Jesus. When overwhelmed by the parts, the self must predict the consequences of continuing on the parts' survival path. The self is also invited to predict the consequences of unhooking from the parts and turning to the Lord for empowering. The self then chooses between the two paths.

The chapter then describes the encountering the Lord block as consisting of two steps. Confessing choices made urges the self to acknowledge the ways it was ensnared in the parts' attitudes, feelings, and behaviors, which took it away from a relationship with the Lord. This helps the self take down inner barriers to the Lord. Encountering the Lord invites the self into a parts-free encounter with the Lord by opening the heart. The chapter shows Kirsten's experience of opening her heart during which Jesus restores her personhood as a gift from God. This experience then becomes a new foundation for future encounters with her daughter.

The chapter then describes the construction of the last two blocks, the Christ-centered perceptions block and the Christ-centered feelings block based on the new empowered state with Jesus. These provide a means for assessing whether the self is in the empowered state and ready to lead the parts. The chapter tracks how Kirsten first developed the blocks and then used them in her encounters with Elizabeth, increasing her mastery to unhook from her parts and return to a grounding with Jesus.

The chapter concludes by showing how the systematic debriefing of the encounters provides the evidence the self needs for confidence and for the parts to trust the self to lead. Self and parts eventually come to see each encounter as a win-win situation—either a win by succeeding or a win by learning or both. Thus Kirsten's self begins to take a more proactive posture.

CLINICAL OUTLINE:
EQUIPPING THE SELF TO UNHOOK
FROM PARTS AND EMPOWER THROUGH JESUS

What follows are the steps in helping a client learn the unhooking and empowering process.

I. Therapist describes the goal of the sequence and helps client assess its timeliness in light of the client's current needs.
   A. The goal of the first block, taking self's pulse, is to construct a tool to discover under pressure when the parts are overwhelming self and to choose either to stay with the parts' strategies or to turn to the Lord for a new approach to the situation.

B. The subsequent blocks invite self to open the heart to Jesus for the needed empowering for the new approach.

II. If client decides to proceed, therapist helps client fill out the pulse block:

  A. Self's emotional state

    1. Client selects a recent experience where parts, triggered by stimuli in column 1, overwhelmed self.

    2. Client identifies the most noticeable (conscious) symptoms, noting physical symptoms because they offer reliable indicators of the overwhelmed state.

    3. Client compares the symptoms to those noted in the first sequence and selects the most noticeable for inclusion in the self's emotional state block.

    4. Therapist helps client recognize new insights, especially if the present emotional state is a reflection of a powerful flashback state of the parts.

    5. Therapist describes process of assessing the self's emotional state as stepping back from parts, then noting the self's current symptoms using prompting from the symptoms listed in the emotional state block.

  B. Comparing to Christ-centered state

    1. If client has had an empowering encounter with Jesus, these sensations are recalled and listed in the block.

    2. If client has not had a parts-free encounter with Jesus, therapist offers help. If client agrees, therapist coaches client in mountain exercise or other exercise to facilitate the self's parts-free encounter with Jesus.

      a. Therapist helps self identify the sensations and the effect of the encounter.

      b. Therapist helps self to encounter Jesus and His unconditional love.

      c. Therapist helps self identify the sensations and the effect of the encounter.

      d. Clients selects the most important effects (especially physical) and lists in the compare to Christ-centered state block.

  C. Predicting consequences and choosing

    1. Therapist helps client anticipate consequences of continuing on parts' spiral versus seeking new options opened by Christ-centered state.

2. Client lists most important consequences of each choice in the block.
3. Client considers the significance of the two routes and chooses.
4. Therapist ascertains whether client understands how to use the steps to assess and choose when entering a situation.
5. Client decides whether to try out the tool in the next situation or to prepare the next block.
6. If client uses the tool, client and therapist begin next session by debriefing the experience and incorporating results onto flowchart as appropriate.

III. Therapist helps client fill out the encountering the Lord block
  A. "Confessing choices made"
    1. The goal is to take down barriers that prevent self's heart-to-heart encounter with Jesus.
    2. Therapist helps client's self to step away from parts to identify the ways self has gotten caught in the parts attitudes, beliefs, and behaviors.
    3. Therapist helps client find the most meaningful way back to the Lord: confessing, acknowledging, disavowing, repenting, making restitution, etc., for behaviors as needed.
    4. Client selects most useful steps and statements for inclusion in the confessing choices made space.
  B. "Opening heart to the Lord"
    1. The goal is self's returning to a heart-to-heart relationship with Jesus for grounding for self's task of leading in the situation.
    2. Therapist helps self settle parts for a parts-free encounter with Jesus, seeking needed love and grounding for self.
    3. Therapist helps client identify empowering effects of the encounter on self.
    4. Client selects most important effects (especially physical) and lists in the opening heart space.

IV. Therapist helps client fill out Christ-centered perceptions block
  A. The goal is to identify new beliefs about self and others to ground and empower self for finding new possibilities for the situation.
  B. Therapist helps client reconsider parts' old perceptions and beliefs in light of the encounter with Jesus.
  C. Client selects most empowering new beliefs and enters in block.

V. Christ-centered feelings
  A. The goal is to identify feelings of Christ-centered state so self can assess when it is empowered to lead.
  B. Therapist helps client recall the encounter with Jesus and notice the feelings.
  C. Client selects the most energizing feelings and lists in the block.
VI. Client decides whether to go directly to the third sequence or to reengage in the situation. If client decides to reengage, therapist and client use next sessions for debriefing and reviewing the important features of the interaction.
  A. Client notices if any new perceptions or responses were utilized and what effect they had on others.
  B. Client notices any entries on the flowchart that were validated and any needing to be changed.
  C. Client notices which entries are most useful and if any shorter routes to the empowered state were found.
  D. Therapist and client may listen to the parts for their input or to inquire whether parts observed any changes and how it affected them.
  E. Client considers any unmet needs for self to lead and whether to go to the third sequence or to return to the unburdening parts process.

EXERCISE: TAKING YOUR PULSE

Make a pulse block for yourself on a sheet of paper, including spaces for the self's emotional state, compare to Christ-centered state, and predicting consequences and choosing (see Figure 7.1). You may adapt the exercise by substituting "God-centered" or another modification of your choosing.

1. Find a place to relax with deep breathing.
2. Select an incident that triggered your parts into blending with your self. If you did the exercise in Chapter 6, you may use the same incident.
3. Return to the situation and reexperience the feelings, behavior impulses, and perceptions.

4. Step back from your parts and list these on a separate worksheet. If you did the Chapter 6 exercise, compare these entries to your present responses.
5. Select your most powerful and noticeable responses. Try to include at least one physical sensation. List these in a few phrases in the self's emotional state block.
6. Consider whether these would alert you when you are in a similar situation and your parts are blending. If there are other sensations that better alert you, add or substitute them.
7. Take note of new insights about the experience of your parts blending with your self. Are your reactions a reflection of a flashback state?

Comparing to Christ-Centered State

1. If you have ever had a parts-free encounter with Jesus or a higher power, recall it and list the empowering effects on your worksheet, including physical effects. List the most important of these on your flowchart. If you prefer a new encounter, go to Step 2.
2. If you have not had a parts-free encounter with the Lord, you may choose to visit Jesus or God for a few moments to glimpse the character of the relationship and its effect on you. You will need to negotiate with your parts to give you the needed space. When you are in the presence of Jesus or God, take notice of His feelings about you. If you sense anything other than unconditional love, immediately stop and check for parts interrupting. Settle them and return. See if you are free enough now to sense His feeling toward you.
3. See if you can open your heart to take this in.
4. What effect(s) does this have on you? Note the most important effects in the Christ-centered state block, especially the physical sensations.

Predicting Consequences and Choosing

1. While remaining separate from your parts, anticipate the consequences of continuing in the overwhelmed state in the situation.
2. List these in a phrase or two in the consequences space.

3. Predict the effects of dealing with the situation while in the Christ-centered or God-centered state.
4. List these in the consequences space.
5. Consider the anticipated consequences of the two paths. Which do you choose and why?

Consider a Field Test

1. Review the three steps in the block. Are you clear enough about the pulse taking and choosing process to try it? If so, select a situation in which to experiment. You may use your sheet or a shortened version to review before and during the situation. Prepare by putting the situation in a room and settling your parts with Jesus or God. When ready, enter the room with parts watching and respond to the situation. Incorporate what you learned from this into your plan for the field test.
2. When ready, engage in your field test. Find time afterward to debrief and notice the results. Did your parts try to overwhelm you? If so, what steps did you take as a response? Did you:

   - Take your pulse?
   - Step back from your parts?
   - Compare your state to the Christ-centered state?
   - Predict the consequences of each path?
   - Choose a path?

3. Note the result of each step on yourself, on your parts, on the situation.
4. Did you experiment with different responses in the situation? What effect, if any, resulted?
5. Did you discover anything more about your parts? Do they need any further response from you? How can you respond to them?

Further Steps

Are you interested in taking steps toward empowerment, using the other three blocks in the sequence? You may turn to the Chapter 7 Clinical Outline and follow the steps listed there.

Chapter 8

Developing Christ-Centered Responses: The Third Sequence in the Flowchart

Love the Lord your God with all your heart, soul and mind and love your neighbor as yourself. The whole law of Moses and the prophets depend on these two commandments.

Matthew 22:37-40

In the above passage from Matthew, Jesus focuses our calling to love self, neighbor, and God. However, many of our clients are unable to do this. Not having been loved, how can they love? Loving comes from a free heart and requires an inner transformation. Jesus opens the door to this transformation when he invites us into a relationship with himself. This results in a new relationship with self, God, and others.

The previous chapter offered a tool to help the self, after separating from the parts, to open the heart to this transforming relationship with Jesus. This chapter offers the Christian a way to love self and others by developing Christ-centered responses. These responses arise from the self empowered by an unconditional relationship with Jesus rather than from the parts' survival reactions.

Because the first two sequences are tools for the self to separate from the parts for empowering, the parts themselves often remain in their state of distress. However, the hard spiritual and emotional work of the two sequences enables the self to respond to the parts' distress as well as to the situation itself. The third sequence incorporates ministry to the parts as well as analyzing and responding to life situations.

In the chapter, Kirsten, having returned to God's love by opening her heart to Jesus, now is invited to love and minister to her parts and to find new godly responses to family and others. She can then return to deeper healing of the parts, which was interrupted by the urgent situation regarding her daughter's reaction to the impending divorce. The chapter then introduces a final application of the flowchart as a tool for the self and for unusually needy parts titled Charts for Parts. The desired result for this third tool is for self and parts together to become increasingly free to love self, neighbor, and God.

SETTING THE STAGE FOR THE WORK OF THE THIRD SEQUENCE— DISCERNING WHERE TO BEGIN

After completing the unhooking and empowering sequence, the self has a new capacity to respond to a current situation and also to the parts who remain distressed by the situation. The client, with the therapist's help, must identify whether it is more urgent to begin with the distressed parts or with the situation. The situation may involve an abusive spouse or complicated work situation. In addition to the threat of actual abuse, the situation may trigger a flashback state in some parts, activating in turn various firefighters and managers. Frequently, not enough time exists to care for these parts fully as well as to prepare for the situation. Self and parts must solve this dilemma by choosing the higher priority.

Typically, self and parts conclude that the greater urgency is to develop new responses, especially when danger of abuse exists. The parts, though distressed, will often give the self space to design new responses and to feel encouraged enough to let the self lead in trying them out. Occasionally, some parts are so distressed they cannot contain their anxiety while the self analyzes and designs new responses. In such cases, self and therapist may need to begin with the ministering block to help these parts feel safe during the encounter. It is usually not necessary for a comprehensive development of the ministering block at this time, and the task can be postponed until the situation is more resolved.

As Kirsten and her parts considered preparing for the next frightening phone call with her daughter Elizabeth, they all decided that Kirsten needed new responses to the situation. Thus they solved the dilemma of how to proceed by agreeing to let the self first design new responses to the situation and then to care for the parts when the situation was resolved.

To follow Kirsten's case as well as illustrating this common pattern, the chapter will begin with the analyzing and designing blocks. The ministering block will be described after these blocks.

ANALYZING THE SITUATION

At this stage, the self, although unhooked from the parts and empowered, is still burdened by the old parts' view of the situation. The self now needs a fresh parts-free look at the situation.

What is the known data about the situation? What clues does the self have regarding the hidden causes of the dynamics? Were there any insights about the situation that came while the self was with Jesus? Is there new clarity about why the situation keeps the parts so hooked?

These questions have both an objective and a subjective dimension. The objective dimension includes the individuals involved as well as the family or social system. The focus begins with the observable behavior of individuals such as speech content, voice tone and volume, facial expressions, and body language. The focus then expands to observable behaviors in the social systems as well as the patterns such as norms and expectations and sanctions for enforcing them.

The subjective features includes the client's experiences in the system such as boundary violations, engulfments, neglect, abandonment, the client's various feelings, and the clues and insights the client has about how the system and its members are organized to meet its needs for safety and esteem.

The therapist invites the self to consider these subjective hunches and insights as well as the known objective data in seeking a better understanding of the situation. The therapist will need to help the client stay in self and not accept parts' views as facts or rush to quick judgments. However, clients often formulate amazingly insightful theories about family and system dynamics that can be tested and substantiated. When clients remain in the self, these theories generate hope for the client and new understanding and compassion toward the others involved.

Beginning the Analyzing Process

The therapist describes the goal of the analyzing block to the client as taking a fresh look at a confusing situation to see hidden dynamics behind the visible behavior and to design godly new responses. The therapist then helps the client into the process by raising questions to sharpen his or her behavioral observations and intuitions about what is motivating the other's behavior. Clients quickly grasp the process as well as the need to test the insights that emerge so as not to get caught up in the parts' perspectives.

Client and therapist need to stay in focus with the analyzing process. Family history and generational patterns can be useful, but they can also lead astray. The therapist, as coach, needs to help the client consider only the data that clarifies the situation at hand.

In Kirsten's case, the purpose of the analysis was to help her respond to Elizabeth's anger and her questions about the divorce. We briefly considered the history of the relationship between Kirsten and Elizabeth and the possible effect of Bihari's sharing of his side of the divorce with Elizabeth. This could result in an alliance between Elizabeth and Bihari against Kirsten and could also affect the complicated divorce process between Kirsten and Bihari.

The next step, selecting the most relevant observations to list in the analyzing block, also helps to keep the scope of the inquiry relevant to the goal.

Kirsten's Analyzing Process

During her previous conversation with Elizabeth, Kirsten was encouraged to see that because she was unhooked from her parts and empowered with Jesus, she was not so intimidated by Elizabeth's angry parts. She was able to acknowledge Elizabeth's need to hear her side of the divorce. Also, she acknowledged her own need to sort out what was appropriate to share with Elizabeth.

Now free of her confusion and fear, Kirsten could see that her reasons for divorcing Bihari were deeply embedded in the dynamics that had characterized the failed marriage of thirty years. She saw her need for a better understanding of that dynamic and how it was currently affecting her relationship with Elizabeth, including Elizabeth's questions about the divorce.

Kirsten decided first to recall her own reasons for her decision to divorce Bihari. With some help from the therapist to stay unhooked from her second-guessing and blaming parts, she recalled her original evaluation that Bihari's infidelities were not the central issue. The main issue, for her, was Bihari's inability to face his own drivenness and needs, which incapacitated him from entering a relationship of intimacy and mutuality. She also concluded that she needed to be free of the relationship in order to face her own internal wounds and to change her second-class posture in life. When she articulated these reasons again, Kirsten found they continued to remain valid. She felt grounded in her personhood and in her decision and was able to quiet her frightened and critical parts. Now she was ready to look at how her interaction with Elizabeth was embedded in the family dynamic.

I asked her what observations she had about the dynamic that could help her to respond to Elizabeth. The following conversation illustrates the analyzing process.

Kirsten: I see that I'm doing some things I could not have done before I had a personhood. I don't get caught by Bihari telling Elizabeth his side of the divorce issue.

Therapist: It's exciting to see your ability to stand back and observe Bihari's behavior instead of getting hooked into it. What do you think the effect is of Bihari telling his side to Elizabeth?

Kirsten: I'm afraid it puts Elizabeth in the middle and makes me out to be the bad guy.

Therapist: That's a valid concern. Why do you think Bihari would do that?

Kirsten: He's used the kids against me before, even getting them to join him in making fun of me or my opinions.

Therapist: Why would he act that way?

Kirsten: I believe it was part of the way he kept me in a submissive state. I cared for his needs, didn't question his unfaithful behavior, and didn't walk out on him.

Therapist: Why do you think he would tell Elizabeth his side of the divorce story?

Kirsten: I suppose he's feeling desperate, so he's trying to figure out how to keep me in the marriage. He's using Elizabeth as another way to manipulate me, to keep me from leaving him.

Therapist: What's the effect of that for you and Elizabeth?

Kirsten: It puts Elizabeth in the middle, and it puts me in a dilemma with Elizabeth. I want to protect my relationship with her and help her face the divorce. I also want to help her as she is preparing for her own marriage to Jeff. Instead, she is getting drawn into our marriage issue.

Therapist: What did you mean when you said you wanted to help Elizabeth prepare for her own marriage?

Kirsten: I am finally learning some things about autonomy that I would like to share with her so she doesn't need to be a second-class person in her marriage like I was.

At this point, Kirsten, in her empowered state of concern for Elizabeth, has analyzed an important dynamic, that of Bihari's using Elizabeth to manipulate her. She also became more aware of how long she passively stayed in her demeaning and depowering relationship with Bihari. This awareness helped her to connect the way she had been "trained" in her family of origin, which had for generations subordinated and depersonalized the females in the family.

Kirsten then understood why she felt it so natural to marry Bihari. Her experience of being subordinate to men fit in with the norms of Bihari's culture. She also realized that Bihari carried his own internal wounds from his family of origin. He was predisposed to look for a subservient wife and a range of sexual partners to fill his internal needs.

Kirsten and I observed that she had been subjected throughout her lifetime to four cultures that depersonalized women: her family of origin, Bihari's family of origin, Bihari's third-world culture, and her own marriage. She saw why it was so radical and difficult for her personhood to emerge and began to understand the value of a primary relationship with God and of being part of an empowering church community. Also, she could understand Bihari's triangulating behavior in light of his internal needs and his cultural expectations. Instead of getting angry and hooked by Bihari's behavior, she was able to return to her present concern about her relationship with Elizabeth.

Kirsten began to consider that Elizabeth needed to be free to identify and work through her own feelings regarding the divorce and that the best way for her to help would be to listen to Elizabeth's concerns and needs. She considered how to share her reasons for the divorce without blaming.

Together we noted that if Kirsten's self was present without a hidden agenda it could help to free Elizabeth from being caught between her mother and her father. We were approaching the "how to" questions. It signaled to us that the analyzing was complete enough to move to the next step.

Kirsten's Analyzing Block

I asked Kirsten to select the most important observations for the analyzing block. I helped her sort them out and she listed these on her flowchart as follows:

- Bihari's purpose is to keep me in the marriage.
- Bihari is using Elizabeth to keep me in the marriage.
- This puts Elizabeth in the middle.
- This puts me in a dilemma with Elizabeth.
- Elizabeth needs to face the divorce.
- Elizabeth and I need to restore our relationship.

I also suggested that she draw a second arrow from the Christ-centered feelings block pointing to the analyzing block. I noted that this indicates that she can choose to proceed directly to the analyzing block (Figure 8.1).

THE ANALYZING BLOCK INVITES THE SELF TO LIFT THE VEIL ON HIDDEN DYNAMICS

The dialogue with Kirsten illustrates the primary goal of the analyzing process: finding the hidden dynamics in the situation. The process usually proceeds from the known observable behavior to the more hidden dynamics. Kirsten started with her dilemma with Elizabeth and progressed to her observation about Bihari's triangulation with Elizabeth. Next, Kirsten connected the triangulation to Bihari's patterns of using her to satisfy his own internal needs. She connected this to her pattern of submissiveness and concluded with the theory that Bihari was again using one of the children to manipulate her to stay in the marriage.

FIGURE 8.1. Kirsten's Analyzing Block

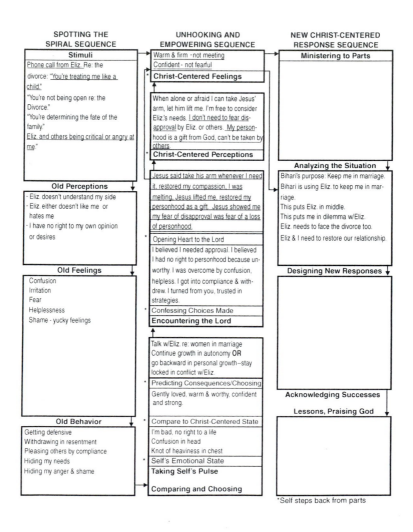

SPOTTING THE SPIRAL SEQUENCE	UNHOOKING AND EMPOWERING SEQUENCE	NEW CHRIST-CENTERED RESPONSE SEQUENCE
Stimuli	Warm & firm - not meeting	**Ministering to Parts**
Phone call from Eliz. Re: the divorce: "You're treating me like a child."	Confident - not fearful	
	* **Christ-Centered Feelings**	
"You're not being open re: the Divorce."	When alone or afraid I can take Jesus' arm, let him lift me. I'm free to consider Eliz.'s needs. I don't need to fear disapproval by Eliz. or others. My personhood is a gift from God, can't be taken by others.	
"You're determining the fate of the family."		
Eliz. and others being critical or angry at me."		
	* **Christ-Centered Perceptions**	
	Jesus said take his arm whenever I need it, restored my compassion, I was melting. Jesus lifted me, restored my personhood as a gift. Jesus showed me my fear of disapproval was fear of a loss of personhood.	**Analyzing the Situation**
Old Perceptions		Bihari's purpose: Keep me in marriage. Bihari is using Eliz. to keep me in marriage.
- Eliz. doesn't understand my side		This puts Eliz. in middle.
- Eliz. either doesn't like me or hates me		This puts me in dilemma w/Eliz.
- I have no right to my own opinion or desires	* **Opening Heart to the Lord**	Eliz. needs to face the divorce too.
	I believed I needed approval. I believed I had no right to personhood because unworthy. I was overcome by confusion, helpless. I got into compliance & withdrew. I turned from you, trusted in strategies.	Eliz & I need to restore our relationship.
Old Feelings		**Designing New Responses**
Confusion		
Irritation		
Fear	* **Confessing Choices Made**	
Helplessness	**Encountering the Lord**	
Shame - yucky feelings		
	Talk w/Eliz. re: women in marriage Continue growth in autonomy **OR** go backward in personal growth—stay locked in conflict w/Eliz.	
	* **Predicting Consequences/Choosing**	
	Gently loved, warm & worthy, confident and strong.	**Acknowledging Successes**
		Lessons, Praising God
Old Behavior	* **Compare to Christ-Centered State**	
Getting defensive	I'm bad, no right to a life	
Withdrawing in resentment	Confusion in head	
Pleasing others by compliance	Knot of heaviness in chest	
Hiding my needs	* **Self's Emotional State**	
Hiding my anger & shame	**Taking Self's Pulse**	
	Comparing and Choosing	

*Self steps back from parts

This process of lifting the veil on hidden dynamics is similar to the column 1 process of lifting the veil on the hidden flashback state. These theories need to be tested by the client by asking the parties involved, when possible, and by comparing present behavior to past behavior and to previous generational patterns. The theories are used to help the client design new responses. Also, the behavioral observations serve as a baseline against which the client can notice any changes in the system resulting from the new responses. The therapist's role is to help clients stay unhooked from their parts and to help them progress to the hidden dynamics.

DESIGNING NEW RESPONSES BLOCK

The self, having analyzed the situation, needs to take the new insights and, empowered by Jesus, consider new responses. The goal of the block is to design a range of new responses and to put the best of these in the response block for use as a coaching tool for the actual encounter.

Clients usually need help to begin identifying new responses. They have been socialized into a limited range of responses by family perceptions and prohibitions. Kirsten had been taught that she had no rights or preferences and should be compliant to others' wishes, especially those of men and authority figures. Like many clients, some of Kirsten's parts dreamed of using anger, force, and intimidation in retaliation against those who had put her in this position. Other parts thought new responses either were not possible or would not be effective in achieving their goals. They had never seen respectful proactive responses modeled. This left Kirsten's self with the challenge of envisioning a new type of response, which was unimaginable to her parts.

In these situations, it is useful to help the self design new responses by pointing to examples or by role-playing. Because Kirsten was familiar with the Bible, I noted that Jesus modeled this style with his life, never seeking to control, diminish, or use others. He moved toward his goal by assertive yet respectful interaction. Such behavior can create a win-win situation, benefiting all parties.

Kirsten brought up the biblical story of the woman about to be stoned for adultery according to the religious law of that time. In looking at the account, we noticed that Jesus did not berate either the crowd or the woman but found a way to interrupt the punishment. He caught their attention by drawing in the sand and presenting his well-known directive, "Let he who is without sin cast the first stone" (John 8:7). Each person felt convicted and dropped his or her stone. Then Jesus offered the woman a fresh start, saying, "Your sins are forgiven, go and sin no more" (John 8:11). The familiar story inspired Kirsten to look beyond her usual options to seek the mind and heart of God for new responses. Then she was ready to flesh out the new options.

Building a Menu of Options

One simple but effective way for the client to explore new responses is to brainstorm, with the help of the therapist, a wide range of possible responses. This signals to critical, skeptical, and fearful parts to withhold their concerns until later and allows the transcendent and creative self to explore new possibilities. If the self remains stuck, role-playing can be used with the therapist taking the role of the client, as needed, to demonstrate new possibilities.

Kirsten could not envision any responses to Elizabeth's anger other than to comply, to withdraw, or to get angry. We decided to role-play. Kirsten played Elizabeth and I played Kirsten. The following illustrates our dialogue:

Elizabeth (played by Kirsten): You've been withholding your reasons for the divorce and treating me like a child.

Kirsten (played by the therapist): I see you're upset. I don't blame you, but when you get angry I feel like you're saying it's all my fault.

Elizabeth: I'm not trying to blame you, Mother, but I guess I'm angry and upset. It seems like our family is falling apart, and I don't want to lose either one of you.

Therapist (out of role): Elizabeth's response has changed. Do you want to look at what happened there?

Kirsten (out of role): Yes, you said something that made me, as Elizabeth, feel different. You acknowledged I was upset. You didn't withdraw from me because I was blaming you. I guess if I didn't need to run from Elizabeth's anger but could stay with her and acknowledge it, I would be taking a step toward rebuilding our relationship.

Therapist: Yes. There was something else in the dialogue, too.

Kirsten: You said, "When you get angry I feel you're saying it's all my fault." Then Elizabeth told you her fears that the family is falling apart.

Kirsten saw that acknowledging Elizabeth's feelings and using "I" statements about her own feelings softened Elizabeth's angry part and invited her self to engage in the dialogue with Kirsten's self.

Kirsten also caught on to the spirit of role-playing and brainstorming as a way to experiment with new responses. We arrived at the following list of possible responses to Elizabeth:

- I see you're upset. I'd like to hear about it.
- When you're angry, it feels like you think it's all my fault. Is that right?
- I'm afraid that your father sharing his side puts you in the middle and that you will turn against me.
- I'm afraid that if I tell you my side it will put you more in the middle. I don't want you to have to side with one of us against the other.
- I hope you know that after the divorce your father and I will have a working relationship with each other and we will still love you.

Kirsten also used role-playing to test what to share with Elizabeth about her reasons for the divorce. Next, she reviewed all the options, selected the best options, and listed them on her flowchart as follows (see Figure 8.2):

- Listen to Elizabeth's feelings and acknowledge them.
- Own my feelings with "I" statements to avoid blaming.
- Assure Elizabeth as needed regarding her continuing relationship with Bihari and me.
- Express my concern for putting Elizabeth in the middle.
- Tell her I forgive Bihari so she sees I'm not acting in anger.
- Tell about my reasons for the divorce without blaming Bihari.

The listing process requires the client to evaluate and select the best options. The response block, indicating the best responses, becomes a tool for the self to use in the next encounter.

The process of selecting responses demonstrates to self and parts that effective and respectful responses are actually possible. This creates hope and brings the self another step toward a proactive stance. It also brings the parts closer toward trusting the self to lead.

After Kirsten completed the response block, she expressed surprise that her angry parts did not jump in and interrupt the designing of responses by suggesting ways to put Bihari in a bad light to Elizabeth. Instead, she actually felt confident that she could tell Elizabeth her reasons for divorce without criticizing Bihari. She felt this was because she had processed her resentments and anger toward Bihari the previous month using the resentment worksheet (see Chapter 5). Kirsten saw that her angry parts were settled about her thirty years of mistreatment by Bihari. However, the parts continued their anger toward Bihari's recent behavior.

When a client has not forgiven and released a wrongdoer and angry parts interrupt the process of designing new responses, it may be necessary to acknowledge the angry parts' resentments and help them set aside any retribution agendas until later when there is time for the resentment process.

Checking on the Parts' Readiness

I asked Kirsten how ready her parts were to let her lead in the encounter with Elizabeth. She was surprised to find that, having thought out her options, the parts were far less afraid and were ready to trust her to lead. Some clients' parts, however, continue to feel nervous and need to be listened to and reassured. Other parts require more care. This is the "ministering to parts" process and will be illustrated in a subsequent episode where Kirsten's parts were quite frightened.

Debriefing Kirsten's Conversation with Elizabeth

The first encounter after the development of the analyzing and responding blocks creates a particularly useful opportunity for learning because, with the exception of the ministering to the parts block, it is a field test of all the unhooking, empowering, and new response skills in the flowchart. The debriefing of this encounter is the primary way to harvest the yield of discovery and experience.

After the client reports the main features of the encounter, client and therapist together focus on two tasks. First, they note the client's capacity to stay empowered to try the new responses. Second, they judge the usefulness of the new responses. In the first task, the therapist helps the client notice ways the self has progressed in unhooking and trying the new responses. If the self has gotten stuck, they track

FIGURE 8.2. Kirsten's New Response Options

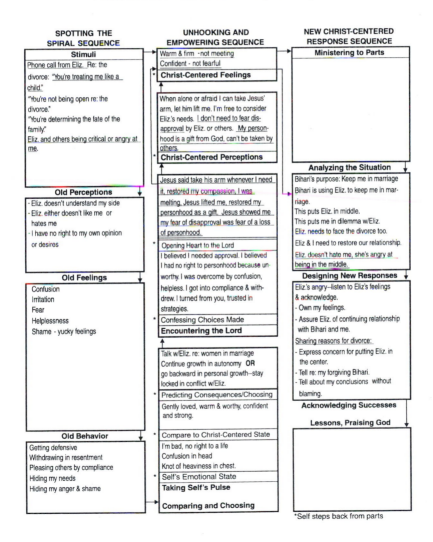

back through the flowchart to find the causes. Remedies can then be designed and incorporated into the flowchart for the next encounter.

In the second task, the client reviews how the other party reacted to the new responses. These outcomes are used to evaluate the usefulness of the new responses. Then client and therapist modify the response block, discarding, changing, or adding as needed. These two processes maintain the win-win quality of each encounter whether or not the outcome goals are achieved.

Kirsten and I followed this procedure to debrief her next phone conversation with Elizabeth. Like many clients, Kirsten expressed uncertainty about how well she handled the interaction. Elizabeth was irritated at several points, so Kirsten told Elizabeth that she felt blamed by some of her angry statements. Surprisingly, Elizabeth said she did not really believe what she said about Kirsten's treating her like a child or wrecking the family. She was hurt and angry about the divorce and wanted to blame someone. Kirsten acknowledged Elizabeth's feelings and Elizabeth reported her frustration and fears of being pulled on her father's side by hearing only his position.

Kirsten apologized for taking so long to get back to Elizabeth with her reasons. When she expressed her concern about Elizabeth getting caught in the middle, Elizabeth was reassured and thanked her. She said that the conversation with Kirsten was helping her stay out of the middle. Kirsten then felt free to tell Elizabeth her reasons for divorcing Bihari. Elizabeth acknowledged that Kirsten's reasons made sense and that she had a right to decide for herself.

When Elizabeth expressed concerns about what would happen to the family, Kirsten assured her that she and Bihari would continue to love each of the children. This led to Kirsten's sharing how she was treated as second class in her own family, which led to her accepting a second-class status in the marriage. This opened the conversation to include the role Elizabeth is taking with her fiancé.

Kirsten's Reflection on This Encounter

I asked Kirsten to consider how much she was able to stay in self and what effect this had on the conversation. Kirsten was surprised to note that she stayed in her self each time Elizabeth became angry. Instead of retreating, Kirsten acknowledged feeling blamed. Elizabeth then retracted her blaming statements and disclosed her own feelings. Kirsten noticed that the way was now open for them to discuss the three most important topics. Kirsten connected her ability to stay in self with the surprising success of the conversation. I agreed and congratulated her.

Next, I asked Kirsten how many new responses she tried and to judge each for its usefulness. She responded that she used them all and that each produced a positive result by meeting a need for both parties in a respectful way. She concluded that the new responses, in combination with her staying in self, opened the way for appropriate and loving dialogue between her and Elizabeth and put their relationship back on track.

Often clients notice that some of the new responses bring negative results. These are examined and either eliminated or corrected on the flowchart and other responses added as needed. Thus the self's repertoire of respectful and productive responses is expanded through experience.

Kirsten and I concluded that the encounter further validated our analysis that Elizabeth's anger was from being caught in the middle and not toward her mother. We also noted that the encounter confirmed that Kirsten, when empowered by Jesus, could use a new style of relating and was free of the old belief of having no right to a life. This was important evidence for self and parts. The debriefing, begun with Kirsten's uncertainty, concluded with positive evidence of how effective she could be when equipped with tools to stay in self and to respond proactively.

STREAMLINING THE FLOWCHART

Facing a challenging situation successfully, as Kirsten did, involves a sequence of skills: identifying the parts' old reactions, taking the pulse, unhooking from parts, empowering with Jesus, analyzing the situation, designing new responses, and calming the parts enough to try the new responses while staying in self.

Facing a challenging situation successfully does not guarantee that one can do it again. The next situation will have variations from the previous one, requiring the client to generalize from the previous success and adapt to the new situation. Some clients quickly internalize the skills and easily adapt them. However, other clients lack confidence in their skills or in their grasp of the sequence and its principles. These clients benefit from a chance to review, adapt, and streamline the flowchart to meet new situations with success.

Knowing that Kirsten would soon be facing the next steps in her divorce, I asked her if she had internalized the flowchart skills and sequence well enough to use it with Bihari or others. She was uncertain, sensing that she had mastered several steps but not all of them. I asked if she would like to review the sequence she used successfully with Elizabeth to note the skills she had internalized. Together we reconstructed the streamlined sequences she had discovered. On the day of the phone call (the stimuli), she noticed increasing discomfort. Instead of calling me, she decided to try the flowchart to come to an empowered state. Because she knew her parts were active, she skipped the first sequence and went directly to the pulse block, avoiding the downward spiral. We represented this by a line from the stimuli to the pulse block (Figure 8.3).

While taking her pulse, Kirsten noted the beginning of the old heaviness in her chest. She compared the heaviness to the warmth and confidence she felt when centered in Jesus (see Christ-centered state block). She realized that the parts were starting to take her into the paralyzing fear. She decided to step away from them and take Jesus' arm (we added this to the opening the heart block). Now she felt warm, confident, and free of the old fear of disapproval. She could consider Elizabeth's needs. We added this to the Christ-centered feelings block. These feelings confirmed that Kirsten was in the empowered state and ready to go to the analyzing block. At this point, we recalled that she had followed the streamlined route once before (Chapter 7). On the strength of this evidence, Kirsten felt more confident of using the technique with Bihari.

Next, Kirsten skipped the ministering to parts block and went to the analyzing block, remembering her theory that Elizabeth was angry because she was in the middle and she needed help. Then Kirsten went to the new responses block and remembered her plan to relate to Elizabeth's anger by listening to her feelings, giving "I" statements about her own feelings, and sharing her reasons for divorcing. Feeling prepared as well as empowered, she took Jesus' arm, got the parts settled, and made the call.

Kirsten also recalled that in the beginning of the phone call some of her fearful parts tried to interrupt her. Each time she calmly reminded them that with Jesus there was nothing to fear because her selfhood was secure. Each time they let her continue the conversation. I asked if she realized what she had done. Looking at the flowchart, she saw that she had ministered to her parts (first block of third sequence) and was amazed to see this calm reminder of her selfhood. We added this reminder in the ministering block (Figure 8.3).

FIGURE 8.3. Kirsten's Streamlined Flowchart

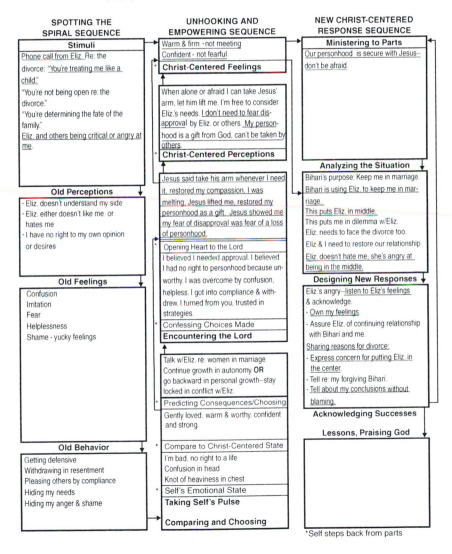

SPOTTING THE SPIRAL SEQUENCE	UNHOOKING AND EMPOWERING SEQUENCE	NEW CHRIST-CENTERED RESPONSE SEQUENCE
Stimuli	Warm & firm - not meeting Confident - not fearful **Christ-Centered Feelings**	**Ministering to Parts** Our personhood is secure with Jesus—don't be afraid.
Phone call from Eliz. Re: the divorce: "You're treating me like a child." "You're not being open re: the divorce." "You're determining the fate of the family." Eliz. and others being critical or angry at me.	When alone or afraid I can take Jesus' arm, let him lift me. I'm free to consider Eliz.'s needs. I don't need to fear disapproval by Eliz. or others. My personhood is a gift from God, can't be taken by others. **Christ-Centered Perceptions**	
Old Perceptions	Jesus said take his arm whenever I need it, restored my compassion, I was melting. Jesus lifted me, restored my personhood as a gift. Jesus showed me my fear of disapproval was fear of a loss of personhood.	**Analyzing the Situation** Bihari's purpose: Keep me in marriage. Bihari is using Eliz. to keep me in marriage. This puts Eliz. in middle. This puts me in dilemma w/Eliz. Eliz. needs to face the divorce too.
- Eliz. doesn't understand my side - Eliz. either doesn't like me or hates me - I have no right to my own opinion or desires	Opening Heart to the Lord I believed I needed approval. I believed I had no right to personhood because unworthy. I was overcome by confusion, helpless. I got into compliance & withdrew. I turned from you, trusted in strategies. **Confessing Choices Made** **Encountering the Lord**	Eliz & I need to restore our relationship. Eliz. doesn't hate me, she's angry at being in the middle.
Old Feelings		**Designing New Responses** Eliz.'s angry—listen to Eliz's feelings & acknowledge. - Own my feelings - Assure Eliz. of continuing relationship with Bihari and me. Sharing reasons for divorce:
Confusion Irritation Fear Helplessness Shame - yucky feelings	Talk w/Eliz. re: women in marriage Continue growth in autonomy **OR** go backward in personal growth—stay locked in conflict w/Eliz. **Predicting Consequences/Choosing**	- Express concern for putting Eliz. in the center. - Tell re: my forgiving Bihari. - Tell about my conclusions without blaming.
	Gently loved, warm & worthy, confident and strong.	**Acknowledging Successes**
Old Behavior	Compare to Christ-Centered State	**Lessons, Praising God**
Getting defensive Withdrawing in resentment Pleasing others by compliance Hiding my needs Hiding my anger & shame	I'm bad, no right to a life Confusion in head Knot of heaviness in chest **Self's Emotional State** **Taking Self's Pulse** **Comparing and Choosing**	

*Self steps back from parts

I asked Kirsten how she was able to minister so effectively to her fearful parts. She noticed that, when she was in her self, she intuitively knew what the parts were worried about and how to calm them as though they were little children. We observed that when she is in self, all her motherly compassion and wisdom from raising three children is available for her in caring for her parts. We drew a line from the responses block and the analyzing block back to the ministering block to remind her that she could stop, even in the midst of a conversation, and comfort her parts.

Kirsten looked over the contents of the blocks in column 2 and 3 and underlined the most important statements. This directed her attention to the key points (Figure 8.3). We observed that she had streamlined her flowchart to six or seven steps by bypassing the parts spiral and mastering much of the second and third sequences. The effect of this streamlining is to create a new chart that highlights only the areas where Kirsten needs prompting. It is an updated learning tool consistent with her new achievement.

The 3x5 Flowchart

Kirsten was still afraid that when encountering Elizabeth or Bihari face to face, she could lose her way. I told her that some clients put their flowchart on a clipboard when using it for an interaction, while other clients write it on an index or 3x5 card. Since Kirsten wanted to try a 3x5 card, I helped her select the key steps and phrases to put on the card (Figure 8.4).

Streamlining the flowchart or putting it on a 3x5 card seems to have several benefits. Making it becomes a self-assessment process, requiring clients to differentiate between the steps they have mastered and the steps they need to master. Block contents must be recorded concisely to serve as appropriate prompts. Using the chart or card requires clients to draw on what they have already mastered. The effect of this is to raise expectations consistent with their current mastery level.

Each time clients use the chart, they get rapid feedback by comparing performance to this baseline. They know which skills they have mastered and can monitor their progress on those they have not. They need the therapist less and less as their skills and confidence grow.

FIGURE 8.4. Kirsten's 3 x 5 Flowchart

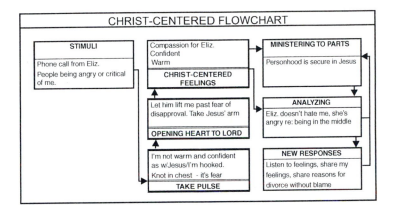

THE ACKNOWLEDGING BLOCK—
ACKNOWLEDGING SUCCESSES AND LESSONS
AND PRAISING GOD

This block is a listing of the lessons the self has discovered in unhooking, empowering, and leading the parts in recent encounters. The debriefing of an encounter is typically a comprehensive teaching and learning experience for the self. These successes may tempt the self to skip the acknowledging block and get on with other business. However, only a few minutes are required to identify the most important successes and lessons of an encounter to guide both self and parts in future encounters. Also, the self and parts are reminded that their new proactive posture comes from the empowering relationship with Jesus. Because the self is now more assertive in leading through life's crises, the parts are tempted to return to their old survival roles and behaviors. It is important that the self shows the parts that the relationship with Jesus is the irreplaceable grounds for the new behavior.

I asked Kirsten to review the flowchart and consider which of the successes and lessons she would like to include in the acknowledging block and how she would frame a statement thanking God for his role in her new posture. She listed the following and entered them on her chart (Figure 8.5):

- Learned to identify stimuli which trigger my parts.
- Learned to avoid a downward spiral by taking my pulse immediately when the parts blended.
- Learned to take Jesus' arm for empowering to use new responses.
- Learned that my new responses can restore relationships.
- I praise God for restoring my personhood through Jesus as the basis for my new life.

FIGURE 8.5. Kirsten's Acknowledging Block

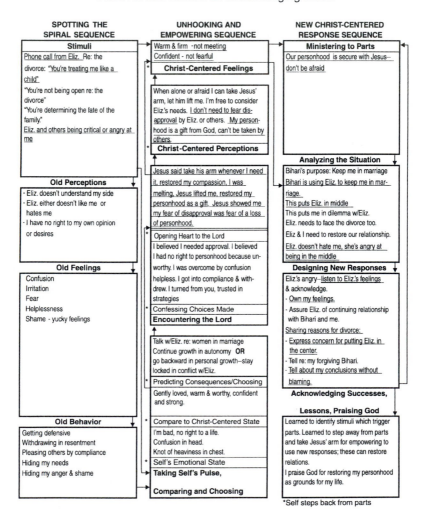

After Kirsten listed these points, I congratulated her on how much she had learned, and together we thanked her parts for trusting her to lead. Kirsten said that the parts all clapped and congratulated one another. Their enthusiasm illustrates how the acknowledging block underlines the growing capacity of the self to lead when the parts co-operate. Also, the parts are praised for their courage in letting the self lead.

MINISTERING TO THE PARTS BLOCK

The client is now in a good position to develop the ministering block unless he or she has already done so at the beginning of the sequence.

The goal of this block is to give the self a tool to provide for the needs of the parts in a frightening situation so they will permit the self to lead. A secondary goal is to help the parts grow in their capacity to manage their emotions in the face of stimuli so they do not lose their trust in the self's leadership. Both goals facilitate the longer-range goal of completing the unburdening of the parts.

Many clients ask why it is so hard for the parts to contain their feelings and trust the self when facing a powerful stimuli. The answer lies in the differential development of the self from the parts. The self has deliberately learned to separate from the parts to develop the needed leadership capacity to face challenging situations. However, at this point, the parts have not been freed and empowered as the self has, and some may feel left behind and fearful. Other parts, distressed and stuck in their old roles, join with the fearful parts to block the self's leading.

This dynamic is illustrated by the client who, after a series of healing breakthroughs, developed a solid relationship with her boyfriend leading to engagement. After the engagement was announced, she immediately became intensely angry at her new fiancé. I asked her to consult her parts about who they were really angry at and why. She instantly had an image of her parts throwing tomatoes at her, saying, "You didn't consult us, you're pushing too fast, and it's too scary." The self, separated from the parts and empowered by Jesus, led in developing the relationship with the fiancé, but the parts did not have the chance to grow and share in the relationship.

The growing self can easily get overfocused on a situation and lose touch with the parts. The ministering block invites the self to return to the parts in a shepherding or parenting capacity. The shepherding metaphor comes from the biblical image of Jesus as the good shepherd who sees the needs of the flock and responds to them. The purpose of the ministering block is to help the self develop this shepherding capacity of listening and responding to the parts.

In situations such as Kirsten's, where the development of the ministering block was postponed due to the urgency of the situation, some parts feel abandoned by the self. Thus the rule must be: do not delay any longer than necessary to listen and respond to the parts.

Developing the Ministering Block

The self must shift from being the assertive leader facing an external situation to the empathic shepherd listening to internal needs. The self now seeks to understand what the parts experience when facing the stimuli and what they need from the self. For the parts to feel the loving regard of the self, it must be free from blending parts.

In helping Kirsten prepare for developing the ministering tool, I described the shepherding role and the shift of focus to the parts' needs. I suggested that she take her pulse to see if she was in the empowered state and ready to care for her parts. She quickly affirmed that she was feeling concerned for her parts and ready to proceed. We noted Kirsten's previous response to her parts when they interrupted her last phone conversation with Elizabeth. "Don't be afraid: our personhood is secure in Jesus," she told them. Now our task was to let the parts show us if this response was what had comforted them.

I suggested that Kirsten let the parts take her back to the last phone call with Elizabeth to show how they felt. They showed her their fear and helplessness and their sense of having no right to be respected or to make an important decision like divorcing. This proved to be a group of parts that believed in Elizabeth's power to take away Kirsten's personhood. Another group said they only wanted to please Elizabeth and receive her approval. These parts gave Kirsten the urge to comply with Elizabeth's expectations while the first group tried to get Kirsten to withdraw from the interaction.

As we looked at these parts, Kirsten and I noted that the first group was previously identified in the first encounter with Elizabeth. Kirsten asked them why they calmed down when she reminded them about her personhood being secure in Jesus. They responded that this reminder reassured them that she could now stand up for her decision. The second group said they felt Kirsten accepted their fears even though she did not have time to listen to them. Kirsten added "listening" to the ministering block to remind herself to attend to the parts' fears (Figure 8.6).

Kirsten's interactions with these two groups of parts illustrates the process of listening to parts' fears and needs and checking with them about what will help them in a stressful situation. Responses to the parts often come from the self's discoveries listed in the heart block, Christ-centered perceptions block, or Christ-centered feelings block. Kirsten's recovery of her personhood was listed in the heart block and Christ-centered perceptions block. The parts noted this and said they were reminded of her new ability to take a stand on an issue.

Some parts, especially when in a flashback state, lose sight of self's new grounding in Jesus. The self's reminders may enable them to trust the self's ability to handle a difficult and stressful situation. Also, Kirsten's discovery that the second group of parts needed a different kind of help illustrates a common need. Many parts need to be recognized and affirmed by the self to deal with their feelings.

Kirsten soon discovered a third group of parts who were not reassured by the self's reminders or attention. They were so frightened that they needed physical safety or protection during encounters. The self can explore various options with them such as sitting in a safe place to watch the encounter, staying in a remote place until the encounter is over, or waiting with other parts or with Jesus during the encounter. Parts quickly identify what suits them best. Also, parts welcome a postencounter debriefing with self to assess the results.

After Kirsten listened to her third group of parts, she added the following to her ministering block (Figure 8.6):

- Help parts to a safe place: watching, hiding or staying with other parts
- Debrief with parts after encounter

She and the parts now felt ready for the next encounter with Elizabeth. I asked her if she could apply her flowchart skills to other situations when the need arose. She felt she could apply them, with help. We did not realize how soon she would need to do this.

NEW FLOWCHART APPLICATIONS FOR NEW CHALLENGES

Since flowcharts are constructed around specific stimuli, do they become obsolete when the original situation is mastered? Actually, the flowchart is intended to be generalized to new situations. The

FIGURE 8.6. Kirsten's Ministering Block

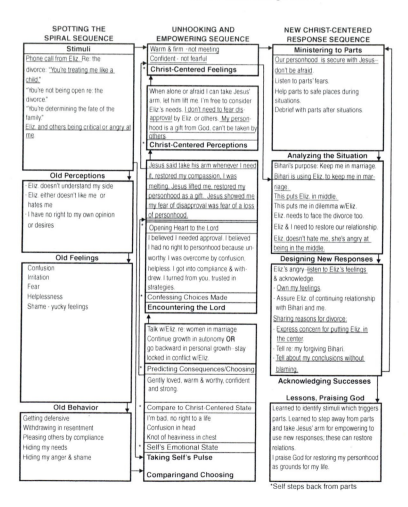

*Self steps back from parts

content is specific to a situation for two reasons: to offer the self a blueprint for behavior and because the self learns more quickly by doing than by theorizing. When the self works through an encounter using the flowchart, it assimilates the experience and is ready to generalize behavior to other situations.

Although the external goal is to adapt the flowchart so the client can be successful in a second situation, an internal goal is for the self to exercise its transcendent capacity in the adaptation process. To accomplish this, the therapist should let the client proceed with a minimum of prompting. This optimizes the client's learning and equips him or her to respond to a wide variety of situations with new spiritual, analytical, and social skills. Clients, now feeling some confidence, frequently open the door for the next challenge. This is what happened with Kirsten.

Kirsten Uses Her Flowchart to Take on a New Challenge

At our next session, Kirsten was very distressed. She said she had decided to travel to India to facilitate her divorce by meeting Bihari face to face. She and Bihari had arranged a flight in three weeks. Since making this decision, she felt overwhelmed, terrified, and unable to sleep at night. She was ready to call off the trip.

This illustrates how a new situation can trigger many parts who overwhelm the self with their anxieties, even though the self had already led successfully through similar situations. At such times therapists are tempted to perceive clients as "regressing" and may lose patience with them. However, it is vital that we take our own pulse and unhook from our own parts so our compassionate selves are available to help clients adapt their flowchart to the new challenge. We can also see how well our client has learned the skills and sequences by observing how well they adapt their first situation flowchart to the second.

Regarding the preparation of the flowchart, if there is space in the blocks to put additional entries, the original flowchart can be easily modified by adding entries specific to the new situation.

In Kirsten's case, there was no room in the stimuli block for the new situation with Bihari. However, Kirsten felt that she did not need to note the new stimuli because the reactions were so similar to the Elizabeth stimuli. Had she desired, the Elizabeth stimuli could have been grouped together as stimuli #1. The new stimuli (about her trip to India) would be entered as stimuli #2. Often the old perceptions, feelings, and behaviors blocks are so similar that new entries are not needed, but when they are, they are designated as #2, showing they are results of stimuli #2. The entire unhooking sequence is often similar enough that no additions are necessary.

However, the response sequence usually calls for additions in the ministering block and, most important, to the analyzing and designing blocks because they involve responses to different persons, settings, and behaviors.

If the first flowchart has no space for additions, the client may elect to make a new flowchart for the new situation. To do this, the client simply reviews the original flowchart and enters only the relevant content on the new flowchart. Having mastered some of the first flowchart, the client can leave out many details and supplement them with new entries specific to the new situation.

Kirsten's Preparation for the Trip to India

Kirsten began her trip preparation by taking her "pulse." She knew she would need maximum autonomy to function on her own. She and her parts saw the trip as a watershed. She could either leave the old compliant victim posture or cave in to Bihari's pleading and remain in the marriage.

I suggested she go as far as she could on her own, with minimal input from me. The following illustrated her process:

Kirsten (looking at her flowchart, Figure 8.6): I'm going to start with the pulse block. I'll step back from the parts. I see I'm pretty overwhelmed by confusion, and I have the knot in my chest. I've lost the warmth and confidence of being with Jesus, and I can predict that if I stay on this track I won't face my fears and go to India to complete this divorce. Instead, I would stay locked in conflict with Bihari. If I turn back to the Lord, I think I will have the courage to go to India and complete the divorce. Also, I'll probably learn a lot about leading my parts if I go. I see that I need to turn back to the Lord. Should I do that now?

Therapist: Yes. I noticed you began by taking your pulse. That's often the best way to begin. Your predictions are right on the point.

Here Kirsten has demonstrated her understanding of the importance of first taking her pulse and unhooking from her parts. I simply underline her judgment.

Kirsten: My parts are bombarding me with their fears. What do I do now?

Therapist: Okay, consider your options.

Kirsten: I guess I should try to get them to step back so I can turn back to the Lord. It would be better to listen to why they are so upset, then I can decide what to do.

Here Kirsten is already feeling empowered enough to listen to her parts.

Kirsten: One group is fearful that I'll cave in to Bihari's pleading and manipulations. Another group feels that Bihari hasn't accepted my decision, so I'm stuck in the marriage. These parts don't believe I can face the world alone.

Therapist: Good work. What's your next step?

Kirsten: I think I will tell them that these are important concerns but that right now I need to get back to Jesus for my own grounding. I'll ask my parts to wait and to watch. They're pretty nervous, but they are trying to give me space. They feel better because I listened to them.

Having settled her parts, Kirsten was free to return to Jesus for empowering. Soon she reported that she found Jesus. This time, instead of lifting her up out of a melting state, she felt a gentle affirming warmth. She filled up with this warmth until she felt fully confident again.

Now Kirsten was ready to plan for the India trip. She saw that the next block was ministering to the parts. She checked with the two groups to see if they would wait until she worked on the analyzing block and the response block. Because the parts were listened to, they agreed to wait.

Kirsten noticed the first point in the analyzing block "Bihari's purpose is to keep me in the marriage." She realized that the Indian subculture was one reason why Bihari could not easily release her. She saw that she needed to face Bihari and her Indian friends in their own culture. Although they loved her, they also reinforced her second-class status in the marriage. Also, she realized that Bihari and the Indian culture reinforced her own family legacy of inferiority as a woman. She saw, in a fresh way, how these influences shaped her internal family so that many of her parts believed she was actually inferior and deserved to be subservient. Thus, for many of Kirsten's parts, the trip to India and her impending divorce were shaking their foundations.

With this much clarity, Kirsten went on to the new responses block. First, she clarified her goals for the trip: bringing her marriage to a conclusion, and saying good-bye to her home and to her Indian friends. She then began to consider new responses. Since she expected Bihari to persuade and to manipulate her to stay in their marriage, she considered ways she could strengthen her capacity to stay in self and be respectful yet firm in her interactions with Bihari. She asked for help to find ways to stay in self. Together we brainstormed the following strategies:

- Lodging outside their home where Bihari was living so she would be able to limit all interaction and conversation with Bihari as needed. Also, she would not be dependent on him for food and lodging.
- Debriefing her interactions every evening with her parts, using the flowchart.
- Journaling and praying every morning to stay centered in Jesus.
- Calling me long distance as needed for consultation or support.
- E-mailing friends for spiritual support and prayer.

Kirsten also brainstormed a range or possible responses to Bihari when he was pleading or manipulating. She selected the best options and listed them as follows:

- Acknowledging that Bihari is upset by her decision and that he doesn't believe it's wise.

- Repeating, in a calm voice without blaming, her decision to divorce to continue healing.
- Reminding Bihari that she has accepted his apologies and is not holding wrongs against him or wishing him ill.
- Noting the need to make some decisions together about various topics.
- Reminding him of the agenda when he is manipulating or off track.
- If Bihari doesn't return to the agenda, she will give him one warning that she needs to end the conversation. If he persists, she will leave.
- If she feels overwhelmed, she will stop the conversation for a moment or excuse herself so she can separate from her parts and reempower her self.

Kirsten and I observed that these responses seemed to be free of manipulations or put-downs and were consistent with her desire to center on Jesus.

Kirsten's New Challenge Calls for New Ministering to Her Parts

Kirsten's parts were growing more frightened as the trip approached, keeping her awake at night with a knot in her chest and confusion in her head. She tried several ways to reassure them. She reminded them of the new responses she had designed and her empowering in Jesus to stand fast against Bihari's manipulations. Also, she reminded them of the gift of her personhood from God. However, the parts refused to be calmed. Kirsten sensed that her efforts were too theoretical for the primitive level of their fear.

Kirsten's parts needed safe places to stay during her anticipated conversations with Bihari. In talking with the most frightened parts, Kirsten sensed that they carried a deep belief in their unworthiness to make such a decision as divorcing Bihari, especially when he opposed the decision. Previously, in similar situations, Kirsten's parts felt they would lose their personhood and melt away.

In our next session we acknowledged that Kirsten had tried all the usual remedies and there was no time for the deeper unburdening work that some of the parts needed. Facing an apparent dilemma, we finally realized it might be time for the parts to meet Jesus for themselves. Many parts were quite afraid of meeting Jesus. Now we realized they had seen Jesus lifting Kirsten up when she was melting and that His gentle love was not diminishing her but empowering her. Kirsten checked with them. Several were ready to meet Jesus. Others, however, believed that, because of their unpopular roles in the internal family, they would be judged by Jesus as failures or as ungodly and would be reprimanded or discarded. A few parts were fearful that Jesus' power would swallow them up.

Kirsten asked the parts if they could imagine a difference between the manipulative relationship they had seen with her parents and with Bihari and the accepting love of Jesus. They could not. However, their interest was piqued by observing Kirsten's interaction with Jesus and His gentle, affirming love for her. With various parts hiding for protection, three parts invited Jesus to come to them. When they looked at His face and felt His interest in them, they were amazed to find that he accepted them and the other parts as well. The hiding parts had varying reactions to Jesus' acceptance. Some felt wonderment and hope, but others were puzzled and cautious. Kirsten invited them to take their time with the new experience.

Inviting the first three parts to open their hearts to Jesus' love, Kirsten had an image of them sitting on Jesus' lap, playfully climbing on him. Several of the other parts were sitting or standing nearby but keeping some distance, while a third group was sitting in the balcony for safety, yet watching closely.

Kirsten asked the first three curious parts if they wanted to ask Jesus to come to India with them. They immediately said they were ready to go if Jesus would come and if they could sit in His lap and watch. Jesus said He would like that. The other parts were more hesitant. Some wanted to watch from behind Jesus while the most frightened parts agreed that it would be safe enough to sit in the balcony. They all wanted to participate in the debriefing with Kirsten and Jesus after each encounter with Bihari. It seemed as though the trip was on.

The next event, however, showed us that more was needed. Suddenly, the image of the parts playing with Jesus disappeared. I asked Kirsten to see if there was another part present. She soon saw a tiny baby crying out, "Don't let Jesus see me; I'm too dirty." As Kirsten talked with her, she revealed that she had been "ruined" by experiencing sexual pleasure and therefore was "worth absolutely nothing." She believed that she deserved her subservient place in the family and in the thirty-year marriage. She could not bear to be with Jesus so Kirsten held her, thanked her for speaking up, and welcomed her into the family.

Over the course of our counseling relationship, Kirsten and I had observed various signs of early sexual abuse. We expected to find an exile part carrying these painful memories. Now this high-stress situation had brought such a part forward past the usually watchful guard of the manager parts.

After the part calmed down in Kirsten's arms, Kirsten asked her if she knew the plan to go to India so she could speak up for herself to Bihari. The part was amazed that Kirsten would treat her so respectfully and that, in going to India, Kirsten was so self-respectful and strong.

Kirsten expressed her desire to get to know that part and to hear her story. However, that process would need to wait until after the trip. The part said she had waited many years to speak up, so waiting a few more weeks would not be a problem. She would hide, as she was used to doing, while Kirsten was with Bihari. Kirsten noted that the knot in her chest was gone and she was feeling confident and warm. We took this as evidence that the parts were fully ready for the India trip.

Amazingly, such young and deeply wounded parts are capable of waiting after they are acknowledged and accepted. However, they may continue to influence other parts to create or maintain dependent and abusive social relationships such as Kirsten's relationship with Bihari. Thus I cautioned Kirsten to be alert to the young part's behavior and consider meeting regularly with her during the trip.

This completed the needed ministry to the parts. Kirsten added a note to the ministering block: "Help parts come to Jesus for acceptance and safety as desired" (Figure 8.6).

Bringing Parts to Jesus

What is the effect of bringing Kirsten's parts to Jesus at this point, and when is this a useful step? Typically parts are individually helped to a relationship with Jesus in the process of unburdening (see Chapter 4). In that setting, relating to Jesus feels natural and voluntary. Each part, which feels the need, receives Jesus' help in unburdening or in filling its inner void. However, in this case, the urgency and fearfulness of the trip created a dilemma for the parts.

Though Kirsten tried all the usual ways of meeting the parts' needs for the trip, they remained extremely fearful. The time dilemma prevented their own individual healing and empowering encounter with Jesus. Thus the parts could not access the available spiritual and emotional resources and remained blocked in their fears. With such a dilemma, it is tempting for the self either to press ahead with the trip as scheduled or to accomodate the parts' fears and reschedule the trip. Instead, client and therapist should consider if there are other ways to help the parts.

In this case, another option emerged as Kirsten and I explored her internal family system. We were aware that the India plan had further polarized the parts. Some parts were afraid to face Bihari in India because the plan could fail, yet others were pushing to bring closure to the marriage so Kirsten could get on with her life.

We also were aware that some parts were fearful of relating to Jesus but other parts were curious and open. We finally realized that, although the internal family was polarized and stuck, it would be possible to invite the curious parts to meet Jesus without violating the other parts. The others would be free to observe and respond with skepticism, fear, or any other response. Giving the parts an individual choice was also consistent with Jesus' character and love because it was a genuine invitation and not a hidden expectation. This allowed each part to find its own level of encounter with Jesus.

The majority of the parts did not block the three curious parts from taking the first steps with Jesus. Rather, they appreciated the courage of the three and felt they all benefited from what they discovered about Jesus. Surprisingly, each part then found some position of safety for the feared encounter with Bihari. In addition, each part had new and personal evidence that there was a source of unconditional love, something they had long wished for. This was especially important for the parts who had grown skeptical and hopeless.

This episode also illustrated the effect of the self acting as a change agent for the internal family. As long as the self does not side with one group of parts against the other, the self, when empowered, may invite the parts into bold new steps to equip them to meet a challenge.

When is it useful to invite the parts to meet Jesus? Usually it is the self who meets Jesus for empowering to lead. In Kirsten's case, the India trip was so stressful for the parts that there was no way to provide for their needs in the usual way. In effect, the situation created a need for a new source of courage which could only be found in Jesus. However, this requires a leap of faith. As long as the self is truly inviting the parts into a relationship with Jesus and accepting the results of the parts' free choice, the parts experience a freely given invitation. This requires the self's willingness to accept the result of the invitation, including the possibility of the parts' inability to meet Jesus or to make the trip. This is the risk of a genuine invitation. The self must value the parts more than the goal and be willing to cancel the trip, if necessary. The parts experience this valuing and sense that the invitation to meet Jesus is genuine. Without this, there would be no encounter because, being true to his character, Jesus would not participate if the parts were forced.

A second observation also underlines the need for the client to stay in self during the parts' encounter with Jesus. A controlling part will, at times, manipulate these encounters either by blocking the interaction or, more subtly, by mascarading as Jesus and using the encounter to advance its own agenda (see Chapter 4). This will create confusion and pain for the parts. Whenever the self, aided by the therapist, observes a part experiencing anything other than loving regard from the apparent Jesus, self must immediately interrupt the process, find the controlling part, and get it to step back, freeing the other parts to encounter the real Jesus.

In summary, facing a stressful situation can be an occasion for inviting the parts to a first encounter with Jesus as long as the client stays in self and offers the parts a genuine choice. This may, as in Kirsten's invitation to her parts, result in some spiritual breakthroughs for individual parts, some increased unity in the internal family, and an increased capacity by the internal family to let the self lead in meeting the challenge.

Using the Future Imaging Technique with Jesus to Prepare Parts for Challenges

Although Kirsten's parts felt more secure after their meeting with Jesus, some of their fears returned as the departure date approached. The parts projected their fears onto Kirsten and she began to experience the sleeplessness and heaviness in her chest again. I decided to tell her about future imaging, a technique developed by Schwartz to help clients and their parts prepare for an anticipated situation. It involves putting the situation in a room and helping the parts release the self to respond to it.

I described the procedure to Kirsten. She put the living room scene of their home in India into the room and invited the parts to look in through a window. The three curious parts came and, appraising the situation, said, "Where's Jesus? We want Jesus with us." Kirsten said they could ask Jesus to stay with them. Soon He was there hugging them. They moved the couch back so they could sit together and watch Kirsten and Bihari's conversation in safety.

Soon the second group of parts came and crouched behind the sofa where they could be close to Jesus, but not too close. Finally, the third group went to a balcony where they could watch in safety. The baby was carried by Kirsten in a backpack.

Kirsten took her pulse and, continuing to feel the confidence of her empowered state, went into the living room and tried her new responses with Bihari. Surprisingly, her parts were able to remain quiet during much of the imaginary conversation. However, at the point where Kirsten imagined Bihari insisting on his way and not staying on the agreed upon topic, several fearful parts began blending and giving Kirsten the sensation of melting. She lost her assertiveness.

I asked Kirsten to step out of the room to figure out what was happening. She saw the blending parts, quickly got them settled, and was able to continue the exercise and try the remaining responses. In addition to discovering that the parts with Jesus were able to allow her to lead, she found that her new responses apeared to be effective with Bihari.

I asked the parts if they noticed any difference in Kirsten. They said they could see that when they gave her space to lead she could be powerful enough to stand up to Bihari.

Kirsten's experience illustrates the usefulness of the future imaging technique to prepare parts to trust the self in frightening situations, as well as giving them evidence of the effectiveness of the self when given space to lead. In addition, the exercise serves as a field test for the client's new responses. Kirsten felt encouraged that, when in the self, the new responses could be respectful as well as effective. Kirsten and her parts felt ready for the big trip.

Debriefing Kirsten's India Trip

After several weeks, Kirsten returned from India, feeling successful but wanting to review the trip. In out next session, Kirsten was quite excited, observing that she managed to stand firm with Bihari in each of her conversations with him. As she had predicted, he tried to persuade her to stay in the marriage by promising, pleading, manipulating, and occasionally becoming angry and threatening. However, she was able to be clear with him about why she was ending the marriage. Bihari told her several times that he did not approve of her plan and, although he is an atheist, told her that God said she should not leave the marriage. Instead of becoming confused and immobilized, Kirsten told him gently but firmly that she was not presenting a plan or a proposal. She was presenting a decision and it was not open for discussion. She also gave her wedding ring back to him, saying she was sorry that she needed to leave the marriage and acknowledging that this made him very upset.

Although Bihari continued to try to persuade and manipulate, Kirsten quietly insisted that they pursue their agenda. Sometimes she terminated the conversation and continued it later. In this way, they came to agreement on many issues including Bihari's visits with the children and various financial and family needs.

Kirsten also said good-bye to various Indian friends, many of whom tried to persuade her to stay in the marriage. She was able to be patient and clear with them. Kirsten felt satisfied that she achieved her goals for the trip, standing firm when necessary without diminishing Bihari and without withdrawing, as she had done previously. She was also pleased that she had not needed to call me, although she had been strongly tempted at points. I congratulated her and her parts for how much she stayed in self and for the courage and wisdom she and the parts exercised.

Kirsten's Use of the Flowchart During the Encounters

Kirsten made a new 3x5 flowchart on the flight to India by substituting the new analysis and responses specific to Bihari for the old content regarding Elizabeth. She easily memorized the 3x5 chart, although she also carried a written copy with her. With this she quickly noticed Bihari's manipulative behaviors and, observing that she was still empowered, skipped directly to the analyzing and response blocks before responding to Bihari.

When Bihari was pleading and crying, Kirsten was able to perceive this as some of his parts trying to get her to take care of them. She recognized that it was Bihari's job to care for them and, instead of getting hooked, she quietly repeated to Bihari her reasons for ending the marriage, waiting to see if he would stop pleading. She used the moment to quiet her own parts. If he did not stop, she selected a more assertive response such as reminding him of the importance of returning to the agenda or she would need to temporarily end the conversation. When she noticed fear or heaviness in herself, she either turned to Jesus until she felt empowered again or excused herself and left the room, using her 3x5 chart to return to Jesus. When energized and ready, she returned to the conversation. This kind of flexibility illustrates how creatively clients can adapt the steps and skills of the flowchart for the needs of the moment.

Using the Flowchart for On-Site Debriefing

Kirsten felt that the flowchart helped her debrief each evening. She tracked various episodes of the day through the flowchart, noticing how her successes in unhooking and empowering affected her ability to try the new responses. She recorded the effectiveness of the new responses in her journal. Kirsten noticed that using the chart for the debriefing helped her parts see the evidence of her successes and discoveries. This reinforced the parts' trust in her leadership.

During the debriefings, Kirsten noticed that her parts were able to let her lead through many of the encounters with Bihari by sitting on the sofa with Jesus or behind the sofa where they could watch her. In talking with her parts, she discovered two important changes that had happened to them in the last two sessions before the trip. First, they had, for the first time, seen for themselves that Jesus accepted them. This began a shift from their dependency on others' approval to a kind of inner assurance by carrying Jesus' acceptance with them. Second, they had seen in the future imaging how clear and powerful Kirsten could be when they gave her space to lead. For the first time, they felt they could survive an encounter with Bihari. The result was that when they were safely with Jesus around the sofa, they were able to trust Kirsten to lead. Kirsten discovered that, for the first time in her life, she, too, felt confident. She could use the flowchart, stay empowered, and not get hooked by Bihari. She now felt she could trust her own judgment about how to respond to Bihari and to her Indian friends.

Kirsten's Use of the Flowchart to Prepare for the Next Day's Encounters

Kirsten concluded each evening's debriefing by preparing herself for the next day's conversations. After centering on the Lord, she incorporated the lessons of the debriefing into the flowchart for the next day, especially noting any changes to the analyzing block and the response block. Then she checked her parts, listened to their concerns or suggestions, and helped them return to Jesus using the future imaging exercise as needed.

Kirsten used her journal to process many of the debriefing and preparation steps because she felt that journaling made them more concrete for herself and her parts. Together, we observed that she had done a creative job of adapting the flowchart to her own needs using her new skills.

Kirsten's encounters in India illustrate how the self uses the flowchart in several ways: preparing for encounters, prompting self during encounters, and debriefing following encounters. When used this way, each day's experience becomes a building block for the next day's challenges. This results in a growing feeling of competence, reinforcing the new proactive posture. Kirsten said she was starting to believe that she could think for herself, make decisions for herself, and trust her decisions. We identified this as growth in autonomy and took it as an outward sign of an inner transformation in progress.

Postscript on Kirsten's India Trip

Did Kirsten and her parts continue building her new proactive style on the foundation of success from her India trip? As with many clients, when the "crisis" was over, Kirsten's old fears and perceptions flooded back into her consciousness. For Kirsten, this happened as soon as she boarded the plane for home. "How can you leave Bihari and think you can have your own identity and manage your own life?" her parts cried out while filling Kirsten with their fears.

Later, as Kirsten and I considered this apparent regression in our next session, Kirsten experienced it as a "window of understanding," revealing how deeply the terror had controlled her throughout her life. Now she felt she was ending one chapter of her life and beginning a new one based on her relationship with Jesus. She sensed a new calling, continuing to stay centered in Jesus, leading her parts, and discovering her talents and how to use them to serve God and others. We noted how this vision fit the pattern of the great commandment, "Love God with all your heart, mind, and soul and your neighbor as yourself" (Matthew 22: 37-39). This validated her new sense of direction.

Charts for Parts

In the following months, Kirsten and I used another technique that illustrates an additional use of the flowchart: making out a chart, not as a tool for the self to grow, but as a tool for the parts to grow.

Following her India trip, Kirsten and I returned our focus to the healing and unburdening of her parts. Many of her parts blossomed as she and Jesus freed and healed them. However, several parts continued blending with her self during stressful situations, continuing to be dependent on Kirsten to help them cope with each situation. As we listened to these parts, we found a fearful five-year-old and a few others who, even though unburdened, had been unable to break free of the old spiral of emotions and reactions. They did not grow past this dependent state as the other parts had done.

We checked with Kirsten's five-year-old on several occasions when she needed much help to get through a situation. There was no evidence of other undiscovered burdens or other hidden internal dynamics affecting her other than a few other parts complaining that she was a "drag" and a "bother."

Many parts when healed and released from the past mature by themselves and often begin to contribute to the self's new proactive life. Some parts, however, having learned in their neediness to depend on others, transfer their dependency to the self during the healing process. Unlike other parts, they do not easily learn to overcome their fears to become more self-actualizing. (This phenomena of parts' prolonged dependency on the self may also be caused by parts carrying preverbal or primal trauma such as birth trauma or by legacy burdens or by destructive spirits such as demons. However, the procedures for these are beyond the scope of this book.)

Stuck dependent parts need help to discover how to mobilize their own inner resources to grow into self-competency. When told about their internal resources and invited by the offer of coaching and learning tools, these parts can become energized and excited at the possibility of learning and becoming more competent. The parts are then helped to construct their own flowchart as a tool for unhooking and empowering and are coached just as the self was.

I told Kirsten about the use of the flowchart as a tool to help parts grow past their dependency and the role of the self as a coach to the part(s) in the process. Kirsten, an experienced parent, saw the process as helping a stuck child learn to use his or her own resources to overcome obstacles instead of always relying on a parent.

Kirsten followed her own flowchart as she would in preparing to minister to her parts. Noting that she felt empowered and compassionate toward the five-year-old, she explained to her the concept of having a chart like Kirsten's to help her find her own way through frightening situations. The five-year-old was interested and hopeful.

The five-year-old and Kirsten selected a recent situation that made the part feel that she was back experiencing childhood abuse. They listed the trigger in the stimuli block on a blank chart. Next they identified and listed her old perceptions, feelings, and behaviors. These revealed how the current stimuli put her in the frightened state.

Next, the part and Kirsten filled in the pulse block so the part could take her pulse and notice when she became hooked. At that point she could choose to turn back to Jesus instead of grabbing and disabling Kirsten. Many such dependent parts, having already been unburdened, are able to turn to Jesus. However, Kirsten and the five-year-old part discovered it wasn't possible for her. Instead, this part had to reenter the trauma scene with Jesus, reexperience it, reexperience the victory, in this case speaking up to the wrongdoer with Jesus, and thus reexperience the resolution.

This illustrates the need for these traumatized parts, triggered into a frightened state by the stimuli, to learn to reenter the trauma itself and come again to the resolution. When self and part find the steps they need, they list these in the heart block as a reminder to the part about how to unhook from the situation. After numerous repetitions of resolving the frightened state, the part establishes such a strong new resolution sequence it needs only to recall it to be freed and empowered to deal with the stimuli.

After Kirsten helped the five-year-old construct and practice her flowchart, the other parts wanted their own charts. They easily adapted the five-year-old's chart so that the one chart served for all. In the next months, they learned to use the new sequence so well that they could face a variety of fearful situations without needing much help from Kirsten. Kirsten then felt more free to take risks of growth since she was less distracted by the parts. She felt they were now like growing children, sometimes even cheering her on and congratulating her after an encounter, much like I had done with Kirsten's self earlier.

The process of helping parts learn how to provide for their own emotional needs is in keeping with Schwartz's discovery that parts have selves and can become centered and less extreme. This process underlines the capacity of parts, when assisted, to provide for their own emotional and spiritual needs in stressful situations. It also helps them move away from the old survival axis and move toward the new life-giving orientation to the self and Jesus.

CHAPTER SUMMARY

This chapter described the Christ-centered response sequence, the third and final sequence in the flowchart. Having unhooked from the parts and empowered with Christ, the self now can see the frightening situation through new eyes, design new godly responses to it, and minister to the parts as needed to enable the self to lead in trying the new responses and monitoring the results. Kirsten's case study illustrates the steps of coaching the client in developing the sequence and using it.

The first step in the sequence is deciding whether to begin with the parts (ministering block) or with the situation (analyzing block). The chapter noted the desirability of beginning by ministering to the distressed parts (the first block). However, because the situations clients face can be quite urgent, the self may need immediate help in coping. For this reason, the chapter offered a second way, proceeding directly to analyzing (second block), then to designing new responses (third block), while promising to return to the parts as soon as possible. The chapter development followed this second plan as did the case study with Kirsten.

In the analyzing block, the steps were described as taking a fresh look at the situation, especially the dynamics and issues past and present that keep the parts hooked. Some of these involve hidden motives and dynamics not just in the family of origin but in the social and cultural systems as well. The client selects the most relevant of these and lists them in the analyzing block.

Next, the chapter described the steps in coaching the self to design effective new responses to the situation, consistent with respectful interaction. The chapter described how the therapist helps the client prepare for and test new options, first with future imagining, if desired, then in the situation itself.

After the client encounters the situation, client and therapist then debrief, assessing the effectiveness of the responses as well as the capacity of the self and parts to implement the responses. The therapist then helps the client's self prepare for the next encounter by incorporating the lessons from the first encounter into a plan for the next. The chapter described the streamlined flowchart as a modification of the flowchart made by highlighting the steps where the client needs prompting to stay unhooked and empowered in the pressure of the situation to try the new responses. This streamlined chart can also be listed on a 3×5 card for the client to use during the encounter.

The chapter described the value of returning to the ministering to the parts block if previously skipped. The goal of the ministering block was noted: constructing a tool to help the self listen and respond to the parts' needs in the frightening situation. Secondary goals were described as helping parts notice the self's growing competence and helping parts grow in their own relationship with Jesus, becoming more self-regulating.

Several levels of responses to the parts were noted: reassurance, physical comforting, helping parts find safety during frightening encounters, and helping parts to their own empowering relationship with Jesus. These are listed in the block for guiding the self in future encounters.

Finally, the chapter described the acknowledging block as a summary of the successes and lessons and a statement of thanksgiving to God for his empowering. This summary is developed by the client through reviewing the debriefings and the flowchart steps, identifying what he or she has learned about the parts' reactions, about unhooking and empowering, about the hidden dynamics of the situation(s), and about how well the self was able to try the new responses and about which responses are effective.

Throughout the chapter, Kirsten is tracked as she develops the blocks and uses them in a next encounter with Elizabeth. Kirsten, in her empowered state, was able to listen to Elizabeth's feelings, own her own feelings, and share her reasons for the divorce without blaming Bihari. This straightforwardness elicited Elizabeth's self, who retracted some of her extreme statements. Mother and daughter came to a meeting of heart and mind, achieving Kirsten's deepest goals for the encounter.

In the debriefing, Kirsten noticed how the encounter strengthened her confidence in her ability to stay in self and validated her analysis of Elizabeth's anger as well as her own new responses. The chapter observed how encounters at the completing of the flowchart become evidence of all the lessons learned throughout the three sequences in the flowchart and how these are summarized in the acknowledging block.

Kirsten's preparation and executing of a plan for a more difficult challenge, the trip to India to conclude the divorce process on Bihari's home turf, is described in the chapter. Kirsten is followed as she adapts her old flowchart to the new situation and prepares her parts for the trip by inviting those who are able to experience Jesus' unconditional love for themselves. This enabled the other parts to observe Jesus' love and to find safety in his protection. They were able to move past their terror to let Kirsten lead in dealing with Bihari's manipulation.

The chapter described the debriefing after the trip in which Kirsten noted the various ways she used the flowchart during the encounter and during regular evening debriefings with her parts and Jesus. Kirsten's excitement was reported in the chapter as she found she was able to stay in self throughout conversations with Bihari and friends, even when they tried to persuade and manipulate her. Kirsten found herself using new and creative responses, patterned after her flowchart entries.

Finally, the chapter described how, months later, after the parts were unburdened and brought to a deeper trust in Kirsten and in Jesus, some parts continued to blend with Kirsten in their dependence on her. This section described a different use of the flowchart, as a tool for the parts to grow instead of a tool for the self—thus the name Charts for Parts.

CLINICAL OUTLINE:
DESIGNING AND IMPLEMENTING
CHRIST-CENTERED RESPONSES

This outline is a summary of the procedure to coach a client in developing and using the new responses tool.

I. Self and therapist consider the place to begin, with the parts or with the situation, using the following factors:
   A. If the situation is not too urgent, client begins with ministering to the parts (first block).
   B. If the situation is so pressing that there is no time for parts, client explains the urgency to them, seeking their support in letting self prepare and lead through the situation, returning to the parts after the event. In this case, client and therapist begin with the analyzing block and the new responses block.
   C. If the parts are so distressed that they will block the self's leadership in the situation, client and therapist enlist the parts to discover the cause of their distress, then develop a plan with the parts for both meeting the situation and meeting their needs for reassurance and safety.

II. Client and therapist develop the "ministering" block.
   A. Therapist describes goals of the ministering block:
      1. Primary goal: Give self a tool to help discern and meet the needs of the parts in relation to the frightening situation so they can trust the self to lead.
      2. Secondary goals:
         a. Help parts observe self's growing ability to care for parts and to lead, further increasing trust.
         b. Help parts grow in confidence of Jesus' unconditional love.
         c. Help parts grow more self-regulating and less reactive.
   B. Self takes pulse (pulse block), follows unhooking sequence as needed until empowered in Jesus and positive toward parts.
   C. Self reviews "survival sequence," noting old perceptions, old feelings, and old behaviors in relation to the stimuli in question.
   D. Self sees that all parts know the plan for self to analyze situation (block 2) and develop new proactive responses (block 3).

E. Self consults parts regarding their fears, concerns, and needs in letting self lead in the situation, including parts in frightened state.

F. Self and therapist consider the various increasing levels of response to parts, consistent with time available before the situation occurs:

   1. Reassurance based on self's perspective of the situation as well as holding and comforting parts.

   2. Safety from external danger such as helping the parts find safe places to hide or watch or a protector to stay with, such as another part or Jesus.

   3. Safety from internal danger such as criticism by manager parts or impulsive behavior from exile or firefighters.

   4. Inviting parts to their own relationship with Jesus for empowering:

      a. Self describes the option to meet Jesus, listening to parts' fears, and responding as needed.

      b. Parts who are ready come forward to meet Jesus; others watch.

      c. Self helps parts experiment with opening their hearts to Jesus to let Him respond to their needs.

      d. Self monitors the encounter to prevent other parts from imposing their fears or agenda onto the encounter.

      e. Self helps parts assimilate the encounter, noticing any physical or attitudinal changes in themselves.

      f. Self invites watching parts to meet Jesus.

      g. Self asks parts how the encounter affects their readiness to let self lead in the situation.

G. Self and therapist fill out ministering block with data learned about meeting parts' needs so the self can lead.

III. Client and therapist develop the analyzing block:

   A. Therapist describes the goal of the block: Taking a fresh look at the situation with a Christ-centered perspective after unhooking from parts and their perspective.

   B. Self, coached by therapist, reconsiders the situation:

      1. What dynamics and issues, past and present, in the situation keep parts hooked?

      2. What hidden motives, power imbalances, system dynamics, or legacies in the situation need to be identified to free the self to consider new responses?

C. Client selects the most relevant dynamics and lists in analyzing block.

IV. Client and therapist develop the new responses block:

A. Therapist describes the goal: Designing, evaluating, and testing Christ-centered responses to the situation. The responses need to be effective in meeting the self's needs without diminishing the other person(s). Secondary goals include self experiencing a proactive style and parts observing self's growth.

B. Self identifies, without criticism, a range of responses using brainstorming, role-plays, etc., with therapist's help as needed.

C. Client and therapist select the best options and list them on the flowchart for testing.

V. Client tests new responses:

A. Therapist checks self's readiness to test responses in the situation, first using future imaging as needed to prepare.

B. When ready, self tries new responses in situation, noting consequences of each response.

VI. Client and therapist debrief the encounter and prepare for the next encounter.

A. Goal of debriefing is to assess effectiveness of new responses and the capacity of self and parts to implement them.

B. Client recounts the events.

C. Client observes his or her ability to implement the new responses and their effect.

D. Client considers needs for next encounter, building upon discoveries of previous encounter and designing additional new responses as needed.

E. Client adds important discoveries or additional responses to the flowchart.

F. Client considers a streamlined flowchart or a 3×5 flowchart to facilitate self's growing skills. Self reviews flowchart, selecting the minimum number of notations for prompting in the situation. Self either highlights these on the original flowchart, makes a new chart, or makes a 3×5 chart.

G. Client and therapist consider any new stimuli presented by new situations. Client decides whether the old flowchart can accommodate these by adding to the stimuli block and to selected blocks or constructs an additional flowchart.

VII. Client and therapist construct acknowledging block:

A. Goal of the block is to summarize successes and lessons to remind self of the base of learning to support future encounters and to remind self to have a thankful heart toward God as the ground for self's successes.
B. Self reviews debriefings and use of flowchart in encounters and identifies successes and lessons. Therapist helps as needed, asking client to consider what they have learned regarding the following:
   1. Identifying events that trigger parts
   2. How parts, when triggered, affect self
   3. Noticing when parts overwhelm self
   4. Unhooking from parts and returning to Jesus for empowering
   5. Identifying parts' needs and helping them unhook from situations and trust self
   6. Analyzing situations
   7. Designing and testing new responses.
C. Self selects lessons and successes for listing on flowchart.
D. Self and parts consider Jesus' empowering role and lists on flowchart.
E. Self and therapist consider if situation in question is adequately addressed so that the focus of therapy can return to the unburdening process.

EXERCISE: ANALYZING A SITUATION
AND DESIGNING RESPONSES

The goal of the exercise is to practice skills of analyzing and designing in a current situation.

1. Make two blocks on a blank sheet. Label the first "Analyzing a Situation" and the second "Designing New Responses." Have another sheet available as a worksheet.
2. Relax. If you desire, ask God for insight and creativity.
3. Pick a recent situation to which you would like to respond better. It can be the same incident you used in the Chapter 6 or Chapter 7 exercises.
4. Recall the situation and select a specific interaction to focus on. Note it on your worksheet as the stimuli.

5. Step away from your parts, take your pulse, see if you are hooked by your parts. If so, explain to your parts your need for space to do this exercise. If they separate, go to the Lord or to a source of your choice for the courage and perspective you need for a fresh look at the situation and fresh responses to it. If your parts are reluctant to release you, listen to their concerns and respond accordingly. You may use the unhooking sequence (Figure 7.3). If they still are reluctant, you may choose to work with them, developing your ministering to parts block (see Chapter 8, Clinical Outline).

Analyzing the Situation Block

1. When you are ready, focus on the situation and consult with your parts on the following questions:
   - What present dynamics or issues in the situation seem to keep your parts hooked?
   - What past dynamics are influencing the present situation? Consider alliances, power imbalances, and organizational, social, cultural, or spiritual dynamics.
   - Make notes of your observations on your worksheet.

2. Continuing to stay separated from your parts, reflect on your notes, looking for any hidden agendas or dynamics either in yourself or in the situation.
3. Select the most important points and list them in your analyzing block.
4. Consider if there is supporting evidence of your observations such as family stories, your memories, memories of other system members. Do these confirm or modify your observations?

Designing New Responses

1. Continuing to stay separated from your parts, brainstorm and list (on worksheet) all the possible responses you can imagine to the situation. Avoid evaluating them as this point.
2. Select the responses that you feel are the most promising, yet respectful, and list in responses block.
3. If you wish to try the responses, consider when and how you would try these.

4. Explain the goal of the field test to your parts, reassuring them as needed. See how ready they are to trust you to test these and to debrief with them after the encounter. You may use future imaging to prepare them first, if desired.

5. After the encounter, debrief with parts, including a friend as desired, noting successes, discoveries, and lessons, and, if you wish, considering God's role in your experience.

6. Finally, consider how you will build upon this experience for the next situation you meet. Note your thoughts and plans on the worksheet.

God bless you on your clinical and spiritual journey.

Conclusions and Questions:
The Christ-Centered Self Leads
in Healing and Life

Kirsten's success in traveling to India and bringing closure to her abusive marriage was a breakthrough in her lifelong victim posture. This returns us to the original purpose for the book, the need for a breakthrough in therapy for stuck and hopeless people.

The book first describes IFS therapy as a new model of understanding and treatment for struggling people. It then introduces CCIFS as the extension of IFS into Christian spirituality. Kirsten's healing journey illustrates how, using these clinical tools and spiritual resources, a determined individual finds healing, empowering, and equipping to begin a new godly, proactive style in her life. What observations and conclusions can be drawn, and what are their implications for therapists and clients?

THE WOUNDED CHRISTIAN'S DILEMMA

The CCIFS model attempts to discover the powerful inner dynamic that keeps Christians, and especially wounded Christians, bound in internal turmoil. The model helps us see how the wounded Christian, having been ensnared by family and social enmeshment, learns to accommodate by employing ingenious yet ultimately self-destructive survival strategies. In carrying out these strategies, the parts take on internally the same drivenness as the family and the society.

This drivenness results in an endless self-centered search for personal worth and security through performance and social accommodation. Personal autonomy and a relationship with God are both eclipsed by this drive. Seeing this dynamic reveals the parts' survival axis, placing parts firmly in control of well-being. The survival coalition of parts, as keepers of the survival core, find that opening the heart and mind to God is profoundly threatening. The model seeks to help the self discover and understand this internal dilemma. How is the wounded Christian in need of God's healing to resolve this problem?

THE TRANSCENDENT SELF
OPENS THE WAY TO JESUS

The CCIFS model introduces up a way, based on the biblical understanding that the individual, made in the image of God, has the transcendent capacity to fellowship with God. The model observes that the transcendent self can stand at the intersection between God and the parts as the agent of transformation for the internal family. The self receives all the grace, wisdom, and power needed to minister to parts too shamed and afraid of God or Jesus to open themselves. The self receives these spiritual riches as an heir, free of the need of performing for God's blessings and thus participates with Jesus in setting parts free.

God, in His respectful love, never forces Himself on the parts; instead, He invites them into relationship and then waits on their readiness to open themselves to Him. From a clinical view, this means that parts can stay chronically stuck. However, the self, when empowered by Jesus, can intervene as a godly agent, bringing resolution to the internal conflicts and the burdened parts. The parts may then give the self permission to open the way to God's healing love, inviting Jesus to help with burdens too difficult to lift and valleys too terrifying to enter. The parts discover that Jesus is the one reliable "redeemer person" through whom they receive their unconditional worth as a birthright and not as something to be earned. This relationship then becomes their grounding and empowering for interaction in the world, led by the self.

The IFS model, a relationship model centering on the relationship between self and parts, is extended to include the relationship of self to God through Jesus and the relationship of God and Jesus to the parts through the self. These relationships meet the parts' needs for belonging as well as their need for healing love and power.

THE CCIFS MODEL OFFERS A ROAD MAP
FOR THE HEALING JOURNEY

The CCIFS model introduces a sequence for the therapist to use in coaching the client: discovering the internal system, restoring the self's relationship to God through Jesus, extending God's love and grace through the self to the parts, and entering into the deepest valleys with Jesus to see and heal the long-hidden shame and anguish. The confidence in entering these valleys is the biblical certainty and the clinical discovery that there is no pit too deep for Jesus.

One by one the parts are invited into their own relationship with Jesus. This invitation is based on the discovery that even parts who have never trusted before can have their own loving encounter with Jesus. This completes the repairing of the broken relationships and illustrates why CCIFS can be called a relationship model. The healing and empowering of self and parts happens through relationships: self with parts, self with God, parts with self, and through Jesus with God.

Extending the Roles of Therapist and Client

The CCIFS model extends the therapist's role as coach to include spiritual companionship, accompanying the self into the relationship with God through Jesus and into the depths with the parts. The model extends the self's role as leader to include self as minister to parts and self as spiritual leader with God.

Wounded Christians can understand this process and, with the coaching and spiritual companionship of the therapist and the grace of God, can carry it out. This enables the self to emerge as the agent of God's transformation for the internal family.

The Christ-Centered Self Leads the Internal Family

When empowered with Jesus, the self can lead the parts through life's challenges in godly ways, not simply falling back on the parts' old survival patterns. This need, the other central concern of the book, is in keeping with the apostle Paul's call to equip the saints. This section of the book, offering tools to equip the self, is based on the discovery that the self, when empowered and equipped, can, even when overwhelmed by parts' flashback states, interrupt the parts' survival sequence and emerge to lead.

The forgiveness process, the survival sequence, the unhooking and empowering sequence, and the response sequence each help teach and empower the self to lead in meeting these challenges.

Like the healing process, these tools are understandable by the self and parts, enabling the self to meet the specific situation at hand and to continue the learning journey. Using the flowchart as a debriefing tool for important encounters, the self observes how well the internal family mobilizes under pressure and notices the results of the new responses. The self uses this data as an experience base for subsequent encounters. Instead of experiencing life as a victim, self begins to experience it as a learning laboratory with God.

Kirsten began to experience this posture after returning from India. Her experience in India released such energy that, in addition to finishing her own healing and caring for her last at-home child, she found love and energy to develop friendships with a local gang member and several street kids who had not yet closed themselves off from help.

The CCIFS Model Invites the Christian
to a New Paradigm of Faith

What is the significance of this new model? It suggests that the point of the healing process for Christians is not just resolving the disabling clinical problems but also restoring the broken relationship with God. This relationship is not only the means of healing but also the means of releasing the entire personality stuck in an arrested state of development. As self and parts systematically abandon the old dysfunctional core axis, they gratefully embrace God's unconditional love, before so threatening, now so empowering. The result: the personality moves to the new empowering axis centered on the relationship with God. The CCIFS model, a new paradigm of healing, thus invites the Christian to a new paradigm of faith, extending rational faith to the experiential and to the continued reorganization of the personality around the empowering relationship with God.

THE HEALING AND EQUIPPING ROLE
OF THE CHURCH

What is the role of the church in our clients' healing journeys? Deep inner-healing processes happen best in the family of God's people. The client needs to see the inner transformation modeled and lived out in a community of faith like the early believers experienced on the day of Pentecost when God's spirit transformed them inwardly and a new loving community life was manifested outwardly (Acts 2). Our clients and their parts, having experienced wounding relationships, need to see and experience the evidence of loving relationships in God's family, sustaining them on their healing journey and testifying that there is in God a trustworthy source of unconditional love.

Where does the model go from here? I hope it can be useful on a wider scale in God's healing and empowering of wounded people. It needs to be used more broadly, refined, and extended to see what further developments God would give.

I hope the model encourages you, as therapists and healers, to get further acquainted with your own internal family's needs as well as your spiritual resources to meet the needs. Also, I hope the model helps you to discover more about helping your clients open the door to God's healing so His transforming power can come more freely through you to your clients.

We know God has a heart for His broken world and wants to extend His healing love into it. I believe He wants to do this through us to our clients and through our clients to the world. I trust God will encourage you and lead you in your own transforming journey as He reaches out to hurting people through you.

Index

Page numbers followed by the letter "f" indicate figures.

Order Your Own Copy of
This Important Book for Your Personal Library!

CHRIST-CENTERED THERAPY
Empowering the Self

_____in hardbound at $49.95 (ISBN: 0-7890-1227-8)
_____in softbound at $24.95 (ISBN: 0-7890-1228-6)

COST OF BOOKS_____

OUTSIDE USA/CANADA/
MEXICO: ADD 20%_____

POSTAGE & HANDLING_____
*(US: $4.00 for first book & $1.50
for each additional book)
Outside US: $5.00 for first book
& $2.00 for each additional book)*

SUBTOTAL_____

in Canada: add 7% GST_____

STATE TAX_____
*(NY, OH & MIN residents, please
add appropriate local sales tax)*

FINAL TOTAL_____
*(If paying in Canadian funds,
convert using the current
exchange rate, UNESCO
coupons welcome.)*

❑ **BILL ME LATER:** ($5 service charge will be added)
(Bill-me option is good on US/Canada/Mexico orders only;
not good to jobbers, wholesalers, or subscription agencies.)

❑ Check here if billing address is different from
shipping address and attach purchase order and
billing address information.

Signature_____

❑ **PAYMENT ENCLOSED: $_____**

❑ **PLEASE CHARGE TO MY CREDIT CARD.**

❑ Visa ❑ MasterCard ❑ AmEx ❑ Discover
❑ Diner's Club ❑ Eurocard ❑ JCB

Account # _____

Exp. Date_____

Signature_____

Prices in US dollars and subject to change without notice.

NAME_____

INSTITUTION_____

ADDRESS_____

CITY_____

STATE/ZIP_____

COUNTRY_____ COUNTY (NY residents only)_____

TEL_____ FAX_____

E-MAIL_____

May we use your e-mail address for confirmations and other types of information? ❑ Yes ❑ No
We appreciate receiving your e-mail address and fax number. Haworth would like to e-mail or fax special
discount offers to you, as a preferred customer. **We will never share, rent, or exchange your e-mail address
or fax number.** We regard such actions as an invasion of your privacy.

Order From Your Local Bookstore or Directly From

The Haworth Press, Inc.

10 Alice Street, Binghamton, New York 13904-1580 • USA

TELEPHONE: 1-800-HAWORTH (1-800-429-6784) / Outside US/Canada: (607) 722-5857

FAX: 1-800-895-0582 / Outside US/Canada: (607) 722-6362

E-mail: getinfo@haworthpressinc.com

PLEASE PHOTOCOPY THIS FORM FOR YOUR PERSONAL USE.

www.HaworthPress.com

BOF00